After leaving the SBS, **Duncan Falconer** opted to live and work in America. This is his first book.

FIRST INTO ACTION

A Dramatic Personal Account of Life in the SBS

Duncan Falconer

A *Time Warner* Paperback

First published in Great Britain in 1998
by Little, Brown and Company
First published in paperback in 1999
by Warner Books
This edition published in 2001 by Warner Books
Reprinted 2001
Reprinted by Time Warner Paperbacks in 2002
Reprinted 2004

A CIP catalogue record for this book
is available from the British Library.

ISBN 0 7515 3165 0

Typeset in Palatino by
Palimpsest Book Production Limited,
Polmont, Stirlingshire
Printed and bound in Great Britain by
Clays Ltd, St Ives plc

Time Warner Paperbacks
An imprint of
Time Warner Book Group UK
Brettenham House
Lancaster Place
London WC2E 7EN

www.twbg.co.uk

God and the soldier all men adore
in time of trouble and no more
for when war is over and all things righted
God is neglected and the old soldiers slighted

to absent friends

For obvious reasons, many of the names, and certain identifying features, of individuals who appear in this book have been changed, and details of certain operations and events have been appropriately disguised.

In particular the names and addresses of IRA or PIRA personnel, or members of any other paramilitary organisation against whom internal security operations have been mounted, or with whom internal security organisations have had to engage, are not their real ones.

Preface

It was not a simple decision for me to write this book. The pros and cons, political and personal, took several months to sift through my conscience. I abandoned the idea more than once, but each time the urge to write a revealing account of life in the Special Boat Service came back to nag at me. But if an accurate story of the unit was to be written, one that examined its faults and excesses as well as its glories, its nobbers as well as its heroes, it would have to include equally revealing stories of the Special Air Service since the two units are joined at the hip. There is an abundance of literature available to the public describing the greatness of the SAS, so I decided to illuminate some of their blunders, just to even things out a little.

The SAS has remained unchallenged as the world's finest special forces unit since its formation during the Second World War (except when it was disbanded for a few years after 1945). Since then it has sustained its superiority by constantly updating its skills, tactics and equipment, getting stuck into fights wherever it could to keep its edge, and maintaining a level of ability, in most climates and theatres of war, at least one step ahead of the competition. The SBS was formed at around the same time and might have maintained a similar prominence, but due to a lack of foresight from its leaders and support from its parent unit, the Royal Marines (a minuscule group compared to the Army, and more traditional and less flexible), it failed to keep up with the times and in so doing lost the confidence of the combined services' commanders in chief. When a specialised military job came along, the SAS were the first, and most often the only, choice. At one time, it looked as if the SBS might never grow beyond a conventional beach reconnaissance support group with an unclear role at operating behind enemy lines. Had the SBS not changed its focus and begun to look as far as decades into the future, it might never have even seen action in the Gulf War, for instance, where it was selected to be the first into action. After the unit identified and focused on a specific arena (Maritime Anti-Terrorism), the SBS's awesome improvements in skills and abilities have overflowed into other areas. Today, the SBS not only seriously challenges the SAS for pole position in the league of world special forces, it has gained the full confidence of the commanders in chief and taken over many areas the SAS once assumed were exclusively its own.

In writing this book, initially wanting to play it safe (from a security point of view – I have no desire to be a whistle-blower), I first thought about drafting a collection of anecdotes, avoiding the politics, opinions and more sensitive material. But an SBS book, the first modern one written by an actual operative, that did not look under the covers to reveal the true character of the mysterious unit seemed pointless.

I could not make the decision alone and sought advice from those whose opinions I most cared about – the men of the SBS itself. I chose men currently serving and others retired, a mixture of senior NCOs and officers, and introduced the book as a purely hypothetical idea to protect them from the Directorate of Special Forces (for reasons I explain later in this preface). I did not avoid consulting men who I felt certain would be against the idea. To my surprise, the vote to write the book was almost unanimous, the abstainers being unsure. Of the dozen I talked to, none gave an absolute thumbs-down. It was impossible to get the views of the entire unit but I was confident I had a majority opinion. That does not mean the book has the blessing of the SBS. The SBS recently (unofficially) sponsored the publication of an official history of the unit that contains more hard facts about the SBS than my book, but it is a characterless record and skips all the juicy details – understandable since it was written by a civilian and edited by a rupert (our affectionate nickname for officers).

The reasons against such a book as this are obvious. The SAS, having produced somewhere in the region of thirty books by actual operatives, have blown so many whistles that their reputation within the corridors of power has been tarnished by the publicity it has attracted – all publicity for special forces being bad. The reasons I got from the SBS members who approved of my book idea hovered around a central point which was rebellious in nature. The target of their dissent was the Directorate of Special Forces (DSF). In 1997 DSF made it compulsory for every serving member and new recruit prior to selection to sign a non-disclosure contract, making it illegal to tell anyone outside of special forces anything learned while in special forces (the breadth of this relationship is not accurately defined since that is impossible). The contract was supposedly initiated to prevent further book publications where members or former members were involved. This was sound as far as security was concerned. However, the non-disclosure clause turned out to be two-pronged.

Apart from seeking to prevent the writing of books, the decree was also a control over civilian employment if it required the use of knowledge and experience gained within special forces. This was immediately seen by operatives as a threat to their future livelihoods since the majority are forcibly retired by the age of forty. For most of them their military skills are all they have. Breaking the contract, which was seen as an addendum to the Official Secrets Act, could result in a fine and/or imprisonment. The DSF were quick to point out that the contract did not mean a man could not do a related job on leaving special forces, it just wanted control over who did what for whom and where. The DSF proposed an organisation, run by people appointed by the DSF that would centralise, assess, and then disperse suitable civilian job offers that required the skills of former special forces operatives. Anyone with a pinch of imagination could see the idea was as flawed, hypocritical, narrow-sighted and unfair as the people who came up with it. One of the more obvious disadvantages for the SBS of this central jobs office was that it was manned mostly by former SAS operatives who, naturally, looked after their own (SAS) first. This became a bit too obvious when certain water-oriented security jobs went to former SAS operatives who couldn't tell the difference between Boyle's Law and an egg recipe. The DSF went on to threaten that any member who did not sign the contract would be kicked out of special forces. Many SBS operatives said they would not sign on principle until their considerations were noted and the contract amended. They were ignored, and by the time the deadline to sign arrived, only two SBS members, two senior NCOs and highly respected individuals, remained steadfast in their threat and refused to put their mark on the paper as it was written. The DSF booted them out without review or court martial. To my knowledge, neither of the men planned to write a book or teach special forces techniques abroad. One of them recently moved to Russia to run security patrols on a river owned by a fish company, and the other is a published poet.

While in pursuit of opinions on my proposed book, I visited a friend at his house one sunny weekend. Stan, a lieutenant who made his way up through the ranks having served some eighteen years in the Branch, was digging in a complex web of pipes throughout his garden. He was putting together an automatic sprinkler system so that in future, when he was called away unexpectedly, and no matter how long for, his lovingly manicured flowerbeds would get all the water they needed. As he put the finishing touches to the system, he explained his argument in favour of such a hypothetical book, hypothetical because the DSF even made it an offence not to report even the suspicion that such a book was being written (it was all beginning to feel a bit like a 'Tolpuddle conspiracy'). Stan's reason was sponsored by the experience of another SBS member, or to be more precise, of his children. Apparently his two boys had been getting a hard time from school friends because their dad was in the SBS, a unit, the friends claimed, that was not really special forces and whose members did nothing other than paddle around in boats all day. The friends also claimed the SAS were the tops and the only special forces unit worth being a member of. This was obviously due to the spate of books, TV shows and press coverage the SAS was getting. It was upsetting for the children, who even began to show signs of doubt about their dad's importance. Stan felt it was about time at least one book by an SBS operative told the facts. It was not the best of reasons since it was purely ego-driven, but it made the list of considerations. Stan's own footnote was that he wholeheartedly believed it was far more demanding to get into the SBS than the SAS, both physically and intellectually, because of the selection process and nature of the job. With that, Stan tightened the last nut on the sprinkler system.

'And now for the moment we've all been waiting for,' he declared as he went into the house to turn the water on.

He joined me as the first sprinkler heads spluttered to life, forcing the air-pockets from the pipes one after the other in quick succession.

'Who needs a plumber, eh? Just takes a bit of ingenuity

and intelligence,' Stan said, tapping his cranium to reinforce his earlier point about the superior intelligence of the SBS.

Suddenly, we noted steam coming off the sprinkler heads and spreading to the grass and flowerbeds. The water had turned boiling hot. Stan had accidentally plumbed into his central heating system. As he charged into the house to turn the water off, I decided it might not be wholly accurate to claim the superior intelligence.

As for the execution of the book, I decided that, since I had been an SBS operative for many years, the reader might appreciate discovering the SBS as I did, which was in rather unusual circumstances. This personal guide through the early part of the book gives it the unavoidable impression of being autobiographical. But once into the world of British special forces, I drift to the wings to let the sometimes tragic, sometimes humorous experiences of other SBS members tell the story. While the book often gives the impression of a conflict and great division between the SAS and SBS, it is really a story of their coming together. For the future of the two great units ultimately lies on a single path.

When all is said and done, I can only feel pride that the two finest special forces units in the world both come from the same small group of islands. After reading some of the cock-ups by both units, a reader might wonder how true that statement is. Bear in mind it's a most dangerous and dynamic business and the rules are rewritten every day. Anyway, believe me, you should see some of the others out there.

1

I was in my first ambush waiting to kill two men I had never seen before. Christmas was not far away and it was cold and wet. I was twenty years old and alone, outside the back door of a stone farmhouse that had been built more than a century ago. I had a partner from the other special forces unit, an SAS trooper, who was somewhere covering the front. The clouds were low and heavy, making it one of those exceptionally dark nights. I was motionless, crouched like a Gothic carving in the blackness, as much a part of the run-down building as the moss caked to its sides. The farmhouse lay in a dip in the drenched Irish countryside surrounded by clumps of bushes and a few trees. Everything was black. Spindly, leafless twigs surrounding me were charcoal streaks against a barely lighter background. Trying to figure out my surroundings was something to do to pass the time while I waited for the men to come.

I was sitting on a mound of earth and roots under a

1

stunted tree close to the back door, gripping my black, rust-proof M16 assault rifle. The safety-catch was off and my wet, leather-gloved left hand gripped the tapered, Toblerone-shaped plastic stock, while my right encircled the pistol-grip. I had cut the index finger off my right glove to expose the finger which rested outside the cold trigger-guard. It had to remain sensitive and unencumbered to find the trigger instantly. The ground all around the farmhouse was a swamp of creamy mud pitted by the daytime traffic of farm animals and humans, every indentation filled with black rainwater. It looked as if an army had recently trudged through.

The air was still. All was silent. A faint wedge of light came from inside the house. A dim bulb had been left on. The back door was an awkward black rectangle a few yards away. I was invisible where I was, the wall of the house only feet from my back. Anyone moving to the back door would pass just in front of me and I would not miss when I pulled the trigger. I had to be that close. Any further away and I would not see them well enough to make my first shots count.

We would never have been sent out with direct orders to kill someone, but some jobs had inevitable scenarios. Going to arrest a desperate fugitive from justice, a known murderer and one who carried a weapon, was prepared to use it and would never surrender was as clear cut as a sheriff meeting a gunfighter in an old cowboy movie. Whoever got off the quickest, most accurate shot won the day.

I had been surprised, though I did not show it, when during orders for the ambush I was told I would be

alone. It was indeed rare, but not unusual for an operative to be alone on an ambush, but it was new to me.
There were several of us at the briefing in the TV room in
our secret base-camp concealed within a regular Army
camp. We were a mixture of SBS and SAS operatives.
The TV was on all day and night except during briefings.
Those who were not involved in the night's op, mostly
admin staff, left for their rooms until we had finished.
They would be back after we left to plonk back down
into the musky armchairs that were never cleaned and
carry on watching TV.

We were trying to cover every lead that came out
of the intelligence office, keeping busy, attempting too
much, which was usual when you took part in this
conflict for only a few months. This tour of Northern
Ireland was the first live military assignment of my
career. Every ambush I had carried out until then had
been in basic training with no fewer than a dozen other
raw recruits. We would lie beside one another, flat on
our bellies in the spiteful gorse, nudging anyone who
started snoring, watching a dirt track in the middle of
Woodbury Common military training area, the lights of
Exmouth a faint glow on the horizon. We waited for the
exercise enemy to come along and trigger a trip-wire
which would set off a blinding magnesium flare behind
them. Then we would open fire on the silhouettes with
blank bullets and keep firing until someone yelled 'Stop'
or we ran out of ammunition.

That was not much more than a year before when
I was just a noddy, a raw Royal Marine recruit. But
now, incredible though it may seem, I was in the SBS,

3

and working alone was part of the job. I could not put out any trip-flares on this ambush because I did not know from which direction the two men would come. My ears, not my eyes, were to be my most important sensory equipment that night.

The farmhouse was just north of Lough Neagh. It belonged to the family of Simon O'Sally, a Provisional Irish Republican Army (PIRA) terrorist, one of the most wanted men in the province. He was an accomplished killer, highly professional, and a man who enjoyed his work. He moved mostly at night and usually on foot across country to avoid the roads and the possibility of running into an Army checkpoint. He carried the same kind of weapon I had with me that night. It was said that he walked with it aimed out in front with the safety catch off and his finger on the trigger. If he was going to meet anyone who had no business being out at night on his turf he intended to be the first to let rip. I had the utmost respect for him as an adversary.

That night he was supposed to come to the farmhouse. It was one of the places he used to rest up and meet colleagues. I did not dare move a muscle in case he was out there, at the edge of my hearing range, watching the house, which is what he would do for at least half an hour before moving forward. I had been there for several hours and knew all the sounds around me. Keeping still throughout the night was going to be difficult, especially for someone as young and energetic as I was. I decided ambushes like this were better suited to old soldiers.

We knew that O'Sally was coming home one night that week with another member of his Active Service

Unit (ASU). We knew because a third member of the same ASU was a tout, a snitch, and was being paid well for the information.

My backside ached against the cold earth, the damp seeping through my camouflaged pants and thermals. No matter where I sat on this mound a root would dig into me. If I had been more experienced I would have brought a small piece of neoprene rubber to sit on, and worn swimming trunks instead of underpants because they dry out quicker, but I did not know about little tricks like that yet. As long as I kept perfectly still I would remain invisible, to anyone without a thermal image detector that is, and the IRA did not have any of those.

My body heat had dried out the black cam-cream on my face and hands. It felt like old mud and it cracked and aggravated me when I moved my mouth and cheeks. I contorted my face in the hope that the more annoying flakes would fall off. Only when it became a distraction would I risk lifting my hand away from my gun to pick at it. The black cream was designed to take the shine off your face – even black soldiers wore black cam-cream. In training I used to apply it as thinly as possible because it was laborious to wash off afterwards. That night I had spread it on like butter.

It started to rain halfway through the night. I was not wearing waterproofs, just regular camouflage clothing. No one had yet invented a camouflage waterproof that did not make even the slightest noise when you moved. It might not sound loud in the daytime, but at night, in these graveyard conditions, it would be like a crisp packet being opened in a dark movie theatre. My nose started to run. I let it. A sniff carried a long way at night, and it sounded like a sniff. I was a little cold, but I didn't care.

'If you can't ignore being cold and wet, don't join the SBS,' an instructor's voice echoed in my mind – words we were told the first day of the SBS selection course. Truer words were never spoken.

O'Sally and his partner would not move across country in the daylight hours, so I would stay in this spot waiting to kill them until just before dawn. If they did not show, my SAS partner and I would sneak off and spend the daylight in a hide about a mile away, then be back before dark the following day. O'Sally would be home one night this week for sure, and I would be waiting to greet him. As I hunched under the tree, listening to every sound, the rain trickled through my short hair, down my face, following the cracks in the cam-cream and off my chin on to my gun. There was nothing else to do at times like this but think. I could drift away a little. My ears would instantly warn me of the slightest change in the routine sounds around. I had been in the SBS only a few months but my senses were already razor-sharp. There's nothing like a live ambush to bring out those old animal survival instincts we depended on so long ago to get through every day. I was virile and unpolluted.

I was the youngest and least experienced man in British special forces at that time, and that's why I was here – getting experience. I was alone, in the dark and rain, waiting for my first kill and when I thought about it, it amazed me. I was nineteen years old when I passed my special forces selection course, eleven months after joining the Royal Marines from civvy street. It is unlikely that the unusual circumstances that led me to be accepted when so young and inexperienced will be repeated.

As a boy, I thought the only special forces in the world were the US Green Berets, but that was because of a John Wayne Vietnam war movie playing in the cinemas at the time. Years later, when I was passing through Fort Bragg (a huge US Army camp in North Carolina) I walked by the Green Berets' headquarters and could not believe my eyes. Right outside the building's front doors was a larger than life-sized bronze statue of John Wayne dressed as a Green Beret. He had never been in special forces. I wondered if they had to get permission from Hollywood to build it.

I had no military ambitions when I was a kid other than playing war-games with Airfix tanks and soldiers on my bedroom floor. I enjoyed military history, mostly of the Second World War, and knew most of the major events of that war, but I knew nothing about the modern military and its equipment, even though the Vietnam War was often in the newspapers. I lived in Battersea with my father in a flat on the eighth floor of a council block that overlooked London. We were close to the railways that passed through Clapham Junction. A train rattled by at least once a minute, hardly noticed after a while unless there was a tense, silent moment in a TV drama. Up until moving to Battersea I had spent the first ten years of my life in a Roman Catholic orphanage run by nuns in Mill Hill in north London. My mother had died a few months after I was born. My father wanted to get away from everything that reminded him of her and so he placed me in the orphanage and took a job aboard a merchant ship bound for Australia. He had been with my mother for ten years, meeting her not long after losing all his wealth, which was rumoured to have been a considerable amount of money, in a business venture. He never told me much about her, or about any other of my relatives I had never seen. All he ever did say was that he was simply a peasant who worked hard for what he had made for himself, and that my mother was the illegitimate daughter of a Welsh nobleman. That has always been the source of some curiosity for me, wondering who my grandfather was. My mother was a beautiful woman and in her photographs with me looks composed and dignified, if a little sad. Perhaps she knew she was dying.

When my father returned from his travels he got a job working nights as a waiter in a hotel on Park Lane. When I came to live with him at age ten, he kept the same job and so I never saw much of him. He usually came home in the early hours, often a little drunk, and went into his room. I got myself up in the mornings, made myself breakfast and ironed my school clothes. When I came home in the evenings he had usually already gone to work. I would make myself supper if he had not left some out for me, which he often did. I would watch TV after homework then put myself to bed. That was my routine for many of my school years. There was a bad patch when I would head out on to the streets at night to get up to no good with school friends – bunking into the pictures or hanging around amusement arcades to fiddle money out of the machines. When I was fifteen I crept into Battersea Park late one night with four friends. Each of us had a brand new air pistol. While we were assassinating passing umbrellas from behind the park fence and coldly executing tramps, someone called the police and reported that there were 'men with pistols' in the park. Things were just beginning to heat up in Northern Ireland at that time with the introduction of Internment, the first British soldier had been killed (by a Protestant), the IRA had begun a serious bombing campaign and had also taken to shooting off-duty soldiers out on the town getting drunk. But I was oblivious to all that. I was also unaware that the police had arrived in force and were lying in wait for us at various points outside the park. As we jumped the fence to go home they sprang at us from all directions. They must have been wearing bullet-proof jackets under their coats because they looked heavy and cumbersome as they charged us, caps in one hand and radios in the other. I was swift and reckless in my efforts to avoid being caught and ran blindly across a busy road to escape, sprinting through the familiar back-streets, pausing to make sure I was not followed, before finally going home. I was the only one to escape.

However, I was grassed on by one of the others and picked up by the police as I arrived at school the following day. I spent half that day in a cell waiting for my father to come and get me. He was not all that angry and most of his lecturing was done at the police station for the benefit of the police. Not that he didn't mean every word of it. He knew I was not a bad kid at heart. Petty things seemed to upset him more, like making holes in the knees of my trousers. After I did that to my first new pair within a few days of having them, it was all second-hand clothes from then on. The air pistol incident put an end to my night activities and, although I had lied to the police that I had ditched it as I ran from them, I threw it away the next day anyway. I could not have imagined that only a few years later I would embark on a career that would see me operating mostly in the dark hours and carrying weapons many times more lethal than that air pistol.

I stayed at home in the evenings after that. I had few friends anyway and no money. I went to an all-boys' school, William Blake Secondary Modern, which was only a mile and a half from my home. I was not into football – I have never liked crowds – and I could not afford to keep up with clothing fashions which seemed to be the main interests of most of the boys in my year: Ben Sherman button-down collar shirts, stay-pressed, two-tone trousers and tasselled loafers. The group I hung out with most were five Jamaicans. It probably appeared to others, the white boys in my school in particular, that what I had in common with them was a lack of money. The truth was the six of us shared a pleasure for extreme mischievousness.

Our everyday aim was to get one another into trouble, and the deeper and more serious the better. While passing through shops one of us might slip something into another's bag or pocket in the hope they would be caught by the store detective for shoplifting. On one occasion we were having lunch in a pizza restaurant and, after the meal, I collected all the money we had between us and went to pay the bill. Moments later they saw me outside, across the street, waving and holding up the money with a sadistic grin. Naturally, on my way out I had told the lady at the cash register that the others did not have any money and she should warn the manager. It was entertaining watching them scramble out of the place, under and over tables while dodging the manager and staff. When we travelled on the underground, none of us would buy a ticket. On reaching our destination, when the automatic tube doors opened, there was a frantic, jungle-rules sprint from the platform, up the escalators and along the crowded corridors. Just before the ticket collector, the leaders slowed to a walk so as not to attract undue attention then jostled for position to get through the gate.

The first through the narrow opening would indicate the one behind, saying, 'He's got the tickets.'

The following person would say the same, and so on, until the ticket collector cottoned on and made a grab for us. The first three usually had the best chance of getting through. If you had not passed through the gate by the time the game was rumbled, you had to run back down and take a train to the next station and try again. If you were caught, it meant being taken to the station office and your parents or the school were contacted. I was blessed with a set of powerful legs and always managed to be one of the first to the ticket collector and was never caught.

In the five years I spent at that school, apart from an Irish and a Polish boy I was friends with, the Jamaicans were the only boys who invited me to their homes for supper with their families. They also liked to come around to my house for a bite to eat because of the food I always had available. At that time, I thought most people, except my poorer friends, ate smoked salmon, pheasant, and rump steak – food my father always brought home from the fine hotel kitchens.

I did not know a single girl by name during my school years. I had not even spoken to one until my last year and that was a few fumbled sentences after she was introduced to me by her brother outside school one day. They were alien to me and gorgeous and I watched them from afar. In that last year, I had the confidence to be head boy of the school but not enough to walk up to a girl and introduce myself.

There were two reasons why one day, at eighteen years old, I decided to catch a bus to Kilburn and London's military careers offices. Firstly, the two dustmen who collected the rubbish from my council estate had engineering degrees and could not get better paying jobs, which made college seem a waste of time to me. Secondly, my relationship with my father was deteriorating and I felt I could no longer live at home. By that time I had finally lost my virginity to a girl from Tooting Bec who had picked me up off a street in France, which perhaps helped make me feel a bit more manly. That trip was my first time abroad. I was sixteen and with my Irish friend, Patrick. He was an artist, sensitive, somewhat frail, though by no means a wimp, and as penniless as I was. We owned bicycles we had built out of second-hand parts and had scraped up enough money, or so we thought, whilst working over the first part of the school holidays, for a two-week cycling trip across western Europe. We visited First and Second World War battlefields in Belgium and France, with a brief stop at Waterloo. By the time we reached Strasbourg we were very short of money, though that didn't faze us. I suppose it was because we were always short of money. To add to our problems, our bikes were vandalised by the Alsatian French. Patrick had covered both our bicycles in detailed miniatures of his favourite subject, the World War Two German war machine, which included details of its hardware and emblems of some of its infamous fighting divisions. Not very smart, but then we did not really under-stand what that war had meant to so many people. We did a bit of shoplifting for food, feeling a little justified since it was the locals who had wrecked our transport. Our luck changed when we were picked up by a couple of English girls in a car on their way back to London having just toured France themselves. The driver fancied Patrick, which left me in the back seat with the girl from Tooting Bec who was slight and pretty. In such close proximity, wedged between baggage and blankets for many hours, I discovered that women could bring out the very best of my wit and entertainment, and that there were heavenly rewards for making them laugh.

I stepped off the bus in Kilburn and headed for the RAF Careers Office. I fancied myself as a fighter pilot after reading a RAF newspaper advertisement and discovering that I had the minimum educational requirements to join, but as I walked around the elaborate showroom nothing sparked in me and my interest dwindled. I left the building and headed down the street wondering 'What now?' Then I saw the little Royal Marines Careers Office.

I stopped at the window to stare at the action-packed posters. I had heard the Marines were some of the toughest and most highly trained soldiers in the world – that was all I knew about them. I began to wonder, if I could get through the training, whether it might do me some good and I could see the world for a few years, after which things might be a little better on the home front. Curiosity nudged me forward and I stepped into the building to look around. The marketing frills were nowhere near as elaborate as in the RAF office. Perhaps that's why I felt more comfortable there. A pleasant old Marine in uniform – a sergeant – approached me and began to chat with me about the job. Before long, I was sitting opposite him at his desk filling out an application form. It was a spontaneous move and I felt strangely free from any doubt. The size of the step I was taking had little effect on me. I would have put more time and consideration into buying a new pair of running shoes.

One of the last things he asked me was, 'Do you think you're fit, lad?'

I had a green belt in judo by then and attended regular classes. When I answered yes he chuckled, as if he knew something I did not. It was a long time before a Royal

Marine sergeant was to be quite so pleasant and cordial to me again.

There was one thing that worried me about joining the Marines, and it was not a small problem either. I thought of myself as something of a coward. There was no one I could discuss it with, nor did I want to. I would get scared before a fight, and when I dreamed of being in one I moved as if knee-deep in mud while the other person pounded me relentlessly. Dare-devil stunts didn't worry me as long as I did not pause to think about them. I once somersaulted from the highest diving board in Crystal Palace without any coaching (I landed badly and burst an eardrum that day) and I performed mindless Evil Knievel-style jumps and crashes on my bike, but the threat of a fist-fight made me go shamefully weak. My strength would drain before it began.

One day at school, my cowardice became public knowledge when I lost control when confronted by a class-mate and I ran away. I didn't stop and continued out through the school gates and down the street. By the time I slowed to a walk I hated myself completely. I could never go back. It was the worst feeling I had ever experienced. As I walked the streets the self-loathing got a desperate hold of me. I have never felt more alone in the world than on that day. What was wrong with me, I wondered? What exactly was I afraid of? I knew so many boys who seemed completely fearless when it came to fighting. How had I ended up with this disability? I had other fears, normal ones it seemed, such as fear of the dark and close confinement. I knew I had to do something about this one though, but what? How do you deal with cowardice?

I took a long and different route home that afternoon while I thought about it. My route led me past a rival school which was emptying out for the day. I was wearing my school blazer and it was not long before I heard a shout, 'There's a Bill Blakey.'

I instantly knew this meant trouble, but something kept me from running. I don't remember making a conscious decision to stay. They were far enough away at first for me to get away. But I walked on, aware they were running towards my back. Perhaps I wanted to punish myself. I had run away enough that day.

They soon arrived and quickly crowded around me, six or seven boys of about my own age, pushing and shoving me between them. I did not say a word. The first punch came and then it quickly escalated into a frenzy of kicks, punches and karate techniques learned from movies. I tried to cover myself as the blows rained down. It seemed to go on for a long time, but it was probably less than a minute.

'Why don't you run?' a voice asked.

When they finally stopped hitting me they ran away laughing. I lowered my trembling hands, trying to shake off the mild concussion and ignore the bruises that felt like they were all over me. I was in pain, but it actually had not been so bad. I took a few deep breaths and walked on. Then I heard shouts and the sound of running. They were coming back. It had obviously been too entertaining for them and they were not fully satisfied. Again I refused to run. I covered myself as the kicks and punches came, with more confidence and enthusiasm this time. I felt fists come through my hands and wallop my face – someone was chopping my neck repeatedly. I could not protect my sides. I had to keep one hand over my balls as someone was repeatedly trying to kick them. There was a general effort to get me down on the ground, and although I was not defending myself I backed up against a wall and had no intention of going down. Perhaps it was my judo skills that kept me on my feet. They broke off and ran away again, but they were soon back. This routine of breaking off the attack and coming back to resume the punching and kicking went on a few more times, I don't remember how many, until they finally left me alone.

I arrived home battered and shaken with my clothes torn in several places. I was not crying, but I wanted to. I was bleeding from cuts and welts all over. My knuckles were skinless from protecting myself. A couple of my teeth were loose and my lips were cut in several places. I think my nose was broken, but I was never sure, and my jaw felt the same, but it was not. My father had already left for work, which was a relief. I did not want to talk to anyone. I set about cleaning myself up.

I was a dab hand at sewing by then and did a pretty good job fixing my torn clothes. But as I put myself back together I felt neither cleansed nor braver. I did note, however, that the body can take a great deal of punishment. It became obvious to me I had to fix my mind, not punish my body. I suppose I was not too bright to go to such lengths to come to such a basic conclusion, but even by going the long way around, I was finding the answers to some questions in life by myself, and that was the whole point, wasn't it? But solving this one was not going to be easy. How do you correct the feeling of being a coward? I wish I had known then how much I was trying to rush things. I was so eager to get out of this irritating stage of life and on to the next. I had no way of knowing it was life's experiences that formed certain parts of a person's character. But I also later learned, as a special forces operative, that a little bit of cowardice – or fear, as I later came to recognise it – was not altogether a bad thing.

The following morning, although I was stiff and bruised, I did not feel all that bad physically, and mentally OK to go to school. My father was asleep and I left the house without him seeing me. As I walked down the road I recognised one of my assailants from the previous day coming towards me. I locked my eyes on him, but nothing stirred in me – no hate or anger. About twenty yards away he recognised me. He was alone and I felt strangely superior to him. If he and five or six of his friends could not break me he did not have a chance alone. He must have come to the same conclusion because he ran across the road through busy traffic to avoid me. It was obvious who the greater coward was and I ignored him.

A month or so after my interview at the Royal Marines Careers Office a letter arrived addressed to me headed Her Majesty's Royal Marines. It was the first letter I had ever received and it contained joining instructions typed on military paper and a railway pass. In six months I was to report to the Royal Marine pre-commando training depot at Deal in Kent. I immediately felt butterflies in my stomach. I was really going to do it. I don't think a day went by when I did not look at that letter on my bedside table. I had left school by then and so, to pass the time, I took a job in a Mayfair hotel as a ledger clerk.

I was four months short of my nineteenth birthday when I stepped on to the train at Charing Cross Station carrying a small suitcase. I had said goodbye to my father at home. He gave me an awkward hug and wished me luck. I think he was about as surprised at me joining the Marines as I was. I still knew nothing about what I was getting into. I had not received any instructions other than where to report – no programme, no descriptions, no list of requirements, nothing. I had not even bothered to find out any more about the Marines. All I knew was what I saw on their posters – they wore green berets and cam-cream. I felt I was embarking on a journey to a new world and I did not have a clue what to expect.

On the train I picked up a discarded newspaper to pass the time. The first article I read was about the North Sea and the huge oil and gas fields that were opening up there. Oil company executives were worried about where they were going to find the divers they needed to work on the platforms. The North Sea offers some of the worst diving conditions in the world because of the cold and constant storms. The thought of being a deep-sea diver one day appealed to me, but I had no idea there were other implications in that article that, six months later, would change my life.

I walked through the train to see if I could spot other likely recruits. I had this idea that I was not quite big enough for the commandos even though I'd been selected to try them out. I counted half a dozen who fitted my picture of a Marine, all much bigger and harder looking than me.

When the train finally stopped at Deal, I stepped off it and headed along the platform to where a large Royal Marine corporal was barking for recruits to come forward and hand him their joining papers. I merged with the converging crowd of young men and held up mine. Those around me looked like boys too and were all shapes and sizes. I don't think any of the men I had selected on the train were amongst them. I did not realise the corporal was reaching for my papers and that my hand was drifting away from his as I looked around. He lunged forward, snatched my papers then lowered his face inches from mine.

'You little germ,' he said, as bits of spittle hit my face. 'You just went to the top of my list to straighten out – if you make it through today that is.'

He kept glaring at me as he collected the rest of the papers. I was already a marked man.

Seventy-eight of us piled into the back of several four-ton trucks outside the station and we headed for the camp. As we drove through the town I looked out the back down on to the ordinary people in the streets going about their everyday lives. I felt different from them, as if I was off to serve some kind of sentence. For all that, it did not seem as if I was in the wrong place. I didn't want to be anyone other than myself at that moment. I found the whole experience fascinating and that fascination stayed with me throughout my career. No matter where I went or who I met, even the rich or famous with their fancy lifestyles, I knew they did not envy me, but nor did I them, not when all was totalled up. Today, when I smell diesel exhaust fumes, I often have flashes of those early days in training as a young man riding in the back of a four-tonner, and inside I smile.

When we arrived at Deal camp we piled out of the trucks and were shouted at by half-a-dozen Marine instructors to form ranks and march. This was our first attempt at anything military and of course we were useless. I was still curious about my new-found colleagues, many of whom did not look like my idea of a Royal Marine Commando. It seemed obvious to me that many would fail and I wondered what would make them quit. I never wondered that about myself. It's not that I had made any deep pledge to myself not to quit, or that I was gung-ho and consciously determined to pass. I just never considered it, nor did I think for a second about what I would do if I failed. I felt as though I was there to observe the Marine Commando course even though I was taking part. I had always felt like I was on the periphery and looking in, and this was no different. I would be there at the end, simple as that.

The first man to quit, about two hours after we arrived, had had his hair cut and styled early that morning in an expensive London salon, presumably believing the Marines would be so impressed with his coiffure that they would bend the rules. The recruit's hair was heavily bonded together with hairspray and I watched the camp barber as he gleefully concentrated on the job of clipping the recruit's hair off in one solid, helmet-shaped piece. He got half of it off before it dropped to the floor and lay there like a bird's nest. The recruit walked out of the barber's shop and straight out of the camp. The next two quitters walked out of the main auditorium a few hours later in the middle of the camp commander's welcome speech. He told us that one of us in the room would be likely to be killed somewhere in the world in the next three years if we passed through training. It seemed there were some recruits who knew less about the Marines than I did. I at least had accepted that, being soldiers, they did, on occasion, die.

During the first two weeks, if we were not doing educational and medical tests, we were sprinting up and down the gym, climbing ropes, or in the barracks-room (grots) learning boot and brass-buckle cleaning, and for some, basic personal hygiene. The Royal Marines were part of the Navy and Navy hygiene was of the highest order. Early morning shaves in the surf on the beach was a favourite way the instructors had to make that point, and those recruits who did not have facial hair had to practise for when they did. Locals passing by appeared to think nothing of seeing a bunch of recruits attempting to shave as the cold waves broke over their heads.

One day I was sprinting through the camp alone to join my troop after having been for a medical examination – recruits ran everywhere or stood to attention, there was no in between. Up ahead I saw a Marine walking towards me in full dress uniform. I was not sure what to do as I sped towards him. We had not been allowed to go anywhere by ourselves as yet and were marched everywhere as a squad. If we passed an officer the squad was ordered to give an 'Eyes right!' We had not been taught how to salute yet.

I didn't want to make a mistake and so I rehearsed it quickly in my mind. As I closed on him I hit the brakes stopping a few feet short of him, came to attention smartly and gave him a stiff salute.

He brushed passed without returning my salute and said, 'Don't salute me, you wanker, I'm just a corporal. And anyway that's how the Yanks do it.'

The purpose of the first two weeks of training was to get rid of the dead wood, and this they did. We were down to about fifty-five recruits when we climbed aboard the four-tonners to leave Deal, this time in uniform, with blue recruit berets (the green ones were presented only to those who passed selection) and heavy boots, carrying sausage-bags filled with our new military kit (we didn't have rifles yet, we hadn't even held one). We were bound for the main Commando Training Centre (CTC) in Lympstone, near Exmouth in Devon. Mine was one of the last troops to do their first two weeks in Deal. The next time I saw the camp at Deal was in photographs several years later, after an IRA bomb exploded there killing ten Royal Marine bandsmen.

Whereas Deal was old and steeped in Naval history, CTC was a huge, modern military complex more like a small town. My first morning there, whilst heading across the camp for breakfast, I reached the top of a wide flight of stairs and found myself at the back of a large crowd of recruits which was only part of a very long, broad queue waiting to enter the galley. There were over two thousand recruits in CTC and nearly every one of them was here in front of me anxiously waiting to shove cereal, fried eggs, beans and sausages down their throats before the long day's workload. It was an impressive sight to see that number of soldiers, and I was just a little speck amongst them. It turned out that the queue was unusual – the duty chef had either lost the keys to the main entrance to the galley or forgotten to open the doors. Someone at the front of the queue started to *baa* like a sheep, and soon everyone joined in. We all *baaed* as loud as we could, all two thousand of us. It was strange to think that only about a third of us would survive the course to wear the coveted green beret. The NCOs and officers, chomping in their own messes, must have wondered what the hell was going on.

When a new troop arrives at CTC to begin the commando training course it begins at the bottom of a ladder, each rung representing two weeks of the twenty-four-week course (twenty-six in total, counting Deal).

This course is for senior recruits, those of seventeen and a half and older. Junior recruits, those who join at sixteen, do a slightly different, extended commando course because they cannot join a regular fighting unit until they are eighteen. As each troop is two weeks apart, the previous troop becomes that much more senior. Whatever the troop ahead of yours is doing that day, your troop will be doing in two weeks' time, and the troop behind you is doing what you did two weeks ago.

When the troop ahead was seen returning to camp filthy and exhausted having been away for a gruelling week somewhere you knew you had that to look forward to. On the flip-side, it was a good feeling when you came back from a week of hell and saw the faces of the troop behind yours as they watched you shuffle back to the grots.

There were six recruits to a room in CTC and when we first moved into the accommodation block we occupied thirteen rooms. Each week the number of recruits in the troop dwindled and survivors were moved to keep the rooms up to six where possible. By the end we were down to five rooms. Recruits in commando training are called noddies because of the way they tend to whip to rigid attention when questioned by an instructor and nod or shake their heads wide-eyed while they answer.

One of the instructors on our training team was a corporal named Jakers. Jakers wore a permanent scowl whenever he was around noddies and made it obvious at every opportunity that he considered us the lowest form of life. One day a handful of us were debating the characteristics of a particular military weapon while we hung around outside the NAAFI during a break, having a wet of tea.

'Ask Jakers,' one of my squaddies said as he pointed up the road ('squaddy' is a term that usually refers to regular Army soldiers, but Royal Marines also use it to describe someone who is or was in their recruit troop).

Jakers was walking down the main drag towards us. I was nudged forward to ask the question. I had already gained a reputation for repeatedly asking questions in lectures until I understood the answer, showing a confidence I never had before. I stepped forward and politely posed the question to Jakers. He didn't slow down as he glanced at me and his nose wrinkled as if I was a bad smell.

'Fuck off and talk to me when you're a Marine,' he said as he passed.

All 'green lids' (green berets – full Marines) communicated with noddies using similar courtesy. It was part of the process – a growing pain. Commando training was one huge serving of hardship with a good-sized helping of fun on the side, for those who were willing to make the best of it. Reality did raise its ugly head on occasion though.

One hot, sunny day, during a twenty-mile run/walk with rifle and full equipment while in columns of three, we passed a recruit lying still by the side of the road. He belonged to another troop up ahead doing a similar run and he was still wearing full equipment. The recruit's head was covered by a towel and he was lying on his back part way up the grass verge with one of his legs turned out in an unnaturally relaxed manner. One of his instructors stood above him holding his rifle and watched us with a blank expression as we doubled past. We all sensed the recruit was dead. I thought of the only other dead person I had ever seen, a nun back in the orphanage. She had been our English teacher. There must have been a shortage of paper in the orphanage because we used to write mostly on the back of old Christmas cards. When you went up to her desk to ask for more paper she would hastily tear a card along its crease and draw lines in pencil across the blank part for you to write on. The lines were never straight or the same distance apart and always curved down the page to the right. One morning, instead of us all walking into the classroom at the period change, we were made to line up outside. There were about twenty of us. I was about eight. None of us knew why we were lining up. We were told to be quiet. We never disobeyed the nuns. The atmosphere was grave. When we finally filed into the small classroom we saw our English teacher lying on her back on several desks that had been moved together to support her. She was at my chest height. Her eyes were closed and her hands were crossed over her chest. After passing around her we were filed back out of the room.

The Marine recruit had died of a heart attack.

When the last week of the commando course finally arrived only twenty-five out of the original seventy-eight members of my squad remained. I stood on the huge parade ground the size of several football pitches in my white pith helmet, white gloves and navy-blue uniform and a Marine band marched and played in the background. I had reached the top rung of the ladder. We were the Kings's Squad, the name given to the most senior troop in recruit training. The occasion was made more memorable by an event that had happened earlier that morning when we first arrived on the parade ground.

Discipline, especially when marching in a column of three ranks in full dress uniform, is iron in the Marines and it's instant death to turn your head, even slightly, to look at something – the white pith helmet would give the movement away. When we marched on to the parade ground that morning the whole troop was straining to look out of the corner of their eyes at something unusual parked in the middle of it. We were brought to a resounding halt, but still did not dare turn to look.

The drill instructor screamed, 'Left turn'na!'

Twenty-five men moved as one and our feet came together with a crack that could be heard across the River Exe a mile away. We had drilled throughout the six-month training course for this day, but this final week had been spent doing little else so that we would be faultless in front of Lord Louis Mountbatten, which we were. It was with some relief that we turned for we could now see what was in the centre of the parade ground.

It was a standard issue, single, wooden bed, sleeping for the use of, and there was a recruit sleeping in it in his pyjamas. During the night, members of his troop had carried his bed, with him in it, out of the grot and across camp to the parade ground without waking him. He must have had a few beers that night. He continued to sleep soundly even with all the heavy marching and yelling of orders going on around him. The drill instructors and NCOs remained poker-faced, none venturing near the recruit. They were all waiting for God to arrive on parade.

The God of any camp is not the commanding officer, as most would assume, but the Regimental Sergeant Major (RSM). He is chosen for his loud voice as well as for his immaculate bearing. Recruits cowered when he walked through the camp. He could spot a loose thread or an unpolished brass buckle at fifty yards. I was once standing with a couple of my squaddies outside the NAAFI during a break (we did a lot of that). One of them leaned back against a wall to support himself and placed a hand in his pocket.

A voice boomed from nowhere, like Zeus shouting down from Olympus. 'You, with your 'and in your pocket!'

We jerked instantly to our feet like wide-eyed chickens having just heard a fox bark. We knew instantly who it was, but we just could not see where he was.

'Christ,' one of the lads said as he indicated with a jut of his chin, 'he must be two 'undred soddin' yards away.'

There was the RSM, silhouetted against the sky way up at the other end of the main drag, standing rigid and alone in his immaculate uniform. Our instincts were to run and hide but that would have been suicide. God would find us.

'Come 'ere!' he boomed. 'At the double!'

The recruit dropped everything and ran towards the RSM as fast as he could. We watched from cover while he leaned back under the RSM's mouth and received a severe bollocking.

Looking down on the parade ground, a hundred yards away, was the officers' mess, and the RSM stepped out of it to survey his empire. Then his eyes locked on to the imperfection in the centre of it. If the camp was the RSM's domain, the parade ground was his hallowed plot. There was no power on earth to help you if you desecrated this piece of terra firma. Everyone watched motionless – if you moved a finger of your white-gloved hand he would spot it, then you might as well faint and take your chances with a medical examination. There must have been 200 Marines frozen solid. If it suddenly poured down and lightning struck the parade ground no one would have moved.

The RSM marched slowly down the gravel path from the mess, digging his heels in, his cane in his left hand swinging parallel with the ground. The Royal Marines have a unique march in the British military. Whereas the rest of the Army, Navy and Air Force, without exception, march in a brisk, tick-tock fashion that looks like a speeded-up silent movie, the Marines march much more slowly with a longer pace and a proud, historically earned swagger. That is why Royal Marines rarely integrate with other branches of the armed forces while marching. Marines arrive at the same time as everyone else, they just do it with more panache.

The RSM came to a smart halt on the edge of the parade ground and stood staring at the bed some fifty yards away.

'Who's sleeping on my fucking parade ground?!'

No one moved except the recruit, who turned in his sleep to get more comfortable. The RSM developed a terrible grimace and marched towards the bed. The clip of his heels echoed as they cut into the ground. I started to feel sorry for the noddy curled up in his bed. The RSM halted by the bed and glared down at the recruit all snuggled up.

'WAKE UP!' he yelled with all his vast might.

The recruit sat bolt upright and for a second had no idea where on the planet he was.

'Your fucking grot not spacious enough for you, then?' boomed the RSM.

If there was ever a man who wished the world would swallow him up it was that recruit.

'Get that bed off my parade ground, you maggot . . . NOW!'

The recruit fell out of the bed and started to drag it away as fast as he could.

'Don't you make a scratch on my floor or you'll spend what career you 'ave left re-tarmacking it!'

The recruit struggled to lift the bed and carry it off. That night his entire troop ran several times around the camp in full equipment, each carrying their own mattress.

Before lunchtime we were awarded our green lids and passed for duty by the Admiral of the Fleet, Lord Louis Mountbatten. My father stood amongst the other parents. It felt odd knowing he was watching me in my immaculate uniform marching as a soldier. It must have felt strange to him too. I almost hadn't called him to tell him about the pass-out parade. It was as if this was my new world, my new life, and I did not want him to be a part of it.

The RSM, naturally, had the last words before we marched off the parade ground as he shouted the immortal phrase, 'Royal Marines! To your duties, quick march!'

My green beret felt good on my head. But I did not

quite feel like a Marine Commando. That would come when I could make important decisions on my own. There were still many things inside my head I had to straighten out. Only a month earlier my section of ten noddies had been spread out in arrow-head formation headed up a barren, rocky slope in the middle of Dartmoor. It was past midnight and we were on an advance-to-contact patrol with live ammunition, expecting to be attacked at any time. The ground was sodden and heavily pitted as if an artillery bombardment had struck several years before. Suddenly the still, misty night erupted in explosions as simulated mortar shells flashed and boomed, tossing earth skyward all around us. A heavy machine-gun nest then began firing from the crest. The instructors supplemented the enemy attack with a continuous flow of thunderflashes (like bangers but several times more powerful), literally throwing them at us. We hit the dirt and rolled away in preparation to return fire once a fire control order was given. My ears were ringing. Our section commander for that exercise was about to direct our counter-attack when the senior instructor put his foot on the recruit's back and told him to lie still and play dead. The instructors had deliberately not told us who was second or third in command, and so for a moment no one was in command and confusion reigned. I lay there, like the others, waiting to be told what to do. Suddenly a voice boomed behind me.

'You! Yes, you. You're in command.'

He emphasised the order with a thunderflash that bounced off my back to explode only feet in front of me, forcing me to roll away as I tried to gather my thoughts.

It seemed to take me ages to recall the sequence of orders and considerations when under attack. We had practised it often on the camp sports field or on Woodbury Common in daylight with blank ammo, but never under these conditions. I stretched my neck to see where everyone was.

'Get your 'ead down!' shouted the instructor.

'Gun group, go left!' I yelled.

'They've gone left,' he continued angrily as he towered directly behind me. 'Move your fuckin' self! Your men are dyin' out here!'

I squinted ahead to look for the enemy position so that I could give a fire control order.

'Section. Pile of rocks . . . !'

'Which pile of rocks, moron?' The instructor was causing me more stress than the guns and explosions.

'To your front,' I shouted. 'Three hundred metres!'

'Bollocks. It's less than two!'

'Section! Rapid f . . .' Before I could get out the word 'fire' the instructor shouted above my voice.

'Cancel that!' Then crouching closer to make his dark words penetrate further. 'You waste of fucking space. God help any section you ever command . . . Harris! Take over.'

I numbly joined the others to assault the enemy position. All I could think of was what a useless bastard I had been. The instructor knew exactly what he was doing, though. The Royal Marines had been churning out professional soldiers for over 300 years. He knew that making a fool of me and letting me see myself fumble under pressure would rile me enough to make sure it never happened again. Several years later, while on my junior command course, seventy-five of us were lined up in a ditch in full combat gear waiting to mount a sweep through a forest at the end of a heavy five-minute bombardment. The instructors had given each of the seven sections orders, but had omitted to select an overall commander to launch the attack. That was only apparent when the deathly silence fell after the bombardment and no one moved. It felt like a scene from World War One – waiting to go over the top. But there were no officers to lead the charge. I had never forgotten my pathetic effort in training. Once I realised no one else was going to, I jumped up on to the lip of the ditch and shouted for each section commander to advance his men in staggered formation. Then I turned and led them into the wood. Although it was just an exercise I knew I would have done it for real. I had notched up another lesson in life. Whenever you drop down, and the odds are you will once in a while, use it to bounce yourself back even higher. But I was never destined to lead a section of soldiers into a battle like that. During my career in the British military, my involvement in every conflict would be in small teams, pairs, or alone.

After the pass-out parade I walked up to my father feeling a little awkward, as he had never seen me in uniform before. When I got to him, the way he greeted me, I suddenly felt like a schoolboy again. He forced a smile and nodded his understanding of the whole cha-rade then immediately moved on to the subject of times of buses and trains back to London. He never asked what the training was like, or where was I headed next. He wasn't deliberately trying to be mean. That's just the way he was. Why did I think my new experiences would change him at all?

2

The second night I waited for O'Sally and his partner to appear, the wind had picked up. I was disappointed they had not showed the night before. Another lesson. Never expect. Patience is a special forces operative's most important virtue, something I for one was not born with. Recognising its importance was easy. Nurturing it into a quality was hard. I was helped along by knowing the odds on them turning up tonight were now greater. I would wait quietly.

As the wind blew erratically through the farm, causing noise and movement, it allowed me to shift my weight a little, which gave my aching backside some relief. But I was paying a price for that added comfort I had wished for. I had lost some of my advantage. The wind meant O'Sally could get closer before I could hear him. Swaying branches were no longer a warning signal. A new noise no longer proved life was close by. The ground around the old farm was littered with obstacles big enough for O'Sally to sneak up to and hide behind. There were piles of rubbish and foliage, pieces of rusting farm equipment and dozens of bushes and trees. A low stone wall came out from the far corner of the house and curved in a dog-leg in front of me. It would be possible for O'Sally to crawl close to my position behind the wall without me seeing or hearing him. A loose object was now constantly banging against one side of the building, like a hinged shutter. I thought through the several possible scenarios that could happen.

The most important thing of all was not only did I have to get off the first shot, it had to kill O'Sally instantly, otherwise, even peppered with bullets, if he was not dead he would hang on to that trigger, set to full-automatic, and spray everything in front of him as he went down. Twenty bullets his magazine held, and it only needed one to hit me. The high velocity of an M16 bullet meant it would make a pinhole puncture in the front of a man and an exit hole the size of a frying pan in his back. That was the main difference between low and high velocity bullets if they hit you. If I did get O'Sally, what about the other man? He would no doubt be several yards behind and would likely bolt the instant there was trouble. I wondered if I should chase him, and if so, how far? Obviously not at all if he headed around to the front of the house, because the SAS lad would destroy him. I could not pursue him far into the fields either because of the danger of running into other special forces in the area. That could prove lethal for the hound as well as the fox.

We were not always briefed on minor details. I was

expected to work out the finer points and make decisions for myself. Regular soldiers are told when to eat, sleep and take a shit. Special forces are given the mission objective and expected to succeed in the best way they see fit, drawing from their experience. But I did not have any. There must have been a reason that the powers that be had decided I would make the right choice. I did prefer to think for myself. I had been doing it since I could remember. I just had to make sure no one else suffered because of my inexperience. I would be the only one to pay the price tonight if I screwed up. But if I could bag O'Sally and his partner, that would be an experience. Then again, killing people did not make you any better at it. Training did that. Every operative in special forces wants that first kill. It's like a baby touching heat – you don't really know what it's like until you do. Afterwards, you either get less sensitive to it or are disgusted by it. I decided I would leave the second man if he ran. He was not the priority; he wasn't even significant. It was the tout-maker who wanted him killed anyway, and I didn't know why. He had given what was called a 'Becket Approval'.*

Tout-makers (handlers they are also called) were a curious breed. This was the only one I met in all my years in the job. His user-name was Mr Tallyho. Like just

---

* The expression comes from mediaeval times when Henry II, frustrated by Thomas à Becket, the Archbishop of Canterbury, made it clear that his own life would be less complicated if the Bishop were dead. It's been a popular form of delegation for people in power ever since.

about everybody in his department, he was a grey, insignificant man, unhealthy-looking, sharp and skittish. He chain-smoked, looked as if he drank too much too often (though I never saw him even slightly drunk), wore a drab suit under a grey coat and sometimes reacted to sudden noises with a flinch. His nerves were somewhat frayed, and understandably so. Tout-makers have the riskiest job in the whole crazy business. They are usually recruited from Military Intelligence, some from the old SIS. They come out of the same school as the Cold War spy-makers. But theirs was a far more dangerous game in Northern Ireland. When handlers recruited foreign spies it was like a chess game and few died as a result. Recruiting an IRA terrorist is like trying to make an ally out of a vicious dog. You never know if it's your hand he's suddenly going to bite. Most IRA touts working for Military Intelligence are pressured into it in much the same way as criminals are offered deals by the civilian police in exchange for information. Others are offered hard cash.

The IRA touts who operate purely for money are generally the most reliable. They are harder for their own people to detect and their information is more trustworthy. Information from these sources is often bought by the pound, the price dependent on its quality. The difficulty for the tout-maker is identifying the men and women who will sell his or her principles for a foreign bank account and eventually a new life somewhere. Recruiting is a risky business for both sides. Finding such people is the tout-maker's job. Who he decides to recruit often depends on a compilation of detailed profiles, educated guesses and luck. The more senior the IRA recruit, the better the quality of information, but the greater the risk for the tout-maker – the IRA would not miss an opportunity to misinform, capture or kill one of them.

First contact with the proposed tout-to-be is the most nerve-racking and dangerous phase. The tout-maker usually has an armed driver who covers his route in and out, but he nearly always makes the actual rendezvous alone and often unarmed so as not to unnerve the potential recruit. The meeting places are, naturally, secluded spots – sometimes even in other countries. The tout-maker is entirely vulnerable to entrapment. He must wonder if he has chosen the target well. Is the recruit truly greedy enough to risk his life to sell out his brothers in the IRA? What if the recruit has a change of heart at the last minute? If the tout is ever found out he can expect to be tortured, then executed. The tout-maker's greatest worry as he approaches this first meet has to be, is it a set-up? He arrives at every rendezvous like a bullfighter, but without a cape to hide behind or a sword to fight back with. He walks up to the bull, stands in front of it in his worn patent-leather shoes and drab raincoat, looks it straight in the eye and makes a deal. The things that must go through his mind as he approaches the rendezvous point would be enough to make a lesser man run screaming for his life. Many end up with shot nerves after only a few years at the front. No one knows how many tout-makers have been killed or have disappeared without trace over the years. They don't officially exist, in life or in death, not in their true capacity. But there is always paperwork. Even top secret operations are documented. There has to be a report, official and unofficial. The official report that ends up in the newspapers might read something like: 'An off-duty army officer was found dead last night shortly after he was seen leaving a popular pub . . .'

When the IRA recruit's first deal has been sealed he or she becomes a 'client'. The tout-maker then keeps in constant touch, mothering him, seeing to all his needs, counselling him, becoming as close to him as possible, assessing the information and constantly squeezing for more. Every tout has a 'career', a length of usefulness, and although most are short term in the scheme of things, the IRA has always been plagued by the suspicion of a high-ranking mole within its organisation, even today. The rumour alone does damage. I heard there were two.

If an operation is concluded with the help of a tout, that tout's cover is most often 'blown' as a result, or is usually considered so. The tout is given the opportunity to move into a protection programme which means money and a new life, often in a different country. Most touts do very well out of the deal, which is what attracts them, and the rumours help to create more touts. But sometimes the tout gets greedy or is suspected of being a double agent, his information becomes dubious and he must be considered a threat to operations and to the tout-maker himself. If a tout finds himself in such a situation he is in danger from all sides.

I had spent the final hours of the first night's ambush desperate to pee but not daring to move, and so before this night's ambush I drank very little and did not eat much, either, because that would have made me thirsty.

It was colder now that the wind had picked up and I became hungry. I did not reach into my pocket for a bit of nutty (chocolate) in case O'Sally stepped into view right at that second. I would lose the draw. He was too deadly to take chances like that. He knew what it was like to kill a man.

Revulsion and fascination are the primary reactions to taking a life. If an operative discovers it to be revolting, he need not expose himself to it again and can quit. If he remains in the unit after taking a life it would suggest he is prepared to kill again. Most men who have ended a career in special forces without at least once being involved in a deadly conflict regret it to some extent.

O'Sally was more than fascinated with killing. He was an enthusiast. We had a few of our own just like him. I wondered how I would react when it was over – I did not expect to lose the conflict.

As for my fear, I knew I was on the road to controlling it when I began dreaming of meeting a would-be aggressor head on instead of letting my fear get a hold of me. I rarely fought as in quicksand any more. The reason behind the change was that I discovered I could re-programme my default instincts by constantly daydreaming of specific dramatic situations and seeing myself react the way I thought I should or wanted to. When the reactions spilled over into my dreams, the windows into one's true personality, I knew I was succeeding. I was pleased there was a way of changing things I did not like about myself. The first dream I can remember having of killing a man was while asleep back in the hide during the O'Sally ambush. It was a dream in which I killed O'Sally. But it wasn't an easy kill. I still moved somewhat sluggishly, whereas O'Sally was slick and efficient. But somehow I beat him to the aim, and, although he fired too, as I squeezed the trigger I ran towards him like a madman and destroyed him from feet away. After he was dead I was not revolted by it. When the day finally came for me to touch the candle, I took two lives at the same time and rarely ever think about it, and when I do I am not revolted.

I wondered how my SAS partner was doing at the front of the farmhouse. We'd hardly spoken in the two days we had been together in the hide. In fact about the only words we ever did say to each other were, 'It's your watch.'

It was an odd relationship. Two strangers waiting to kill two strangers.

In the hide we took it in turns in four-hour stints to sleep while the other kept watch. When we were not sleeping we ate or read a book. We could not leave the hide during daylight. We peed into an old gallon milk container, and crapped into plastic bags. The urine we could empty out on our way to the ambush, but there was nowhere secure to dump the bags of shit en route so we kept them in the hide to take back to the camp after the op. On extended jobs, where a food drop was required, the shit bags were handed over in exchange for the food.

My SAS partner was not the talkative type, but I

assumed his lack of conversation also had to do with toeing the SAS party line. There was animosity between the two special forces groups. We felt the SAS were planning to take over our area of operations, which was the sea, coastlines and hinterland, and they did not want us even thinking about muscling in on theirs. The SBS were growing fast in size and ability and there were overlaps between the two units in several arenas. Both units felt threatened, and their feelings were justified.

For the SBS, rumours had been flying around that the Royal Marines were being considered for the chop. The Ministry of Defence was planning to disband the oldest and most battle-honoured regiment in the world. If the Marines were disbanded, then so would be the SBS, as we drew our manpower solely from the Marine commando units. An intervention by Lord Mountbatten apparently saved the Marines. Once the Marines were secure for the immediate future, the SBS had to move to establish themselves. Not only was terrorism on the rise, but in conventional warfare special forces were still highly favoured. The obvious arena for the SBS was everything to do with the sea, rivers and coastal areas. The SAS were well established and completely secure compared to us, but our growth was evident and we were already competing for jobs. It was like a corporate war between us.

One thing the SAS were a little concerned about was that the 'A' in Special Air Service looked like it was fast becoming obsolete and the 'B' in Special Boat Squadron was coming into its own very strongly (a more broadly descriptive name for us might be Special Water Squadron). The sea had long ago been the element to control, but after World War Two the skies became the most favoured territory for special forces infiltration. Parachuting was easy, quick and somewhat clandestine. But by now, even the smallest banana republic had radar sensitive enough to detect a plane dropping parachutists. Not even the most sophisticated powers can watch every inch of its coastline. Smugglers can attest to that.

As if to aggravate the SAS further, the SBS made a point of training themselves in the art of HALO (high altitude low opening) jumping, but it was not to irritate the SAS. Parachuting into the sea to rendezvous with a ship or submarine was a viable stealthy option.

After decades of relative stagnancy, the SBS wanted to become the foremost special forces unit. But we had a long way to go before London would take us seriously enough to risk using us on anything important. As for being first into action ahead of the SAS, our only chance, it seemed, would be if the operation was completely water orientated. But even then it was not a foregone conclusion that we would be selected.

On a more local note, a reason the SAS were a tad upset with us at that time in Northern Ireland was because we had almost caused them a major embarrassment. Some months earlier, during a previous SAS tour without the SBS, an SAS team had gone for a long walk over the border into the Irish Republic. It was not their first such venture, but this time they were caught by the (Southern) Irish police, which caused a little 'incident' between the two governments. The SAS did not want to admit they had got lost, but then could not explain what they were doing invading the South. Wrists were slapped and the SAS were warned not to do it again. The Irish government was concerned on more than one level, as a few years earlier two SAS troopers had popped south of the border for a private operation, a little bank robbery which they bodged up, ending up in a Dublin jail. Their commanding officer had to fly in and take them out, after which they were promptly dismissed from the service. This incident raised a laugh when it was reported in the local press.

Near the beginning of my tour, late one night, two SBS men were driving a van full of heavily armed, blacked-out SAS men to a drop-off on the Northern Irish border to watch a cross-over point. The SBS stopped the van in a dark, country lane to check the map while the SAS sergeant prepared to let his team out.

'Don't open the door,' said one of the SBS lads, 'we're not at the drop-off point.'

'Where are we, then?' asked the SAS sergeant.

'A couple of miles south of it – I think,' the SBS man replied sheepishly.

'How can we be a couple of miles south of it?' the SAS sergeant asked irritably. 'That would put us . . .'

The SAS sergeant saw his career flash before his eyes and was very precise as to the report he was going to file if the SBS did not get him and his men back into Northern Ireland as uneventfully as they had brought them out of it. After a few more wrong turns and a couple of Southern Irish villages later they arrived back in Northern Ireland without being seen. But the SBS were in the doghouse.

I never knew the exact time throughout the ambush. I could not look at my watch. In the darkness the luminous dial would appear like a beacon if I unclipped the leather flap that covered it. Boredom was making me long for the terrorists to arrive. But doubt also began to creep into my mind as time dragged on. I found myself looking for the subtle change in light on the horizon that meant dawn was coming and I could get off my damp, uncomfortable mound and walk away.

On this second night of the ambush, O'Sally did not turn up and the dawn did eventually move me on. I stood up like an old man and rubbed my stiff knee-caps and my cold, damp arse. I walked carefully out of the yard, treading slowly to reduce the sucking sound of my feet as they drew out of the mud. The same small light was on inside the house. Nothing had changed. I don't think anyone was home or had been since I first arrived. I met my SAS partner at the pre-planned location fifty yards from the farm and we trudged back to our hide. We would return the following dusk.

It was not until a few days after I had finished Marine Commando training that I saw my first Special Boat Squadron poster. It was pinned up in a hallway of the headquarters building and was a picture of two men, heavily armed and camouflaged, paddling a canoe through the jungle. The canoes were similar to the canvas and wooden types that made the SBS famous in

the Second World War, now made by Klepper, ironi-
cally a German company. The men had been called the
Cockleshell Heroes in that war (cockleshell was the
nickname for the canoe), after their most famous raid
against German merchant ships in Bordeaux, where they
placed magnetised limpet mines on the hulls below the
waterline. Out of the ten men in five canoes who went
on the operation, only two survived. Mountbatten, the
man behind those first amphibious operations, said no
attacks were more courageous or imaginative. No doubt
this was the reason he was so fond of us. Those invaders
who worked behind enemy lines in that war defined one
of the most important roles for special forces, which is
to get in close enough to accomplish what technology
cannot from a distance. The Royal Air Force had tried
repeatedly to bomb the German ships in Bordeaux and
failed. In the Gulf War the SBS carried out operations
against targets smart bombs could not find. Paddling
into harbours in little boats to blow up ships was not
a new idea for the British. The technique had first been
used over 350 years earlier.

In 1587, a year before Drake destroyed the Spanish
Armada in the English Channel, he took on an even
larger Spanish fleet while it anchored in the port of Cadiz.
On board one of Drake's ships was a sergeant (a Marine
one might say, but it was to be another seventy-seven
years before the Royal Marines were officially born)
who came up with a high-risk, low-cost plan to destroy
several Spanish ships while they lay at anchor. Drake
liked the idea and let the man go ahead. Under cover of
darkness, he rowed a small boat into the harbour and in

amongst the Spanish fleet. Between two enemy galleons, he screwed a keg of gunpowder to one just above the waterline. Unfortunately, the same choppy weather that covered his infiltration prevented him from lighting the fuse. The mission was unsuccessful, but the general idea, so imaginative and daring, was to catch on. Drake later went on to destroy the fleet anyway.

Why would the SBS use the two-man canoes in their poster nowadays, I wondered? I imagined they were a little out of date. I would eventually find out the answer for myself after spending weeks in them, often several days at a time without once getting out – cooking, eating, sleeping and evacuating from them. They can quickly be broken down and packed into bags then carried hundreds of miles to be reassembled. They move silently, can take tremendous punishment, be parachuted out of aircraft, launched from submarines in minutes, carry several hundred pounds of equipment such as explosives and are easily repaired. A heavy machine-gun can be mounted on the front and fired whilst on the move, and it can even accommodate a light mortar, positioned and fired from in between the two canoeists. They can be rigged with a sail for long sea crossings, some have been rigged with small engines, and they can carry a passenger in between the canoeists, a technique used for dropping off spies and agents during the war. Made of wood and canvas, there is still nothing to compare with them in today's hi-tech world.

Throughout my regular commando training there were wild rumours, many of them ridiculous, about that most mysterious, élite group known as the SBS.

Some suggested they were the government's top secret hit squad, others that they did not exist at all. There was always some noddy declaring how he intended joining them as soon as he had completed the minimum requirement of three years in a commando unit. The ones who bragged about it never seemed to carry out their boast. As for me it was not even a fleeting daydream. The SBS were out of my thoughts as soon as I walked away from the poster. In three years, which was the length of service I had signed up for, I planned to be back in civvy street and looking for a career. Before I joined up I did not altogether disagree with the popularly negative view that most civvies seemed to have of the military, and especially of soldiers – 'Join the Army, go to distant countries, meet new and exciting people, and kill them' was a well-known T-shirt slogan. I was in the Marines to get what I could out of them and then leave, and if a war happened along in those three years the excitement might be an added bonus. But the more I learned and the harder the commando course became, the more I experienced a growing appreciation for the soldier's life. When it comes to pay, promotion, education, pension, job security and being ordered about, the military offers a freer and kinder existence than most corporations. And only a few civilians can turn up to work on any given morning to find they are off on an another adventure somewhere in the world. The one drawback is longevity. Most soldiers find themselves on the street after twenty-two years, having to carve out another life. But that's a worry for the old soldier, not the young one.

A few days after receiving my green beret I met the Personnel Selection Officer (PSO), whose job it is to plan the first step in a new Marine's career. His task is to balance the manpower within the corps by distributing new recruits to the various units, and also maintain a flow of apprentices to the various administrative and support departments, such as cooks, drivers, mechanics, carpenters or illustrators. The PSO noted in my file that I had worked in a Mayfair hotel as a ledger clerk. He thought that was an excellent background for an administrative clerk. What? I said to myself. A pen-pusher? I baulked. He sounded like a car salesman as he explained how the corps was short on clerks and that there were great advantages to be had in becoming one. For instance, if I wanted to be a sportsman I would have loads of time off to train, and promotion was quick and guaranteed. I grew concerned as I listened, even a little panicked. Now that they owned my life, could they actually force me into any career they wanted?

I whipped myself to a rigid attention – I was still essentially a noddy – and blurted out, 'I want to be a fighting Marine. I didn't join up to be an office boy, sir!'

He was unmoved. Of course no one wanted to be a clerk; no one who wanted to be a real soldier, anyway. But he had quotas that had to be filled and was used to having to hard-sell this particular berth. He insisted I would be a soldier as well as a clerk. Clerks, he maintained, did everything regular Marines did, even parachute courses. He asked me to look at being a clerk as an added responsibility, on top of being a soldier. I suddenly saw myself charging up a beach, gun in hand, carrying a large desk on my back.

In an effort to convey how much of a soldier I wanted to be and how little of a clerk, I declared, 'I want to join the SBS one day, sir!'

I could see the letters, SBS, hanging there in front of me like large slabs of concrete challenging me to eat them. The thought of joining the SBS had never entered my head before that moment. I had daydreamed about it a little, just like everyone else who saw the posters or heard the exaggerated stories about the squadron. But I had never for a second thought seriously about joining them.

The PSO scoffed at my outburst and explained what I already knew, that I required a minimum of three years as a regular Marine Commando before I could even think of applying for the lofty heights of the SBS. But he went on smoothly to suggest I could become a clerk then apply to join the SBS after three years, but that, of course, would require signing on for the full twenty-two. At the time I did not know I had the choice of flatly refusing the posting, but he never even hinted at that, letting me think it was as good as an order. However, I could not bring myself to buy his package and so he finally sighed and told me to go away and take a few days to at least consider it.

As I left the office I was confused and depressed. I didn't want to be a shiny-arse. I decided my primary goal was to get myself into a regular commando unit, and not as a clerk. Surely they could not force me.

Later that evening, my troop was meeting down at a

local pub as part of an end-of-training farewell bash. In a few days most of us would bomb-burst to the various commando units which at that time were 40 and 42 in Plymouth, 41 in Malta and 45 in Arbroath, unless any of us got a draft to a Royal Navy ship or a career course, such as a cook or clerk: then we would be off to one of many training establishments to learn the necessary skills. I was not particularly close to any of the other recruits, even after six months of arduous training in which teamwork was encouraged as the key to success and survival. But the hardship and attrition had created a unique bond between us.

One of the lads had organised a competition for that evening and we had all chipped in a pound towards the winning prize, which was a candle-lit dinner for two. The winner would be the man who turned up with the ugliest date. The entrants would be judged by the whole troop. The lad who won, or lost, depending on how you look at it, was the smallest in the troop, weighing in at around nine stone. He entered the pub with a broad grin, holding the hand of a nineteen-stone, no-neck behemoth in a flowery dress. She had no idea what was going on and smiled sweetly while everyone applauded them as the undisputed winners. The lad had spotted her at a bus-stop in Exmouth on his way to the pub and wooed her to come and have a pint. The poor girl looked around at the sea of ghoulish, laughing faces and her smile faded as she realised what it was about. She was not amused. Her huge, blubbery arm must have weighed only a little less than her date when it hit him with the force of a sledgehammer, after which he needed to be taken to the sick-bay with a suspected fractured jaw. We found out later that the lady was a notoriously proficient bouncer in a nightclub in Exeter.

The following day I was called back to the PSO's office. It looked like he wasn't even going to give me the full few days to think about it. I was aware I might eventually lose the fight but I had prepared a detailed argument nevertheless – a speech on wanting to be the best I could be and all that crap. I was OK at thinking up speeches in my head, but when it came to actually making them they always turned to fudge. I was rehearsing it over and over in my mind as I approached the HQ building, when I spotted Corporal Jakers walking up the main drag of the camp towards the main gate carrying his backpack and kitbags. He looked like he had all his belongings and was leaving, having obviously got himself a draft somewhere. I adjusted my brand-new green beret on my head, called a 'flight deck' at that stage, because it was still a little rigid and stuck up on one side (the trick was to soak the new beret and put it on wet, adjusting it to perfection, then keep it on until dry), straightened my uniform and called out to him.

'Where're you off to, Corporal Jakers?' I said, thinking he would be different towards me now that I was a Marine.

He glanced at me long enough to recognise me, and said, 'Fuck off and talk to me when you're a man.'

I should have expected a comment like that from him. Mister Angry, we called him. As I watched him disappear up the road, I wondered if I would ever bump into the bastard again.

I gathered myself, had a last few seconds of anti-clerk speech rehearsal, and entered the PSO's office, but before I got a chance to open my mouth what he said shut me up completely.

'Due to a sudden shortage of manpower, I've been informed that the SBS is allowing a handful of recruits fresh out of basic training to attempt the selection course. It's some kind of experiment, and one I don't approve of, I must say.'

He did not look pleased, but it was the PSO's job to fill the slots presented to him and that is what he now had to do.

'Since you have declared your desire to join the SBS, you're to report to Royal Marines, Poole and attend an acquaint. If you pass that you'll attend the SBS selection course the following month.'

It was not until I left the office that it fully sank in and I went into something of a mild shock. By the time I was walking back down the main drag it had turned into a kind of euphoria. But as the day wore on and the realities of what I had got myself into set in, I became worried. After six months of ball-busting Royal Marines commando training I was, almost immediately, to attend probably the hardest special forces selection course in the world, equal in content and intensity to SAS selection, but including extensive diving and sea-canoeing, both conducted in wintry and stormy weather conditions.

I did wonder what he meant by, 'Due to a sudden shortage of manpower.' Had something terrible happened?

The reason, I was to find out later, was connected to the news article I'd read on the train to Deal six months earlier. When oil platforms had started appearing in the North Sea, pumping vast amounts of wealth into the country, the SBS, aware that the platforms were a target for terrorists, had evolved ways of assaulting and recapturing them in case one was hijacked and its crew held hostage. No other country's special forces had yet considered the threat or were doing anything serious about it. The SBS had had to start from scratch, and it was a great way to help put the unit on the map.

The platforms were enormous, exposed and in the middle of nowhere, difficult to get to without being seen and in seas which averaged near storm conditions seven out of every eight days of the year. You had to be an expert diver, a fearless climber, have the stamina of an athlete, and sport a fair-sized set of nuts before you even got on to the lowest deck a hundred feet above the water to pull out your gun and become a soldier. That's why they are called special forces. When SBS operatives first surfaced from beneath those terrible swells, they defied driving winds, rain and sometimes snow and ice to climb the immense, razor-sharp, barnacle-covered, slippery, towering steel structures armed to the teeth. But the oil platform executives did not see them as a potential rescue force, only a pool of resources from which they could recruit much-needed divers. The executives were propositioning the SBS members even before they had caught their breaths, offering them irresistible wages. In a short time the SBS lost over twenty per cent of its operatives. The Navy reacted by increasing diving pay, which was then followed by special forces pay. It still did not compete with the oil companies, but it reduced the flow to a trickle, and one of mostly older members on their way outside soon anyway.

This exodus from the SBS of those mainly older operatives did have a positive side. British Special Forces is a dynamic organisation, growing more high-tech each year. Twenty years ago, when a special forces operative went out into the field, he carried equipment no more than a few hundred pounds in value, the most expensive items being a pair of binoculars, a rifle, camera, his diving equipment, a canoe and a Morse code radio set. Today the same operative can expect to carry equipment worth hundreds of thousands of pounds. Night-viewing aids, satellite navigation systems, laser-guided weapon-sighting systems, satellite communicators with secure and coded signals and microwave wireless surveillance systems. Add to that list mini-submarines, high-speed surface craft and other specialised vehicles and delivery systems, all operated by SBS ranks themselves, and the value of the equipment entrusted to a single SBS operative zooms into the multi-millions. The squadron was going to need not just tough men with high physical and mental stamina, but educated men with the technical awareness to operate and understand these new sophisticated systems.

When I revealed to my squaddies that I was on my way to attend an SBS acquaint, instead of mocking me, to my surprise two of them, Andy and Dave, both tough and intelligent young men, went directly to the PSO and put themselves forward for the course. Looking back, Andy and Dave were far from ordinary as regular Marines. They were well-educated, Andy had a degree, and both were articulate in speech and sophisticated in manner and dress. So much so that out of uniform they were often mistaken for young officers in training. I never asked either of them why they were not.

A week later I trudged out of CTC carrying my kit-bag and suitcase, having added a few uniforms to my worldly possessions, and headed for Poole. I had a week-end's leave, but I didn't want to go home to London and my father. I didn't want him to know I was attending an SBS selection course either, not that it would have meant anything to him. He had been a soldier himself, in the Second World War, a conscript, but he knew nothing about soldiering today. I decided to send him a postcard when I got to Poole just to say hello. Poole was not far away, but I took the whole weekend getting there, catching buses and stopping off at a couple of coastal bed-and-breakfast places on the way. I was more unsure of my future than ever, but for some reason the world was starting to look quite a beautiful place to me.

3

By the third night of the ambush I started to have serious doubts about whether O'Sally was ever coming. I had lost the razor edge I had arrived with the first night. The muzzle of my weapon had drifted off the critical arc of fire I had set for myself. I shifted a little too noisily. I often took my hand off my weapon stock to reach into a pocket for a piece of nutty. I began to realise why they had given me this ambush. It was because the odds on O'Sally coming home were really very low. 'Let the sprog have that one,' I could hear them saying. Otherwise they would have sent their best people on a kill like this. And what had the SAS trooper around the front done to deserve getting stuck on this job?

Then I heard a noise close by – a stick breaking underfoot. My senses screamed into focus, my head went tight with concentration, I stopped breathing, my heart virtually stopped beating and the world moved into slow-motion.

Seconds later it came again. Definitely a footstep, followed seconds later by another. My heart kicked in again. It felt like a lead weight bouncing hard inside my rib-cage. Someone was slowly approaching down the hedgerow. My mouth was slightly open, an instinctive reaction that improves the hearing. I took shallow breaths. Adrenaline pissed through my veins. I carefully moved my weapon to aim at the end of the hedgerow just yards from me. Another footstep. My finger was lightly touching the trigger, a little more pressure and a burst of bullets would roar from it. I wanted to hit him in the head first shot, but what if he was crouching? What if I aimed too high and missed his brain? I aimed lower, my plan being to move it up and unzip him from belly to forehead. It would not matter if he had a bullet-proof vest, not with this weapon. You would need three-quarter-inch steel plate to stop 5.56mm high velocity at this range.

The footsteps paused. He was listening. I could not afford to even blink or swallow now. If I could not see his face, he could not see me yet. How long would he wait to step forward? As soon as I could make out the remotest outline I would let rip at it. What if it wasn't O'Sally? Tough shit. I'd find out when I shone a torch on his dead face. No one else was supposed to be out here anyway. It was not my SAS partner. We had a signal worked out if one needed to approach the other. A few days earlier, on the border near Forkhill, a duck-hunter had been shot and killed when he turned the corner of a field to face the point-man of a Marine patrol. The Marine simply saw a man carrying a gun and cut him in half. No one blamed the Marine. Duck-hunting in bandit country was not the brightest of pastimes. Anyway, this had to be O'Sally. He always took point. I had the drop on him. I was going to shoot the son-of-a-bitch right through his message centre, stop the signals from moving down his cerebral cortex to his finger so he would not pull that trigger and kill me. God, I hoped I would not fuck up. I did not feel like a soldier at that moment, never mind an élite soldier. I felt no different from when I was at school, a kid, as if it was only the other day. School *was* only the other day. Looking back on that moment and others like it, the rush one gets from deadly conflict, they were the most thrilling of my life, what I like to call rocking-chair moments, to look back on when you're old and all you have left are memories.

A soft, squidgy sound came. He was shifting his weight. Nothing could move quietly in that mud. I suddenly feared my safety-catch was on. No matter how hard I squeezed the trigger the gun would not fire and I would die. My right thumb quickly found it and it was off. Of course it was off.

'Come on,' I kept saying to myself. 'Take the step. Show me just a piece of yourself.'

The step came and I could make out his face. He was low, on his knees, and he was growling.

How I did not blow it away I'll never know.

It stood there on the end of the hedgerow looking at me and snarling continuously, pausing only to take a quick breath. It was six feet in front of me. Maybe it belonged to O'Sally. It looked like a Rottweiler. Its head was huge.

My eyes and ears scanned the area like lightning. Had O'Sally sent it ahead to flush out anyone waiting for him? If I fired at it O'Sally would see my muzzle flash and fire towards that. Maybe it was a stray dog. Whatever it was, if I shot it the operation would be blown – locals would hear the report – the word would be out before dawn – O'Sally's house was hot – he would never come home, and my name in special forces would' mean shit. His first ambush and all he shot was a dog. What a nobber. My brain needed more information. The dog came closer. Christ, it wanted to have a go. I could not afford to get into a hand to hand with it, either. I was screwed either way.

Then I had an idea. I carefully reached into a breast pocket and pulled out a laser torch. Laser torches were designed to be used with light amplifiers such as passive night-vision goggles (PNGs), otherwise the light is invisible to the naked eye. The laser beam is harmless to flesh, except areas as sensitive as the retina of an eyeball, which it will burn if concentrated on for several seconds. I flicked on the beam and aimed it at the dog's face. I could not see the beam and had to guess it. The dog continued to growl, but then began blinking and shaking its head. I was on target and the laser was quickly taking effect. Its eyesight was deteriorating and it had no idea why. Within a few seconds it stopped growling, let out a whine, and backed away. I had blinded it. It turned around, disorientated, and walked off into permanent darkness. I heard it bump into bushes as it headed back into the countryside.

Silence fell. I was fully alert once again. I chastised

myself for relaxing. This was not a game. No matter how long the odds are of something coming off you never relax, especially when you're the only one on watch. War graves are dotted with those who did.

I would not normally have been carrying a laser torch. They were not standard equipment unless you had the PNGs to go with them. PNGs fitted over the head with lenses positioned over the eyes that extended like binoculars and were balanced by a counterweight on the back of the head that allowed the hands to be free. They were not practical for ambushes because the batteries did not last very long and they had a binocular effect which distorted the true distance of objects. If you were to stand and look straight ahead you could not see the first yard of ground immediately in front of you without looking down at your feet, which then looked further from your body. An inexperienced user walked in a kind of goose-step fashion. The reason I had the torch was because a few nights earlier I had been on a reconnaissance job with Sam, an SAS trooper.

We had been sent to check out a building in the middle of a large farm complex suspected of being used by the IRA for hiding arms. There was a ground frost that night and we had to avoid the hundreds of puddles and water-filled hoof-prints that had frozen over. Country folk, especially those fighting for the cause, are vigilant, often to the point of paranoia. They will notice any small thing out of place. They might not know one footprint from another in a busy farm, but they could tell if someone had been snooping if, in the morning, the thin film of ice that had formed in the night had been freshly broken.

We would not be able to use regular torches inside the dark building so Sam had brought along a pair of PNGs. I was lookout while Sam, an experienced trooper, picked the padlock. He signalled he was ready and I closed in. Sam pulled on the goggles and tightened the strap on the counterweight. The lenses extended four inches from his eyes, making him look like a giant insect. The high-pitched whine of the tiny transformers was barely audible.

'Open the door,' he whispered.

I opened the door and we both stepped inside. I closed it behind us and put my back to the wall. It was so dark I could not see a hand in front of my face. I could feel Sam beside me searching his pockets.

'Shit!' he hissed. 'I can't find the fuckin' laser.'

The PNGs needed a small amount of light to amplify, though much less than the human eye needed to see. In total blackness, such as inside a closed vault without a single light source, the PNGs would not work. There was just enough starlight coming in through a single dirty window for the PNGs to amplify, but a laser torch would have looked like a powerful light beam to him.

'Do you think you dropped it somewhere?' I asked.

'Dunno. I 'ad it when I got in the car.'

He scanned around. 'I can see enough to do the job. This looks like some kind of tool-shed. You stay 'ere while I 'ave a skeg.'

I was not about to go anywhere. I might as well have had a blindfold on.

I felt Sam step away from me and then a second later there was a crash followed by a painful-sounding moan.

'Sam,' I whispered. 'Sam, you all right?'

The moan came again and sounded like it was below me.

'Sam?'

I could hear him moving slowly.

'Uggg. This ain' a fuckin' storage shed,' he said painfully. 'It's a fuckin' garage.'

I crouched and stretched forward, feeling the floor. I felt an edge where the floor dropped away. Sam had fallen into an inspection pit.

Something landed beside me with a clatter. I felt around and found the PNGs. They were badly buckled.

'Fuckin' PNGs. Useless piece of crap,' he mumbled. ''Elp me out of 'ere, for fuck's sake.'

I reached down into the darkness, found his hand and helped him out of the deep, narrow, greasy pit used for servicing the underside of vehicles. He did not seem to have broken any bones, but every joint had been well rattled and he was filthy. There was no point in continuing with the recce. The goggles were bent out of shape and so was Sam. I helped him outside and propped him up against the building while I replaced the padlock. He leant on my shoulder, and as I helped him through the complex I radioed for the pick-up car. We looked like a pair of drunks hanging on to each other as we staggered down the deserted lane. Half a mile from the target, well away from any other structures, our car stopped alongside us. I helped Sam into the back and we drove off. Something was digging into my butt and I pulled it from under me. It was the laser torch. Since the PNGs were no longer any good I kept the torch issued with them rather than handing it in. As we passed through a town, by the light from the streetlamps, I saw Sam's face. He must have hit the bottom of the inspection pit face first, because the bruise around his eyes was oval-shaped like a Lone Ranger mask.

After the dog had gone it began to rain gently and I sat motionless once again, hunched under my stunted tree holding my gun. I stayed that way until the first hint of dawn. Once again O'Sally had not come. I met my SAS partner at the usual place and we walked back to our hide. The next night was our last night in that ambush, and it was to be the last night anyone would have to wait outside that house for O'Sally ever again.

As I arrived in Royal Marines Poole for the SBS acquaint I had mentally prepared myself to expect just about anything – I had nothing to go on but the exaggerated stories from recruits at CTC. The rumour that bothered me the most was one about having to hold your breath for five minutes underwater. I was relieved to discover that was not a requirement. But some tales were not exaggerated.

I was initially surprised by what I took to be lax security around a camp that housed such a secret organisation as the SBS, but it was there. It was invisible. The SBS protected themselves with the most effective security system there was. Anonymity. Unlike the SAS, the SBS wore exactly the same uniform and cap badge as regular Royal Marines and could not be told apart. And they shared the large camp with several other regular Marine departments such as Driver Training, Ships Detachment courses, R Company, which was responsible for recruiting and laying on displays all over the country, Landing Craft Company, Royal Navy ranks and several other smaller departments and schools which altogether consisted of several hundred non-SBS ranks and their structures. I was impressed with what I thought was a deliberate ploy – the SBS's covert existence hidden within the overt structure of the Royal Marines and Navy. The truth behind the SBS's set-up and organisation was a bit disappointing. I did not piece it together for many years, by which time many aspects of our structure had improved, and many had not. But since I was still unaware of all the politics and bullshit as I took my first tentative steps into the world of the SBS, I'll leave those revelations alone for now.

As I walked through the camp, that same feeling of inadequacy I experienced on the train to Deal grew in me again. Anyone who looked hard and ruthless I assumed was SBS and I wondered what I was doing here.

At the headquarters building I met Andy and Dave. I was relieved to sense that they were uncomfortable too. Together we went to locate our quarters, which we found in one of several recently built three-storey barrack-room blocks. The selection course took up three of these buildings at the start, each capable of sleeping over fifty men. Marines were arriving for the course from the far-flung corners of the corps, loaded with baggage and looking for their assigned rooms. It was a hive of activity. There was an endless cacophony in the corridors and stairwells, Marines shouting for pals or looking for the galley or bedding store. But beneath the surface of all this normality there was an air of expectancy. It was safe right now, with some Marines even confident enough to exude a bit of macho bravado, but very soon the pain and hardship would begin and no one could honestly say they were eagerly looking forward to it. We would live in these barrack blocks for as long as we lasted the selection course, by the end of which the buildings would be ghostly quiet and empty, the few survivors being able to fit into just two rooms with beds to spare.

There were six beds in our ground-floor room and we were the first to arrive. We unpacked our kit into our lockers and sat around, talking quietly. The next thing to look forward to was lunch. We were all a little nervous. It was like our first day at Deal all over again. We didn't know exactly what we were getting into. All we could be sure of was it was going to be a damn sight harder than the commando course. The window beside my bed overlooked an empty field in the centre of the camp large enough to accommodate several football and rugby pitches. A large helicopter was parked to one side. Poole Harbour was half a mile away. Beyond the sound of men settling into their rooms around me I could sense the peacefulness outside. This place was a stark contrast to the bustling soldier factory that was CTC. The ghosts of those who had gone before us haunted the room. A daily programme sheet was pinned into one of the lockers and bits of survival packages such as sutures, fishing line and hooks were left in drawers. It was rumoured that the selection course had an average pass-rate of only one in sixteen. Pinned on a window-frame, partially hidden by the curtain, was a photograph of three course members climbing into a landing craft, having just completed a gruelling survival exercise on Little Cumbria Island in the wilds of Scotland. They had been stripped naked, then dumped on the island with nothing but a pile of hessian cloth to make clothes from. They lived off seagulls and their eggs, kelp, rabbits, if they could find a way to snare them, and vegetation they had been taught was nutritious. Every waking hour was spent in the pursuit of food and firewood and by the end of the week they looked pale and feeble. One of the men in the photo was named Arthur, and though I saw him once or twice around the squadron it would be two years before we would have our first words together and then it was in unusual circumstances.

We were startled by the door to the grot being kicked open, and when we saw who stood in the doorway under the weight of his personal baggage we leapt to attention. As a regular Marine you never came to attention for anyone entering a room other than an officer or warrant officer, but our noddy buttons had not quite dropped off yet and there were still people who could push them. It was Corporal Jakers.

He recognised us, but did not acknowledge it. Assuming he was in the wrong building, with his customary scowl he shuffled back out. We breathed a sigh, irritated with ourselves for leaping to attention. We had to stop doing that. We were Marines now, not noddies, and on an SBS selection, for Christ's sake. What was Jakers doing here, anyway?

The door burst open again and Jakers stormed into the room. We leapt to attention.

'What are you arseholes doing in here?' he shouted. 'This is for SBS selection ranks only.'

'We're on the SBS course, Corporal,' we said in an unsynchronised chorus.

He stared at us in total disbelief. Then he completely lost it. He started raving about how he had applied years ago for a crack at the SBS course and how he had done nothing but crap jobs such as teaching wankers like us at CTC while he waited for his chance and that we had not been in the corps a dog's watch and here we were on the same course as him. He was going to see someone about this. Someone had made a mistake. And no way was he about to share a grot with a bunch of noddies, especially us. He took all his kit and slammed the door behind him.

We all exhaled and dropped our shoulders in relief that he had gone. We actually sympathised with him. It did seem unfair that he had waited all those years to join and here we were, fresh out of the factory. But as Jakers was finding out at that moment we were all SBS noddies now, him too. He was soon back. He threw his bags on the furthest bed from us, and as he packed his kit into his cupboard he mumbled on about how the corps was going down the toilet. But we were stuck with each other. As if life was not going to be hard enough for us in the coming months.

The SBS acquaint, designed to weed out the obvious no-hopers before the main selection course, lasted from Monday to Friday. Its aim was to see if we had basic map-reading skills; if we enjoyed the wet and cold, long mud runs, crouching in sodden bushes all night with thousands of ravenous mosquitoes; if we could run a mile in five minutes, swim twenty-five metres underwater and sit on the bottom of the deep end in a small, dark chamber (simulating a submarine lockout) without face-masks and sharing one aqualung between three without getting panicky or claustrophobic.

Several hundred Marines took part in dozens of acquaints held over a period of months, out of which 134 mustered for the main four-month-long selection course at the end of summer. That final number included fifteen Marines straight from CTC, Andy, Dave and myself amongst them.

The first few weeks of the main selection course were designed to wear us down mentally and physically and get us to a level of fatigue the instructors would then control throughout. The map marches, done individually whilst carrying up to one hundred-pound packs, grew longer each time until we were covering up to thirty miles in a single march. Sleep was kept to a minimum and often interrupted after the first few hours for mud runs and initiative tests. These periods of extra-curricular activity were known as 'beastings' and were frequent and innovative. Over one third of the selection course was spent in the field sleeping out. On long marches the directing staff (DS) liked to surprise us and do things such as give us one minute to consult our maps, memorise compass bearings, distances and the lie-of-the-land of the next four or five miles, then take our maps away and send us on. If you were caught with a spare map, the punishment would far exceed the crime. Speed as well as accuracy was important when moving from A to B. Those who did not make a rendezvous before it closed were likely to be off the course. Fail twice and you definitely were.

Every soldier knew what he was getting himself into before he arrived in Poole for the course and should have been prepared for the worst. Daily programmes were available in commando units months before, detailing the aims of each stage of selection and what was required of a man to pass it. But as with my regular commando course, many men quit in the early stages. It was obviously more intense than they could have imagined. On top of the physical tests, by the end of selection recruits were expected to know the Morse code, to be able to calculate radio attenuation, know diving theory – including Boyle's law and Dalton's law of partial pressures – Archimedes' principle, explosive theory, including the Munroe effect, electrical and igniferous detonations, basic sea navigation, and photography, which included developing film in the field. During the diving phase we covered miles underwater, day and night, in mostly zero visibility and freezing conditions using re-breather bubbleless diving sets. The sets were fine until they leaked. The first warning sign was that, instead of air, you sucked up a caustic soda cocktail (sea-water mixing with the carbon dioxide absorbent powder), which was a bit like drinking a glass of fizzy antifreeze. If you were in deep water at the time you choked to throw it up as you made your way to the surface, without being able to take a breath, and havinf to remember to exhale to avoid an embolism. The safety boat always carried a bottle of vinegar to pour down your neck when you surfaced to neutralise the alkaline soda, which was as delightful a drink as the cocktail, but at least it eased the burning.

We rarely had sufficient sleep and never time to fully recover between phases. This strategy was vital to the SBS selection. A man's limits can only be assessed when he is physically and mentally exhausted.

'What you go through on this course, fatigue-wise, physically and mentally, I hope you will never experience the equal of in combat,' an instructor once said to us. 'But if you do, well, you'll know you can handle it.'

The fitter you were at the start of the course, the longer you could go before having to switch over to sheer willpower to get you through. By the end of the first month we had lost over half our numbers. By the end of the second we were down to about forty. And of the fifteen raw Marines from CTC there remained only three – Andy, Dave and myself. It was more than just coincidence that the only noddies left were from the same troop. We seemed to provide moral support for each other when each of us most needed it. All it took was a smile or a wink when times were hard. But although we were unified, the course as a whole was not, and us three nods were the cause.

The regulars on the course made a point of making the three of us feel unwelcome, especially our room-mate, Corporal Jakers, who constantly reminded us of our inexperience and, most important, our ineligibility. Regardless of what the SBS had decided, we made a mockery of the system. The sooner we quit, the better for the others.

Most mornings we would wake up to one of Jakers' caustic comments such as, 'Are you lot still here? I'd quit today if I were you, it's gonna be a hard one. Why go through all the aggro?'

The one comment that niggled me most was, 'You don't really believe they're going to let a bunch of noddies into the SBS even if by some freak accident you do get through the course, do you?'

The others would rarely talk to us unless they had to. We were referred to as 'the nods' and were fully expected to quit any day soon. But as the days rolled on and the numbers dwindled we were not amongst the quitters. Looking back, it's possible this added pressure from within the course made us more determined not to give up.

I was teamed up with Jakers for most of the canoeing phase, much to his consternation. The Directing Staff did it deliberately knowing it would piss him off. The partnership turned out to be to my advantage, though. Jakers was a very experienced canoeist. He had once competed in one of the most demanding canoe races in the world, the Devizes to Westminster, which was 124 miles in one paddle. He gave me the usual hard time at every opportunity, but as he did not want to do all the work on the long, arduous paddles he also gave me sound instruction and advice. On one thirty-mile paddle in a horrendous storm with the canoe fully loaded as if for an operation, we were capsized by a massive wave as we changed direction. We carried out the proper drills and climbed back in with the help of the other pairs who had formed a raft. Our equipment, including backpacks and weapons, was strewn outside the canoe attached by lines and we fought against the heavy swells to get ourselves back in order. Several stringers (the wooden skeleton of the canvas boat) were broken and we tied splints as best we could. The weather deteriorated further. A coastguard helicopter appeared low overhead after being called in by a civvy who had seen us from the cliffs. The crewman hung out of the cabin and vigorously waved us towards shore. We gave him the bird. As the helicopter flew away he signalled to us by spinning his finger around his temple. We pressed on and in the early hours of the morning, canoeing past the deserted beaches of Sandbanks, we entered the relatively calm waters of Poole Harbour. After that experience I felt I could paddle a canoe in any conditions.

With a month left to go we were down to about thirty drained and numb Marines which included the three nods. The others were less concerned with giving us a hard time by now. Everyone was consolidating their energies and concentrating on getting through the last and most difficult phases of the course.

The final exercises were not designed to support high numbers and the pressure by the DS to reduce the course to a more manageable size increased. However, this was in conflict with the aims of the SBS training officers who, sitting in the blind comfort of HQ most of the time, wanted higher numbers to pass. Orders from above were that the SBS was not only to make up its losses to the oil platforms, but to increase its overall manpower. The obvious method would have been to run more courses each year, but that was expensive, and in any case the Marine Corps could only provide so many volunteers each year. Few people if any (I never knew one) joined the Marines just to join the SBS. Hardly anyone had heard of the SBS outside of the Marines anyhow. The only other way to increase the number of Marines passing selection was to make it easier.

The DS, all NCOs, were generally more interested in maintaining the high standards. They didn't care about the numbers game, nor exchanging quality for quantity. But how else were the SBS, and the SAS for that matter, who were also expanding, going to swell their ranks? There's a natural law at play here – given one or two social factors such as peace-time, the population can only provide so many soldiers of such a standard. An argument from the HQ office was that the SBS course was too hard on men as it was. Too many potentially good operatives were being lost to injuries that could have been avoided. There was a lot of truth in that. I can recall at least two men on my selection who I thought were very good soldiers but who had to come off the course due to serious injuries. One did his back in while running with a waterlogged log across his shoulders after being ordered to by one of the DS. The instructor had no idea how heavy the log really was. But the man carried it without hesitation until he collapsed under its weight. The other Marine was carried off while running down a steep bank with a large, steel oxygen bottle weighing about seventy-five pounds – we were all running with one – when the soldier behind tripped and dropped his bottle on the leading Marine's ankle. In that respect, selection courses were destined to become more controlled and more manpower-conserving. Unfortunately for me and the rest of my course, those changes were still a way down the road. Our DS were from the old school and things were going to remain the way they were, regardless of any requests from HQ Training to be more lenient. If the DS felt at any time the pressure was slipping, due to long spells of good weather for instance, they were brutally swift to compensate.

An example illustrating their methods came in that final month at the end of a long, tiring canoe paddle over several days. We came ashore, thirty of us in fifteen canoes, at the planned rendezvous, a lonely riverbank miles from nowhere. We expected transport would be waiting to pick us up. Instead we were met by one of the DS.

In a typical DS team of four to six men one would play the nice guy. He was more lenient than the others and almost human. We could relax a little whenever he was in charge. The rest of them were indifferent, cold and did everything by the book, all except one. He was Mister Nasty, heartless and devoid of pity. This was by design of course, similar to the good-cop, bad-cop routine. Mister Nasty usually administered the extra-curricular activities. When you woke up to a light flicking on in your grot at three in the morning, having been in bed only an hour or two, and saw him standing there, you knew he had not come to tuck you in and read you a bedtime story. His job was to make our lives hell. Mister Nasty, by design, was an impossible man to please.

A few selections after mine, certain members of a selection plotted to kill their Mister Nasty by tampering with his diving set. He survived, which was even more unfortunate for the course since he uncovered the plot.

It was our Mister Nasty, the symbol of pain, who had come to meet us instead of the truck. There were sighs and curses when we saw him casually approach, alone, with his hands in his pockets and a thin smile fixed to his lips. He stood on a mound and, looking down on us, explained that the four-tonner could not get this far due to poor road conditions and so we would have to walk a mile or so to meet it.

'And don't forget to bring everything with you,' he added.

That meant our canoes, backpacks, weapons – the lot.

We broke down the canoes, each weighing 110 pounds (dry), and bagged and secured them to our already heavy, wet packs. Together the load weighed around 175 pounds. There is a technique for getting these loads on your back and on your feet. It is virtually impossible to do it alone. After the bagged canoe is secured to the backpack, it is left on the ground while the soldier lies back on it and threads his arms through the straps in the normal way. Once the man is strapped in and looking like a beetle trapped on its back, the pack is lifted from either side until he is on his feet and bearing the full weight.

When we were all loaded and ready to go we looked like a troop of two-legged tortoises.

'Just a couple of miles,' Mister Nasty said as we followed him up the road.

We had heard the rumours that the course was too fat for this stage of selection. The word was they wanted to cull twenty more. That's why Mister Nasty was here.

It was not long before the straps began to cut into our shoulders. If you twisted your ankle with this load you might break it, and if your knees had not fully recovered from previous hard yomps you were in trouble – this was sure to take them to their limit.

We shuffled up the steep road like mules. It was pointless and unrealistic to expect the truck to be where Mister Nasty had said it would be.

Two miles up the road Mister Nasty stopped to check his map.

'Seems I've made a mistake,' he said. 'The truck must be a little further on. But don't worry. I know a shortcut.'

We bet he did.

'Come on, then. Don't dawdle.'

We followed him through a farmer's gate and into the wide open countryside leaving the solid road behind. We crossed ploughed fields, pushed through thick under-growth and along narrow, treacherous sheep tracks that were rutted and uneven. Stiles and barbed-wire fences were the most difficult, but you could also ease the pain for a moment while waiting your turn by leaning forward and supporting your hands on your knees, or even better by leaning back on the fence and letting it take the weight for those precious few moments. This had its drawbacks, though. One of the men leant back on a rock wall while he waited for the rest of us to cross a stile and the wall gave way and he fell back through it. We all had to rebuild the wall without removing our packs.

If someone stumbled and fell en route those close by had to stop and lift him back on to his feet – he could not do it alone. Those who did not complete this yomp were off the course and so teamwork was, as in everything else we did, essential. Teamwork also meant sticking together to encourage each other and give moral support.

The load cut deeper into my shoulders with every mile. The vertebrae in my neck were stinging and felt like they were separating and the muscle around them tearing. The skin at the base of my back was slowly being worn through by the pack. To counter the weight you walked leaning well forward. I spent most of the time staring at the ground or watching my feet or the heels of the person in front. Every so often I shifted the load a little to the left or right to relieve sore spots. After several hours I stopped the shifting. It was painful everywhere. The callouses on my feet, which I had developed since CTC, had softened the last few days after being wet the whole time. They rubbed off in solid chunks in the early miles to expose the tender pink tissue beneath. I could feel when they began to bleed. When the pain signals started coming in from all those parts of the body at once it was time to switch off and become an automaton.

'You can't crack me, I'm a rubber duck,' was a saying the course had adopted. I heard someone chanting it softly to himself, and to encourage the others.

After ten miles, Mister Nasty led us on to another narrow country road and stopped while everyone caught up. He had lied about the truck being here too.

'It's another five miles,' he said coldly. 'Get going.'

We trudged on past him as he eyed us, one by one, looking for cracks.

The road was harder on the knees but there was less chance of tripping. More importantly you could slip into a hypnotic rhythm more easily by staring down at the uninterrupted tarmac. I tried to shut out the pain and occupy my mind with something else but it was difficult to lock on to any subject for long. I had not tied my canoe as well as I should have and it was starting to slip back a little. I was having to compensate for it by leaning forward even more. My head was getting lower to the ground. I did not want to stop and adjust it, but if it slipped down any further I would have to drop my pack and rebuild it quickly. To get it up on to my back and rejoin the group meant someone would have to stay and help me. I thought about sherpas who carried as much weight up the sides of mountains. They supported the weight by passing a line under the bottom of the load and up over their foreheads which took the weight off the shoulders and placed it on the stronger neck muscles. We could not do that because of the tactical disadvantage – we would not be able to turn our heads and look from side to side. Not that any of us cared what was going on around us at that time. This was deliberate mental destruction and not a tactical march. Dave saw I was having a problem with my slipping load and moved alongside to study my pack.

'How's it look?' I asked.

'Not good.'

He took a line that was dangling from the back of my load, a canoe bow-line, and tossed it over the top so that it dangled in front of my face.

'Try pulling on that,' he said.

With a bit of a shuffle while I yanked down on the line the load came up a little. I could walk more upright now, although it meant I had to apply constant tension to the rope. But overall it was easier and as long as it stayed that way I did not need to stop. I wrapped it around my hand, held it tightly to my chest and got back into rhythm.

After five more miles, Mister Nasty stopped again and waited for those in the rear to catch up. No one had wrapped yet. That did not please him. There was no truck. Anyone with any sense knew what was coming next. I kept stone-faced even after he said it.

'Did I say five miles five miles ago? I must have meant ten.'

Some expressions turned to pain and teeth were gritted in anger. I knew what some were thinking. Comments had already been muttered on the last leg.

'This is sadism.'

'Are they allowed to torture us like this?'

I wondered if any recruits had died on previous courses. Perhaps the SBS had a death allowance for the selection process.

Mister Nasty ordered us to get going. A few members seemed to hesitate, but when the first few got going the others trudged on behind.

All comments of encouragement tossed between individuals earlier had by now ceased. The yomp was everyone's personal ordeal now. We plodded on in our own worlds. Some were starting to lag further behind, but as long as they kept on going they were part of the course. The DS were looking for tenacity and willpower, not fitness. Jakers noticed some stragglers had lagged too far behind and whispered for those of us in front to slow down. The concept of team unity and looking after one's buddy is paramount within the Royal Marines and therefore the SBS, unlike in the SAS. To leave a man behind is out of the question in the SBS. Over the many years I worked with 'the regiment' I grew to feel many SAS troopers experienced a cold aloofness when insinuating their calm acceptance of a fellow trooper 'written off' as a cost of a mission. Some talked about their oppos lost in battle in the same way macho men discuss their scars.

It was getting dark.

I was beginning to think the plan was to walk us until we literally dropped. There were some who looked close to falling apart. All they had to do was stop. That's what was unique about this slavery and abuse. It was voluntary. We were not being ordered to do anything. All the pain and injuries were self-inflicted.

No one shouted at you and told you to get going. There was no encouragement. Quite the reverse was true. The DS were always inviting individuals to wrap. And if a person quit, no one would tell him off. There would be no punishment. The reason was simple. In special forces you had to be self-motivated to the point of self-destruction, but not quite kamikaze either – the training was focused on getting operatives out after a job as much as it was getting them in to do it.

You could tell when a man was losing control of his pain. There are signs. Shortened breath and darting eyes, or eyes that blink quickly as if trying to focus. Or no reaction to anything, even when asked a question, or looking as if he would walk off a cliff if one appeared in front of him. Another was to move out of character, to suddenly become talkative but in a hyperactive way, asking how far you thought it was and how much longer it could last. An indication that the end is close is a sudden spurt of effort that cannot possibly last. The worst scene is once a man has severely cracked and wrapped, when he curls up and sobs uncontrollably, out of either guilt or self-pity, because his limit has been exposed, not only to others but to himself. Most men give in before those stages are reached. I had seen it all since I arrived in Deal, and I found it curious. Watching someone you know crack up is like watching a deformed person walking towards you. It's uncomfortable and impolite to stare.

It was completely dark an hour later and we were heading up a steep, painful incline when the beast-master paused once again. We leant heavily on to our knees, watching him through our eyebrows, waiting while the stragglers caught up. I had stopped sweating a long time back and was thirsty. I had a water-bottle and had drunk most of its contents, but I was saving the last few mouthfuls. You always did that. If you emptied your last drops when you did not know when your next resup would be it was the beginning of the end in a way – a mental gauge to yourself. Mister Nasty shone a torch in each of our faces, searching for those signs he also knew so well.

'There is no truck,' he said and let the words sink in.

'Ten miles further on is a pub. If you get there before last orders you can have a pint. If you're not there by closing time you're off the course.'

I was trying to calculate my time and distance. We had about three hours. Four miles an hour was normal walking pace. I could do it, in theory, if I was completely fresh. But in my present condition and with this ridiculous weight hanging off my arse I would have to say no way.

'Those who don't want to go on can wait here and transport will come and pick you up in the morning. You can get into your sleeping bags and keep warm. Make yourself a nice cup of tea and get your heads down.'

He made it sound like a great idea.

'Otherwise, get going.'

I stayed bent forward for a moment, taking a few seconds more of a breather before gathering myself to push on. As I pushed my hands off my knees and pulled down on my rope to move on there was a thud behind me. Someone had let his load fall off his shoulders.

'Fuck this for a game of soldiers,' the Marine said as he plonked down to sit tiredly on his pack.

When someone quits, it often has a ripple effect, especially if others are close to cracking. All it needs is someone to set it off. It happened just like that. Several other packs hit the road.

'I don't need this crap,' another said.

Mister Nasty had a glint in his eye and looked at the rest of us, inviting more to quit. His appetite was just getting whetted.

Another pack went down. It looked like Mister Nasty might hit the jackpot.

I think Jakers was the first to move off. The rest of us shuffled off too as another pack dropped behind me. We left six men behind with their packs at their heels, watching us walk away.

I would do the next ten fucking miles if that was what they wanted. We looked like a chain-gang the way we dragged our feet in jagged file up the road and around a steep bend. Earlier on the course during a beasting session in a muddy estuary we had passed a group of civvy hikers who stopped in horror to watch us. They were so disgusted they telephoned the camp and insisted on speaking to the commanding officer. They got the adjutant, who listened while they gave their eye-witness account, exposing how we were treated like Roman galley slaves. The adjutant assured them something would be done about it. When he hung up the phone the complaint was promptly filed in the dead registry – the wastepaper bin.

As we turned the bend in the road a hundred yards

from the last stop, to our surprise there was the truck. Old Noah the driver climbed out to greet us with a flask of coffee. Noah was the oldest Marine in the corps, never interested in promotion, who had been everywhere the Marines had in the last twenty years. He had been a driver for the SBS the past few years, a job he wanted to keep till his time ran out. He always felt sorry for those on selection, as if we were prisoners and had no choice. Although it was strictly prohibited, he operated like a resistance worker against the evil DS and sneaked us a sip of hot tea and a sliver of useful information whenever he could.

'This is it, lads,' Noah said. 'You've cracked it. I'm here to take you 'ome.'

The pub and the next ten miles was a last-minute bluff. Even Mister Nasty had his limitations. I'll never forget the relief when I let my pack drop from my shoulders. I thought I was going to float up like a helium balloon.

'How far did we walk, Noah?' someone asked.

'They were going to pick you up after fifteen, but no one had wrapped, so they kept you going. This is twenty-one miles.'

In the back of the truck, on the journey home, we all had our boots off and were tending to our feet. You did that every opportunity, cleaning and sterilising them, then applying plasters for protection and powder against foot-rot. If your feet fell apart then so did you. The DS knew our feet would be in a bad way and so they would give us a couple of days' light PT before the pressure went back on. The men who had quit sat stone-faced in a group at the back of the truck. There was an invisible wall between us now. They never bothered with their feet. It did not matter any more. They would have all the time in the world to recover. The relief of dropping their packs minutes before the rest of us had cost them their dreams of a future in the SBS. Quitting is a hard thing to live with and a hard thing to admit to afterwards. I knew something of how they felt that moment seconds before they quit. About six weeks into the course I almost quit myself.

I don't know what had got into me that day. I was not tired, mentally or physically. We had just got out of bed after a full night's sleep and the course was mustering outside for the usual early-morning workout. It was icy cold and, as per normal, we were not allowed to wear any more than shorts and short-sleeved T-shirts. We were going for a run which would include frequent stops for sit-ups, push-ups, pull-ups and throw-ups, and end with a swim across a frozen-over quarry lake a quarter of a mile from the camp. The ice covered its sixty yards' width as it had every day that week. On reaching the other side it was a stiff run the last leg back to the grots past main-gate sentries who either thought we were mad or toyed with the idea of having a go themselves one day. I had done it a dozen times already. We had done far worse. Perhaps I was low on energy or had been bitten by the quitting bug that flew thick that morning. Eight had voluntarily withdrawn (VWed) that morning and had gone back to their cosy beds. The ripple effect had been at work. There were no second chances once you quit. If you were not on the road doing PT you were off the course and on your way to a commando unit soon after. I sat on a toilet listening to a couple of quitters outside justifying in soft voices why they had done so. I checked my watch. There was barely a minute to go before the others would set off on the run. If I was not with them I was with the quitters. I examined my thoughts. When I thought I was a coward I tried to solve it; in the orphanage, wondering why I felt alone in the world, I came up with a helpful philosophy; when I ran away from home at sixteen intending to board a merchant ship because I hated my home life I talked myself into staying and finishing my education. But the difference was those times I had been looking for a way to get through, to succeed. This time I was sitting there looking for a reason to fail. The seconds were ticking away. I sat stubbornly, staring at nothing. Time seemed to have been suspended.

Suddenly the door to the bathrooms banged opened and I jerked out of my thoughts as someone called my name. It was Andy.

'Duncan? You haven't time to wipe your arse, the course is heading off.'

All thought of quitting disappeared as if it had never existed. It was like a nudge back from the edge. Without hesitation, I hurried out of the toilet, past the quitters, who eyed me suspiciously, and joined Andy as we sprinted to catch up with the course. I have often wondered if left to my own devices I would have nudged myself out of that dream state in time. I wonder what I would have done with myself if I had not. Maybe I would have ended up a clerk somewhere, keeping my failure on the SBS course and my disappointment in myself a secret.

That was the only time I ever came close to quitting. From then on, if I was going to fail, someone else was going to have to fail me.

With three weeks to go and just over twenty of us left, we were standing in a jagged line in full field kit in a thickly wooded Army training area. Our faces were streaked with black and green cam-cream. We stood like the trees, emulating them, blending with them, silent as them, soaked through to the skin. Rain dripped down our faces and off the ends of our fingers. It was midnight and a storm had been raging for days, but at least it was not freezing. We had just completed an exercise with a ten-mile infiltration to blow up a dummy target with live explosives followed by a ten-mile exfiltration across several deep rivers. Bright green ferns sprouted from gaps in the dense carpet of dark mauve heather that was everywhere. The DS were gathered a few yards away discussing something in low voices as they often did. We just waited quietly. By now we were lean and hard, numb to pain and coiled like springs. With the wearing down came an increased sensitivity and greater self-control. We were like prisoners fed on bread and water who can now see clearer than ever before. I never felt more like a Dog of War than at that time. If they tossed us dead rats for supper we might have eaten them without a word. But behind those pale eyes was a calculating alertness, waiting to spring like a bear-trap. If someone shouted 'ENEMY FRONT!' we would explode into position. A gun-group would automatically take a flank to give cover without a command being given. Smoke would go down to obscure our movements. Someone, anyone, would quickly order an assault and sweep through. Teams would automatically pair up. We would leap-frog relentlessly forward – not everyone moving at once – laying down controlled, accurate fire. The gun-group would set down an endless barrage just yards ahead of us to keep the enemy's head down as we advanced. And God help any bastard who got in our way. We were close to what the DS wanted us to be. But not quite.

It was Friday night and there were rumours, according to Noah, of a rare day off the next day. We would believe that when it happened.

A shout went up from one of the DS to pick up our backpacks and we followed him in single-file in the rain.

Every twenty yards one of us was halted and told to wait. When we were all dispersed about the wood the instructor yelled that we had five minutes to disappear from sight, but we could not move from where we stood beyond a radius of twenty feet. We had done enough of this sort of thing by now and it was becoming second nature.

I quickly dumped my pack, took out my heavy field knife, slammed it hard into the earth and cut a line in the heather four feet long. I pulled up one edge of the heather as if it were a rug stuck to the floor and worked my hands in under it, separating the roots from the earth but being careful not to pull the weave apart. I lay on my back and worked my feet under, sliding in until my whole body was beneath the heather blanket. I pulled in my equipment and worked myself in even further until the opening flap could meet the ground again where I had cut it. I had made good time and had a minute before a whistle would blow indicating silence and cessation of all movement. In the blackness I pulled a waterproof off my pack – I knew where every single item was in my pack, webbing and pockets and could find them blindfold – and slid it over between me and the heather as best I could. I lay there in the fresh soil as the rain dripped through and felt confident I was hidden. The whistle blew. Everyone stopped moving. The only sound was the rain.

I could feel the damp creeping up through my wet clothes. I wiped some of the dirt from my lips and did not give a damn. One of the DS who had been watching me came over and prodded me through the heather with a stick.

'Good,' he said, and walked off. A rare compliment.

We knew at least one of them would remain to watch us throughout the night as we lay in our cramped hovels spread about the wood. An army could have marched through and not found us. I doubt if anyone slept. There was nothing to do but think as the rain trickled in through the heather. If you could form a block of stone by thought alone for each hour of lonely, silent wakefulness, by your career's end in special forces you would have enough to build a castle.

A whistle blast came with first light. It meant we had seconds to muster on the track in full equipment ready to go. I ignored my stiff joints and muscles and, with ligaments as taut as violin strings, burst out of my lay-up position (LUP), pulled on my pack, grabbed my rifle and formed up with the others on a track. We followed the DS at a brisk pace up a steep incline that led out of the wood and on to an old, worn, narrow military road. A hundred yards away was a four-ton truck with its back to us and tail-gate down. Our transport home. The camp was twenty miles away.

'From now until tomorrow morning your time is your own. There's the truck. If you don't get on it you walk back to camp.'

That would take us most of the day.

'Go!' he shouted.

As we set off, the truck gunned its engine and moved slowly away. It matched our speed, the driver watching us in his side mirrors keeping a distance from us as a tease. We broke into a run because it was expected of us, though by now we knew what game was being played. The truck increased its speed to match ours. It was obvious we were not meant to catch it, but we had to show determination. Our equipment bounced and rattled on our shoulders as we loped along. Something clattered to the ground – a weapon magazine – hands went to pouches in case it was theirs. The man who had dropped it quickly went back for it then hurried to catch up – you never left any equipment behind. If the DS found so much as a Spangle wrapper they would terrorise the guilty person, and if he could not be identified, all of us. I had emerged as the fittest and fastest on the course by then and as we pounded along the road, chasing the back of the truck that remained fifty yards in front of us, I was suddenly possessed.

Without thinking about it, I increased power and accelerated away from the others. I had decided to catch the truck. I don't know why. To this day I cannot identify what motivated me at that second. I simply broke into a sprint. I was not angry, nor had I lost control in any way. I just knew I wanted to catch it. I moved directly behind the truck so the driver could not see me in his mirrors. I was going flat out and gaining on it. My arms pumped, my heavy pack bounced on my shoulders, my rifle banged against my side. I had halved the gap. If the driver did not go any faster, if I did not stumble or drop any equipment, I might make it. I was an animal at that moment. The back of the truck was yards from me now. All I had to do was reach out, put on a spurt, grab it and pull myself in. The old military road was coming to an end and once the truck joined the main road the driver would speed up and head back to camp, empty. I put everything I had into it and reached out for the truck. I would be the only one to get in it if I did. The others had not increased their pace and were many yards behind me. Then, just as suddenly, something else came over me which seemed out of my control. I ignored the back of the truck and ran past it down the narrow gap between its side and the trees. This was not an expected reaction for me. My conscious thoughts were always of personal survival – get yourself through the course. I'd always been a loner and my only concern previously was looking after number one, not in a malicious way, but instinctively. Had the Marines' dictum, 'look after your buddy and he'll look after you' finally worked its way into my subconscious?

As I drew level with the cab my strength started to fade. My mouth was wide open, sucking in as much air as it could. My arms pumped and my pack was a ridiculous appendage slamming up and down against my back. My rifle with its attached strap fell off my shoulder, down my arms and into my hands but I kept going. I glanced up at the driver. It was old Noah and he had no idea I was there below his passenger door. I turned in front of the truck and with a final effort threw myself forward to sprawl on the road like a sack of vegetables. Noah slammed on his brakes and the truck screeched to a stop a foot from me. I was totally spent and just lay there sucking in air. Noah revved the engine, honked his horn and shouted at me out of the window. He did not mean a word of his cursing, but he knew the DS were watching and wanted to put on a display.

The DS were quickly upon me, shouting and kicking me to get up. Their plan was going awry. I did not have to feign limp exhaustion. They dragged me out of the way and tossed me and my equipment into a ditch at the side of the road. Noah was ordered to quickly get going. He gunned the engine and the truck accelerated past me. When I looked into the back of it from the ditch I saw the last course member and his backpack being dragged on board. The others were looking down at me as they drove away. The course officer, a lieutenant, appeared on the road above me. He was a tall, hawkish South African. His expression was not angry but curious. He lifted his radio to his mouth and ordered the truck to stop.

'Get on board,' he said. His manner was cold but I could sense what I can only describe as a sort of veiled niceness, if that doesn't sound too much.

I grabbed my pack and rifle and made my way to the truck. I climbed on board with help from the others and Jakers made a space for me on the bench beside him. The truck pulled away. For the first time ever Jakers was not wearing his usual scowl when he looked at me. He nodded then looked away. Others glanced at me as they breathed heavily.

Everything was the same on the course after that except for one thing. Though I was still a punk nod, hard as it was for them to admit, it seemed I was, after all, all right. Psychologically that point was the end of the course for me. I'd been beginning to think it was going to be harder to be accepted by these men than by the SBS. That part was over now.

The final exercise was the last two weeks of the course. We were divided up into teams and Jakers chose me to be in his, and what's more, as his canoe partner.

'This doesn't mean we're mates,' he warned me.

When the final day of the course arrived it was like the first day of spring after being buried underground for the winter. The survivors were mustered in the squadron lines to be officially dismissed by the DS. Out of the 134 who began the course, nine of us were left including Andy, Dave and myself. There were actually ten of us counting the only officer to pass, Smith, who was virtually there at the end. Although we have had many fine officers, there was always a shortage, so when one looked even remotely suitable his failings were often overlooked. Today the SBS, having expanded, is so short of good officer material the vacant positions (mostly administrative) have had to be filled by SAS officers.

For the three of us nods it had been virtually a year of continuous selection conditions since leaving civvy street. But it was not quite over. Not for us three. As we waited outside the HQ block for our final assessment the others were relaxed and joking with each other. They knew they had passed. The three of us stood quietly waiting to one side. Even though we had got to the end, the rumour was that Andy, Dave and I would only eventually be allowed to join the SBS after spending a couple of years in a commando unit. I did not want that. Not after all I had been through. Yes, I was inexperienced, but I would make up for that if they gave me the chance. But we were, after all, an experiment, and perhaps that was all we were ever meant to be.

We waited while the other six, in turn, marched into the SBS headquarters building and within a few minutes exited cheerfully and walked away. The three experiments were kept till last. I was called up first.

I was nervous as I marched into the office and stood to attention in front of the course officer while he remained seated. It dawned on me that this was the most important moment of my life so far. He told me to stand easy. He casually went through the phases of the course telling me my strengths and weaknesses, but all I wanted to hear were his final words.

When he finished he stood up, offered me his hand and said calmly, 'Welcome to the SBS. You achieved the third highest assessment on the course.'

He never mentioned anything about my inexperience or being a nod, or going to a unit for three years first. I was in.

I left the office in a mild state of euphoria. I walked down the corridor lined with honours, photographs and memorabilia of a special forces unit that had seen action in every war and confrontation Britain had been involved in since the Second World War without a blemish to its name. I wanted to shout, 'I fucking did it!' But that would have been egotistical, and the faces of the old and bold that lined the walls were a reminder that this was just the first step, and losing self-control was no part of this job. I had no idea what the future had in store for me but one thing was certain. I was not going to be a civvy in two years.

As I left the building, Dave and Andy stared at me for any sign. I remained poker-faced, knowing that if I was in, they were too. As I passed by I winked and said, 'Welcome to the SBS.'

Corporal Jakers came top of the course and maintained his high standards throughout his career. He is still an active member of the SBS with the rank of major.

Soon after selection Dave had to leave the SBS, and eventually the Marines, due to a knee injury sustained on the selection course. He had surgery on it but the operation was unsuccessful. When I said goodbye to him he needed a stick to help him walk out of the SBS lines. Andy left the SBS a few months after that for personal reasons. The last I heard he was a civilian working in security somewhere.

No other Marine has since been allowed to attend the SBS selection course straight out of recruit training. For whatever reasons they scrapped the whole idea after my course. I was in by the skin of my teeth.

I had changed substantially since I had left home, physically and mentally. It's as if I had grabbed an express train and crashed out of adolescence and into adulthood. Life seemed as if it was all about getting to the top of one ladder to find oneself at the bottom of another. But there was no doubt which direction I was headed. I never gave a thought to the dangers of the job. I never stopped to think how the chances of biting the big one were many times greater than as a civilian. I was soon to get my first lesson in that fact and would receive reminders once or twice a year throughout my career.

The first SBS operative to congratulate me was also the first SBS member I talked with before the course. I had been placed on camp guard duty. His name was Chris and he was the duty corporal in charge of the guard for that night. He was one of the new breed of soldiers in special forces, an intelligent man with a broad, hungry outlook on the squadron and its future. He had been surprised when I told him I was in Poole to do the selection course. He knew I had just come from CTC, but he was genuine when he wished me luck. The day I passed the course he grinned as he shook my hand warmly. He said he liked to see the system bucked now and then.

'You can take my place. I'm out in six months,' he said.

I did not know him well, but I was immediately disappointed. Here was I doing everything I could to be accepted, and here was a man where I was aiming to be who was not content with his lot. The reason turned out to be simple and understandable. His wife was pregnant with twins and he wanted to be with them as they grew up. He was studying to be a youth probation officer and would have a job waiting for him the day he went outside. He explained that, although life in the SBS was great, it would not allow him to spend enough time with his family. I'll remember him as the first Marine to make me feel welcome within the corps as well as the SBS. A few months later I saw the entire squadron gathered in one place for the first time. It was at Chris's funeral. He had died while pioneering a dangerous infiltration technique from a submarine only weeks before he was due to go outside.

The last night outside O'Sally's house was more windy than previous nights. Noises and movement surrounded me. Each night increased the odds on O'Sally and his partner coming and still they had not shown. I was growing old fast.

A clicking sound alerted me. It was the pre-arranged

signal from my SAS partner. I returned it and he walked out from behind the building and came towards me. He approached casually, his weapon held low, as if somehow he knew there was no danger.

'The op's been pulled,' he said. 'We have to break down the hide then head to the pick-up.'

'Why?'

'O'Sally ain't comin',' he shrugged, not knowing any more than that.

I climbed off my perch and, as I walked away, I looked back at the spot where I had spent hours of my life, all for nothing, it seemed.

In the pick-up car an SAS sergeant was seated in front beside the driver. My partner and I sat in the back, wrapped in civilian coats, wiping the worst of the cam-cream off.

The sergeant leaned around and said, 'According to the tout, O'Sally has been home twice. Three nights ago and tonight. Both times were just after midnight.'

I could not believe my ears.

The sergeant looked at me when he said, 'And he used the back door.'

My partner threw me a look.

That got my back up instantly.

'Even if I had fallen asleep O'Sally would've had to step over me to get into his house,' I said.

The SAS sergeant's look was not accusing. 'It ain't you, mate. Something's fucked up.'

I sat there in disbelief as we drove on.

At the debrief in the TV room we learned we had been sitting outside the wrong address. RUC Special

Branch was blamed as they had provided the intelligence. O'Sally's house was the next one along, less than half a mile down the road.

I spent much of that night awake in my caravan, thinking about it all. What if we had been given the right address? O'Sally would be dead by now, I told myself. I would have had him. I was certain. I had played up his toughness in my head too much, as I always did. I would have seen him seconds before he would have seen me, and I would have blown his head clean off before he squeezed that trigger.

I remained convinced of that for many months until I heard news that caused me to wonder all over again what my fate might have been. A few miles from where I had spent those nights waiting for O'Sally, he had faced two men from special forces in a similar situation. He killed one and seriously wounded the other.

4

When I first saw Northern Ireland it was through the cabin window of a C130 transport aircraft. I did not look upon it as a country of lush, green beauty, rambling hills and winding roads through quaint towns and villages that were centuries old. To me the commanding hilltops hid snipers, hedgerows were booby-trapped and country roads invited ambush. I doubt I will ever see Ireland any other way, certainly not as long as the Troubles continue.

That first year in Northern Ireland had begun badly for special forces when Robert Nairac, a liaison officer (non-badged) to the SAS, was kidnapped by Provo and IRA sympathisers while leaving the Three Steps Inn near the border in South Armagh. The fact that he should not have been there, alone, posing as a local, is by the by. He paid dearly for his adventure and, as usual, the press provided some highly creative reports of the incident.

Revenge was never a factor even when we lost one

of our own. Not generally, anyhow. We had a job to do and it had its pros and cons. One day it was in Northern Ireland, another day somewhere else in the world. But in Northern Ireland the job was different from other places because we had to play by a specific set of rules. The referees were world politicians and the media. Points would be deducted for foul play, on our side only, and the IRA could do anything they wanted as long as they eventually said sorry. We were aware that in the eyes of much of the world England was the bad guy and its special forces lurked in the shadows of Northern Ireland like the trolls of Mordor. It did not bother us in the slightest. We knew it was not who we were or what we did that defined our image. It was where we did it. In the Falklands and Gulf Wars, for instance, we were heroic. It seemed that the media pretty much controlled how the average person perceived the situation. We had little respect for journalists. Throughout my career, reporters always seemed to invent what they did not know and misinterpret what they saw.

There was some bitterness when rumours circulated about the torture Nairac went through before the IRA killed him. We knew all about the IRA's interrogation techniques, which they practised most often on their own people. The first torture victim I saw had been a tout. He was hanging by his wrists from the rafters of a barn and had been slowly killed with an oxyacetylene torch applied to various parts of his naked body, the majority of the burns being on his penis and testicles.

Nairac was an SAS man as far as the Provisionals were concerned and the temptation to get information from him during his interrogation was irresistible. In war, when a captive is known to hold valuable information, he can expect to be interrogated. The quality of the interrogation depends on the sophistication and malice of the captor. Nairac's capture was not a major security concern. It was standard procedure to cancel every operation remotely connected to an operative who had been taken alive. The IRA knew that. They operated in the same way. We expected Nairac's body to turn up when they had executed him, but when, after several days, it did not it was because the IRA had elected to hide or destroy it for what they obviously considered to be a sound reason. Nairac's body has never been found to this day. There was no advantage in withholding the body apart from some minor bluff tactic. If anything, it was damaging to the IRA not to hand it over as it denied his family the chance to give him a Christian burial which Catholics everywhere found deplorable. The IRA did not give up the body simply because of the brutality to which it had been subjected. It might have had an adverse effect on the media attention the IRA was constantly enjoying regarding the 'tough treatment' of their own 'political' prisoners.

After arriving at base camp, I paired up with the SAS trooper I was to have my first outing with. Norman was his name. He was an interesting man of few words with the stoop and facial expressions of early man. I looked forward to learning something from this experienced trooper. After a ground orientation period of a few days I was called to a briefing with Norman. I was excited to be going on my first job. It was midnight when we set off together in the back of a civilian van driven by two SAS lads. The entire province was covered in a thick fog. Norman was in charge as I was the new boy on the block, though I don't think he knew how new I was. I squatted opposite him on the cold floor of the van as it trundled over bumpy, narrow roads that wove through the countryside. We didn't exchange a word. We were dressed in regular cammies over thermal longjohns and our faces were blacked out. Our backpacks contained spare radio batteries, extra warm clothes, a sleeping bag, medical supplies, and food and water for several days. Our job was to relieve two operatives in a long-term observation position (OP) passed on by the previous SAS tour that had left the province the day we arrived.

Norman peeked through the curtains at the front of the van, between the driver and passenger. He compared what he saw with his map and told the driver to drop us off here. The van slowed to a crawl, I slid the door open and we climbed out with our equipment. The van was still moving as I slid the door nearly closed. The passenger's job was to hold the door closed from the inside, but without slamming it locked, until the van was out of the area. The fog was thinner here with visibility at fifty yards. I crouched in the darkness on the short, narrow pavement against the wall of the only house in the area and scanned around. It was as quiet as a grave after our van left. Both sides of the road were lined with hedges. Directly across the road was the only other structure, an old derelict stone cottage with a broken thatched roof. Norman's brow was furrowed and his bottom lip was wrapped up over his top one as he scanned around. The lesson I learned that night was, no matter what your responsibility is in a team, be it the lowest in rank, in a plane or on a boat or at the rear of a battalion snake, always have a map of the area and know exactly where you are at all times. I did not know exactly where I was and I was curious as to why we had dropped off against an occupied building.

'How far are we from the target?' I whispered as I pulled my pack on in preparation for an expected mile or so yomp across country.

'This house is the target,' he said, indicating the one I was leaning against with its lights on inside.

He pointed to the derelict cottage across the road, the only other structure around, and said, 'That's the OP.'

Headlights approached in the distance so, before I got a chance to ask the obvious, we picked up our stuff and hurried across the road and around the back of the derelict cottage. We climbed up the back wall and in through the partially collapsed roof to find the SAS trooper and my SBS colleague we were here to relieve. They had seen us drop off in front of them and my SBS colleague gave me a questioning look which I did not wish to answer in mixed company.

As I removed my pack there was a pounding on the bolted front door of the derelict building. We snatched up our weapons and spread back inside ready to return any fire.

A man's voice shouted, 'Would you SAS get the fock outta moy shed. Der's nottin' for you to see here.'

He walked briskly across the road, into the house opposite and slammed the front door shut. I don't know why he thought we were SAS men. We had done nothing to suggest we were soldiers of that quality.

It was not the last time Norman was to drop off in the wrong place. His next time, a few years later, was to be far more memorable and only just missed by millions of people all over the world. He was one of the SAS entry men on the Iranian Embassy siege in London.

There are two conflicting versions to this story. They both begin in the same way, with Norman alongside the rest of his SAS team, many of them the same lads I shared my first Northern Ireland tour with. They were all in the Pagoda Team by then, on one of the balconies of the Iranian Embassy, ready to go in. Seconds before 'Go! Go! Go!' Norman fell off his balcony and landed on the one below. He got to his feet and realised he was alone with no hope of climbing back up to the others in time. Suddenly all hell erupted as explosions signalled the combined entry of the various teams surrounding the embassy. Norman made an instant decision to storm this part of the embassy alone. With his MP5 levelled he burst in through the balcony windows. It is from this point on that the two stories differ.

The following is Norman's version.

On crashing in through the balcony windows he saw, across the far side of the room, a masked terrorist with a pistol held at the head of a desperately frightened hostage. Norman confidently went for the difficult head-shot, immediately aimed and squeezed the trigger of his MP5, but the first round in the chamber was faulty and failed to fire. The odds on this happening are apparently one in 10,000 for this type of bullet (the very same thing happened to me on a rehearsal many years later – I still have the bullet as a reminder). The terrorist took advantage of Norman's misfire and moved his pistol from the hostage's head to aim it at Norman. Norman moved like lightning and, with a dexterity that comes only with years of practice, let go of his MP5, letting it swing on its harness under his left arm while his right hand swiftly reached down for his 9mm pistol at his right hip. Before the terrorist could squeeze off a round, Norman drew his pistol, slick as any Wild West gunfighter, and fired a double-tap straight through the terrorist's head, killing him instantly. The hostage broke down and thanked Norman for saving his life.

The second version comes from the hostage.

As the explosions rocked the building, Norman burst into the room with his primary weapon on aim. The hostage was standing with his hands in the air assuring Norman that all was well and indicated the lone terrorist, lying face down on the floor across the room, shaking in fear, with his gun tossed away. Norman let his MP5 swing aside, pulled out his pistol, casually walked over and shot the terrorist in the head.

It's a strange phenomenon that allies a hostage with his would-be executioner against a man risking his life to rescue him, and it's not an uncommon one, either.

Norman was decorated for his uncommon bravery. I bumped into him a few times over the years after my first job with him, all in different parts of the world. He actually came down to Poole once to do part of an SBS course and to learn something about us pond-dwellers.

111

He was a likeable bloke. He eventually died alone in Northern Ireland one night, drunk behind the wheel of a car, after crashing into a bridge.

One afternoon our liaison officer brought in a tip-off about a weapons cache discovered hidden in the cemetery of a small village way out in the countryside. It was dark by the time an SAS and SBS team dropped off half a mile from the location and moved cautiously in to inspect it. There was always a possibility that the IRA had set up the tip-off themselves and booby-trapped the cache. Live ambushes were not the IRA's style and they were especially cautious if a quality unit was operating in their area. (When the Paras or Royal Marines moved into an area for their four-month stint, the IRA bad boys usually moved out until they had gone. A member of the Provisional IRA once told me the Paras and Marines are more aggressive than other regular Army units and react more positively when attacked.) The inspection of the cache had to be done quickly, quietly and in darkness. After the area had been checked for booby-traps, weapons were indeed uncovered in a hole under a concrete slab behind an old gravestone.

The cache consisted of a selection of pistols and rifles in mint condition, wrapped in plastic and placed tidily in a canvas weapons bag. But the hide had not been weather-proofed for long-term storage. That meant either the weapons were being taken out and serviced regularly, or they were in transit and this was just a temporary, short-term location. Perhaps they were being

kept serviced for an upcoming close quarter assassin-
ation (CQA) in the immediate area, or they were on
their way to an ASU in another part of the province.
Either way it was likely someone would come for the
weapons soon. It was too late to mount a full surveillance
operation which would have been ideal to discover the
weapons' ultimate destination and the players involved.
The only option was to mount an immediate ambush on
the site for that night, while a plan of action was devised
for the following day.

Open ambushes at night in Northern Ireland are technically more complex than in conventional wars for
reasons both physical and political. The ambushers have
to find a place from where they can clearly identify targets but without the risk of being seen themselves. This
means no obvious locations and away from all possible
routes to the target area. The ambushers must also have
a clear view of the target, not just to identify characters,
but to identify precisely what they are doing – do they
have weapons and are they a threat? The observers must
ascertain beyond a doubt the target's legal eligibility for
lethal engagement.

If a courier arrived to pick up the weapons, he (or she)
would probably observe the hide for a while and circle
it before moving in, and this they can do nonchalantly,
especially if they are locals, since they have every right
to be there. The courier might arrive with an accomplice
for cover, posing as a courting couple, for instance.
Ambushers, therefore, not only have to maintain a clear
view of the target, they have to be hidden from view
from every approach.

113

There was a very good chance an amorous couple arriving in the graveyard might be genuine as it is the national pastime of the Northern Irish to 'bag off' in the open air at night. Families in Ireland are generally large, and especially in small towns and villages it is not unusual for offspring to stay at home until they are old enough to get married themselves. This means the houses are always relatively crowded. Bearing in mind that there are often religious restrictions, any member of the family wanting to engage in sex had to do it outside and usually under cover of darkness. A car parked in a lonely spot with two people in it is not an uncommon sight in Northern Ireland. In some towns, where out-of-the-way car parks are in short supply, you can expect to find the few there are fairly packed with cars, especially soon after pub closing time, many of them rocking and squeaking. These are ideal places for special forces drop-off vehicles to park up and wait. Some operatives found that night-scopes helped pass the time in these situations, and it was sometimes necessary to get your own car rolling a little so as not to be the odd one out.

The 'Troubles' are not a war, they're a police action and every soldier is essentially a deputised police officer used to carry out tasks the police are not trained for. Special forces were originally sent over because the sectarian killings, on both Protestant and Catholic sides, were getting beyond the control of the regular Army and RUC. Since the recent Troubles began in 1969, in the years before special forces 'officially' arrived in early 1976, there had been over 1,400 killings. But the SAS and SBS in their conventional modes were not the ideal force for this politically sensitive conflict and were often the proverbial bull in a china shop. Understandably, we became the IRA's number one priority to eliminate, because destroying them was our only reason for being there. Killing any of us would give them kudos and make them look more deadly and more professional. What's more, we were politically safe in so far as there is little pity from the general public for special forces lost in Northern Ireland, only curiosity. Unconventional soldiers operating secretly and independently have a romantic aura of expendability.

There were strict rules of engagement to adhere to before shooting an IRA terrorist and breaking them could result in jail. Rules are designed to make games more sporting and the rules for engaging the IRA appeared to have been designed with that in mind. The IRA naturally saw themselves as soldiers and insisted that we did, too. Fortunately for them, we didn't. Our rules obliged us to treat them as regular criminals, which means they were innocent until proven guilty in a court of law. This worked greatly to their advantage, for if they had been given true enemy soldier status all we would have needed to have done was pull them in off the streets (we knew who most of them were) and place them in POW camps. We had the upper hand in training, equipment, manpower and technology, but that was balanced out by the IRA always being allowed to make the first move. Overtly killing members of the IRA by the rules was almost as difficult as it was for them to kill us (which most often was purely by chance encounter on their part).

The only way we could legally kill one of them was to catch him in an act that could reasonably be judged as an immediate threat to life. It was within the murky confines of that particular rule that we lurked, waiting patiently, ready to bring down the axe without hesitation the instant the opportunity arose.

That is why, in the early hours of the morning, still pitch-black, when a lone figure stepped out from the trees, climbed over the low stone wall into the grave-yard and towards the weapons cache, he came under our heartless gaze. There should have been a skull and crossbones to warn him, like those on the edge of a minefield. He strolled through the graveyard like the neophyte he was, his senses dull, alerting him to nothing. His experiences of the Troubles were obviously limited to riots, in a crowd of hundreds, throwing bricks and petrol bombs at troops lined up behind plastic shields. He had no doubt heard of the SAS, but he would have nothing to do with them until he made the big league and joined an ASU, if that is what he dreamed of. As he walked between the headstones, his silhouette was in the night-sights of two assault weapons in the hands of two men who could easily take on hundreds just like him. I say easily because he was only fifteen years old.

The SBS and SAS operatives could not have known that, not in the cold, green fuzzy light of a weapon's night-scope. They were simply watching a suspected terrorist in a graveyard heading for a cache of weapons, waiting for him to comply with a rule of engagement which was to hold a lethal weapon in his hand. Once he did that he was a threat to life. It was unlikely he intended to shoot anyone at that very moment, but how many more rules do you give to the other side? Do you let him run away with the gun and risk losing him, or do you wait for him to shoot someone first? How much more of an advantage do you give them? If we played by their rules we would grab him now, beat and kick him near unconscious on the ground until most of his teeth were knocked out, bundle him into a car and take him to a lonely spot, then drag him into the middle of a field where his gurgled pleas could not be heard. In the dark of night we would surround and beat him some more with fists, boot and pistol-butt until his face was shredded and broken, until flaps of hair-covered skin lifted to expose his white skull in places, until one of his eyes had burst and was hanging out, and the mud around him turned crimson with his blood. Then we would ignore his hardly discernible plea for a priest to hear his last confession as he knew he was about to die, alone, filthy and surrounded by men who hated him wholeheartedly. Then one of us would place a pistol against his head and fire empty chambers and be amused each time he flinched, until the last two chambers, which were loaded, blew his head apart. That's what we would do if we were like them, for that is precisely what they did to Robert Nairac.

It was a standard tactic of the IRA to employ children to carry arms. During the riots in the cities, it was not an uncommon practice for a sniper, after shooting a soldier, to drop the weapon and run, making him an unarmed target and therefore illegal to shoot. A child

117

was instructed to pick up the gun and run away with it, his instructors knowing full well that soldiers, even though adhering to the strict rules laid out in the yellow card which every one of them carried, won't shoot a child, even one holding a gun.

The choice of using this particular kid in the grave-yard to pick up the weapons was especially sad as he was mentally retarded. He knelt by the gravestone and struggled to move aside the concrete slab. The crossed hairs of the two night-scopes focused on him as he reached deep into the hole. He struggled to pull out the heavy sackcloth and plastic-wrapped bundle and let it rest on the ground. He was putting a lot of effort into getting closer to his own death. If he had left the bundle tied up he would have been safe. He could have carried it away as it was and he would have just been followed and the operation moved on to another stage to catch the recipients. But he was simple and curious and perhaps he had never seen a real gun before. He untied the string and let the bundle roll open. The ends of each weapon were placed in pockets to hold them in position. He touched the rifle that took his fancy most and slid it out of its pockets. He picked it up and gripped it in his hands. His life belonged to us now. There was no question of a reprieve. The kid lifted the rifle into his shoulder to see how it felt. The pads of two index fingers, neither of them his, touched the crescents of two black triggers and took first pressure. In seconds the kid's soul would be homeless. Whatever he saw in the night sky through the sights of his weapon was the last thing he saw. The quiet was shattered by two sharp reports. One bullet passed through his chest as another took the side of his head off.

When the operatives closed in to check their work, any satisfaction they felt faded when they saw they had killed a mere boy.

The true irony of it all came to light during the police inquiry that follows all incidents. It turned out the retarded boy had nothing to do with the IRA whatsoever. His family was in fact Protestant. He had found the arms cache by accident that morning while playing in the cemetery and had run off home to tell his father. The father ordered his son never to return to the cemetery and then did what he believed was right and phoned the police, who in turn handed it over to us.

It seemed there were often long periods of inactivity on the IRA's part, but the truth was we were getting less and less information from the RUC's Special Branch, who were growing disenchanted with the increasing number of SAS (and SBS) cock-ups. During these quiet times and to justify us being in Northern Ireland, the ruperts would scour the lower level intelligence trails in the hope of finding something we could build a task on and create our own operations. To my knowledge we have never had any real success at that level without the help of the RUC or Military Intelligence. Some of these self-generated operations were nothing more than job-creation schemes. The SBS seemed even more desperate than the SAS to find things to do since we were going through an identity crisis at the time anyway. If an operation was anywhere close to water we had to go way over the top and make it more difficult than it was just to prove we were the only unit for the job. One operation consisted of two teams which canoed in from a submarine drop-off to recce a coastline when it would have been a great deal easier and safer to yomp in across country. That fact was proved when one of the canoes capsized on landing, resulting in the team having to be extracted over land the following day (by the 14th Intelligence Detachment) because they were suffering from hypothermia. Another SBS operation involved setting up a series of OPs on the small islands and coastline of Lough Neagh to log the movement of boats, in the hope that we might see one off-loading arms. Nothing came out of it after hundreds of man-hours in sodden, water-logged positions freezing our nuts off. It was not the conditions that made it so boring as much as the ever-present feeling that we were totally wasting our time.

A fine example of one of the more bone-headed joint SBS/SAS tasks where the comedy matched the execution occurred when myself and an SAS lad named Paul set up an OP in a barn.

An empty weapons cache had been found by an army patrol in a lone barn, way up on a hill in a field, some distance from its parent farmhouse. The weapons cache was a tailor-made-for-the-job brick space nicely concealed in the brick floor under the muck and straw. It contained a weapon-cleaning cloth, an old tin of gun oil, but no weapons. The ruperts decided it looked fresh and could be used at any time, and since it was discovered using our own resources, and nothing better was coming down the pipe, we would plan and prepare it as a long-term operation.

The plan was a simple one, not well thought out and badly executed. The bales of hay, over a hundred of them, stacked nearly to the roof of the barn, were to be removed. A pre-fabricated wooden frame eight feet by four feet and four feet high would be placed on the floor of the barn and a video camera (hidden in the ceiling) would be attached via a cable to a monitor within the frame. Paul and I would climb into the frame along with all our OP gear, weapons, food and video equipment replacement batteries to last us several days, and the hay would be replaced to hide the frame. The displaced hay would be taken away and a reaction force installed nearby to wait for us to trigger when the boyos came to load the cache.

To prepare the hide in one night and in complete darkness was going to require a lot of manpower. About fifteen SBS and SAS operators, including Paul and myself, arrived in a civilian truck at the gate to the field where the barn was. We all traipsed a hundred yards through the muddy field up to the barn and began the first stage, which was to remove the hay. None of the SBS or SAS operatives looked as if they were taking it seriously except the rupert responsible for the idea (who was rumoured to be a Lord and nicknamed 'Lord help us') who walked around directing the show enthusiastically.

The technicians put in the video equipment while Paul and I made ourselves comfortable inside the frame, which was placed in a corner of the barn, and the blocks of hay were re-stacked around us. By the time the stack had been rebuilt dawn was approaching. But what to do with the other bales? As there was straw all over the barn anyway it was decided a little more would go unnoticed, and so a bale was broken up and evenly distributed. After that success it was decided to try another one. It was pure laziness and lack of interest that caused all the remaining bales to be broken up and distributed around the floor of what was a not very large building. Meanwhile Paul and I, oblivious to all this in our straw room, arranged our equipment, tested the video, which had a little movement and zoom, and tested communications. The hide had been placed tight against a rust-thin part of the outside wall which we could kick through in the event of an emergency. This was to be our home for several days.

As the others left and all fell silent we sat opposite each other in the stark glow from the monitor thinking the same thing.

'Well, this is a right load of bollocks,' Paul said.

We decided to eat as little as possible so as to limit the necessity to take a shit, an activity neither of us was looking forward to in this cramped, airless space. We only had sandwiches as we could not cook, for obvious reasons, which denied us our main OP leisure activity. In OPs, food is not usually troughed down just as a necessary fuel. Many operatives became mini-gourmets, often bringing along herbs and spices to add to the otherwise bland ration-pack meals. Recipe-swapping and tastings were a part of OP social life. We could not even read as the light from the monitor was too low, and the only thing on TV was the open entrance to a barn.

The SAS are always tight-lipped and introvert when in a group, the senior members always exerting a seemingly telepathic control over the others, ensuring they maintain the stern image. But get almost any of them alone and they soon become your normal squaddy – chatty, complaining and humorous, even in the most harsh conditions. Before long Paul and I were nattering away.

We talked in low voices and whiled away the hours discussing all kinds of things – where we came from, what we did before we joined up, family life, how we ended up in special forces. Paul told me about life in the SAS and I told him what little I knew about life in the SBS. I was surprised he didn't know much about us. Between us we worked out, for instance, that when it came to anti-terrorist room-entry procedures, we spent a similar amount of time training, had similar procedures and demanded the same levels of proficiency. The SAS were the first to pioneer anti-terrorist and room-entry hostage drills and the first in the world to create a 'killing house', which is a training building designed so that the rooms can be altered to resemble civilian habitats, offices and aircraft cabins. After the SBS took what the SAS had learned in that department and built its own killing house, they adapted what they needed for maritime anti-terrorism and continued to improve on it in their own direction.

I took first watch while Paul got his head down. The monitor was the only indication that dawn was coming.

I turned down the monitor's sensitivity as the early light came in through the barn door and got brighter as it crept across the floor. I wondered if sitting and watching that screen for several days was going to do my eyes any good.

It was during my watch the following morning at about 6:00 a.m. that a man stopped in the entrance to the barn. The view of him was angled from above and he was featureless because of the strong back light. I squeezed Paul's boot to wake him and we watched the man, who was slightly stooped, wore a flat cap and had a walking stick, as he looked around. It was the farmer who owned the barn. His family had run the farm for several generations and he had stacked the hay that summer with his two sons. It was quite obvious to him that someone had dismantled his haystack then put it all back together, and untidily too, and that a dozen or so extra bales had been broken up and spread on the floor. He looked around outside and obviously wondered, as the ground was churned by footprints, just how many people must have been involved in this odd exercise. He went to the top of his field and saw the fresh track, sprinkled with hay, leading down to his gate by the road.

He came back into the barn and we watched him as he started searching around, poking the hay and pushing his stick between the bales. It was clear we were going to be blown and so, on a nod, we kicked out the emergency escape hatch and, with our weapons at the ready, divided up and ran around the barn to confront him.

The poor old fellow was in mild shock at first, but soon calmed down. In fact he looked relieved when he realised we were British soldiers. He thought it was the work of robbers or gypsies who had hidden something like a car under his hay. He assumed we were from the local Army unit. We would not have told him who we were anyway, and were content to let him blame them for the amateurish OP.

After we radioed in to get picked up, we questioned the old man on what he might know about weapons being hidden anywhere in the area. He swore he knew nothing, but the subject jogged his memory.

'You boys'll appreciate this,' he said and smiled as he led us directly to the concealed cache in the floor of the barn.

'It's something of a talking piece around here. A little bit of history,' he added.

He showed us the cache we had gone to all this trouble to observe. It had been used during troubles in the 1920s and not since, obviously, as everyone for miles knew about it.

'There's even an old oily rag and oil tin from those days,' he pointed out.

Then he asked what we were doing in the barn. We declined to discuss it.

Paul was another SAS trooper who later came down to play with the SBS on some of our exercises. He was also one of the eighteen SAS lads lost in the Falklands when their helicopter crashed into the sea after engine failure.

*   *   *

Although we were experienced at being wet and cold for long periods, that didn't mean we looked forward to it. Any fool can be uncomfortable. Many of the operations, such as my first ambush, required standing off during the day and moving in to the target at night. This was because either the target was extremely vigilant and the immediate area was searched during the day by the enemy, or there was not enough close cover from view to insert an OP.

If the weather was constantly bad over a period of time it could drain the hardiest soldier. We had to be able to react instantly and effectively to any developing situation or threat, but our efficiency would be seriously impaired if we were cold or soaked through to the skin and suffering from hypothermia.

Early on in the tour, the quartermaster put in a request for some experimental waterproof suits. When the first batch arrived, four of them were dished out to myself and three SAS troopers prior to going out one particularly foul night on a stand-off operation.

One of the SAS lads in the team was a giant Kiwi. He was six-foot-six and built like a rugby forward with long, black straggly hair on a head the size of a pumpkin, dark eyes and a thick, black hombre moustache (standard SAS issue) that covered his top lip and curved down to his chin. Because of the need for manoeuvrability, and to house the extra clothing needed to keep warm, the suits were designed to be extra baggy. Kiwi, naturally, received an extra, extra large one. The suits were black and one piece and zipped up from crotch to neck. The feet were massive to fit over heavy-duty field boots and ties were fixed at intervals around the torso and limbs to take in the slack. It was claimed the suits were watertight to the neck with large patches of Gore-Tex to make them breathable and so that we could stand in a river for hours in them without getting wet (or cold, if you wore enough underneath).

In my caravan I donned my suit over heavy thermals. After loosening the straps I pulled on my webbing, which contained emergency supplies and spare magazines, buckled my 9mm in its holster to my right hip and picked up my M16. Now I looked like a troll. I was sweating within minutes and happy to get outside, where it was pissing down and blowing a gale. When Kiwi appeared I could only stare at him and think, 'My God.'

Kiwi did not like the cold and had taken full advantage of the spacious suit by wearing plenty of extra clothing underneath. His feet looked like those of Frankenstein's monster and the ties along his arms and legs gave him a mummified appearance. He wore his hood up over a woolly hat and it was fully tied up so that only his eyes, big nose and mouth were visible. He looked eight feet tall and if I hadn't known him I would have guessed he weighed some 400 pounds. All he needed to complete the look was a bolt through his neck. To finish it all off, his favourite primary field weapon was a heavy 7.62mm general purpose machine-gun (GPMG), suspended horizontally across his waist by its carrying strap with an extra-long ammunition belt that curled from its breech and over his shoulder.

Our job that night was to watch a farm suspected of

being used as a safe house by an IRA fugitive. The four of us left the drop-off point a mile away and walked at an easy pace in the howling rainstorm along hedgerows and through muddy fields towards the farm. We took our time walking to avoid overheating and eventually stopped at the top of a field where we could look down on the well-lit farm a hundred yards away as the wind and rain pelted us. The suits were everything they promised to be. I felt nothing of the harsh elements and the rain that ran down my face was, if anything, refreshing. We sat down on the muddy ground without a care and leaned back and observed. The suits were a little noisy, which is why they would have been impractical on something like the O'Sally ambush, but for a stand-off they were fine. We gave a radio check to inform ops of our arrival on target and they got back to us minutes later requesting us to move straight in and flush the main house ASAP. They had received information that several wanted members of the Provisional IRA might be inside.

We quickly formed a plan to cover all four sides of the house in case anyone tried to escape through a door or window while Kiwi went to the front door alone. Each operative was responsible for one side of the house. Around each corner was another man's field of fire so each man had to stay his side of the building or risk being shot by an oppo. When we were all in position Kiwi stepped out of the shadows of an outbuilding and walked across the floodlit concrete yard towards the front of the house.

He banged hard on the door several times, then

gripped his heavy machine-gun, aimed the thick, black barrel at the door and let the belt trail over his arm like a python. I stood at my corner and levelled my weapon along my side of the building, waiting for someone to come out of a window. Whoever climbed out, if they had a gun, they died, and if they did not have a weapon I would convince them not to run – I was not about to chase anyone the way I was dressed unless I wanted to give myself a heart attack.

The front door was opened by the owner of the house, who was an old IRA militiaman and veteran of past campaigns. Kiwi's huge figure filled the door-frame and was back-lit by the floodlights. The old man shuddered as he took in the size of the monstrous, black, dripping thing that faced him with its awesome weapon aimed at his face. God only knows what the old man thought had come to pay him a visit. He had an instant heart attack and collapsed and died there in the hallway. The RUC were not impressed but no legal action was taken.

By the end of that four-month tour I'd had enough of Northern Ireland. After that visit, the SBS tapered off their involvement in the province and went on to other things, although they continued to provide small teams for joint ops with the SAS as well as individuals for undercover duties. If I ever had to go back I hoped it would be in that latter capacity and no other. I was to get my wish.

5

A Royal Marine commando unit or Para regiment could have done most of the jobs the SAS and SBS teams were tasked to do in Northern Ireland, to the same standard we were doing them. Our shortcomings stemmed from the limited time we spent over there. It felt to us like we rushed in, scurried about doing anything we could fit in, and then hopped back to the mainland. The RUC were also getting tired of the short-term cycles of hard-hitting special forces trundling through the province, ill equipped for long-term intelligence-gathering and trying to win the war in their four-month tours. What was needed was a specialised, long-term unit committed solely to the conflict that could provide the delicate touch and patience required to take on an enemy also committed to a long-term struggle. There was such a team: it was highly clandestine in its activities, subtle, well equipped for the job, and patient – all the things we were lacking – and it was growing in effectiveness each year. It would eventually nudge the ill-fitting conventional special forces into a more secondary role.

An undercover unit that operated from the early 1970s was the Military Reaction Force (MRF). The MRF was the root of this new undercover unit. By the time of my first visit to Northern Ireland this new unit, called the 14th Intelligence Detachment (14 Int, or 'the Det'), had replaced the MRF. After some early successes using their 'softly, softly catch a tiger' philosophy, RUC confidence was restored in the Army's intelligence-gathering operations.

The SAS, along with the Army Intelligence Corps, trained 14 Int operatives, who were recruited from all branches of the armed forces. The Intelligence Corps provided surveillance techniques learned from years of spying on foreign diplomats and the SAS developed and taught field-craft and pistol-handling tailored to the needs of an operative working alone and undercover in a hostile environment. Locals could never be fooled for long by put-on accents or cover stories, something that Nairac found out the hard way (Nairac was a maverick and did not work for any undercover units). The SBS had provided manpower for the MRF in its heyday and continued to do so for the restructured 14 Int as well as providing the occasional instructor. The SAS were not permitted to provide men for 14 Int because London was keen to dissociate them from activities in Northern Ireland, even though everyone knew the SAS were over there, including the newspapers. It was in this area that the SBS's anonymity proved advantageous to its operatives. Few people had heard of us, and any publicised operations conducted by the Branch were credited to the SAS anyway. And so SBS operatives were permitted to join 14 Int. If the government was accused of putting in SAS undercover men they could honestly deny it.

14 Int was taking on a heavy workload and, although highly effective, their history of successes is dotted with the names of operatives killed in action. One of the earliest incidents for this revamped and newly named group occurred a few months after I left the province and was directly related to a loose string of my own.

Two operators from 14 Int had set up an OP in the countryside in an area close to where I had been working on my tour. They were hidden in a hedgerow that ran the length of a field and were watching a house a hundred yards away. Regular soldiers were not allowed into the immediate area, except in an emergency or as part of a pre-planned contingency, for obvious reasons: one group might engage with the other.

As the two 14 Int men sat in their OP they suddenly saw a dozen armed men walking down the side of the field towards them. This means instant, screaming action-stations with minimum movement and noise. The rush of adrenaline is very much appreciated in assisting muscles and joints to work effectively, having moved little for days in the wet and cold. Safety-catches are flicked off and weapons brought to bear. If there is time, a 'standby' message is sent over the radio to the operations room.

The two operatives waited for the men to draw closer before opening fire. They did not feel confident to remain hidden, especially since the patrol appeared to be alert and searching. Seconds before they squeezed the triggers they realised that the armed men were not terrorists but British soldiers. The soldiers themselves had not yet detected the two men hidden in the bushes and the immediate problem for the operatives was how to alert them to the OP's existence without prompting them to open fire.

There was nothing else for it. One of the operatives cried out, 'Halt! We're British soldiers.'

The soldiers instantly went to ground but did not open fire. It turned out they were members of the Ulster Defence Regiment (UDR), the Army group tasked with patrolling this county.* They had strolled into the out-of-bounds area, but as it turned out later, their intrusion was far from accidental. They had entered the out-of-bounds area deliberately after discovering the exact location of the OP by a breach of security and simply wanted to have a look.

As special forces are small organisations and spread thinly on the ground, they do not have the manpower to provide their own Quick Reaction Force (QRF) to support their own operatives in the event of an emergency. They rely on the regional Army group to provide a temporary standby troop for the duration of each separate operation. A standby troop, usually made up of three sections, provides one section at a time, about eleven men, on an eight- or twelve-hour rotation. They

---

* The UDR were a purely Northern Irish Army regiment formed after the B Specials were disbanded in 1970.

spend that entire time together in a room, fully armed and dressed and ready to 'go' at a moment's notice.

Operational secrecy is of the greatest importance to special forces but the local QRF need to know where to go in case they are called. To satisfy this requirement while maintaining the secrecy of the operation, a detailed map and description of the OP location, including the number of operatives, is placed in an envelope along with special instructions and then sealed. It is handed to the Army commander responsible for providing the QRF at the start of the operation with instructions to be opened only on the order of the undercover unit's commander. If the envelope is not used, and it rarely ever is, it is collected at the end of the operation when the QRF are stood down.

It transpired that the UDR's QRF that night, having sat around staring at the envelope for several hours, were overcome with curiosity. They steamed open the envelope and read the 14 Int OP details. Word quickly spread throughout the camp and before long most of the company knew the whereabouts of the operation.

Steaming open the envelope to find the location of the OP was bad enough, but for a troop sergeant to then take out a patrol to look for it was nothing short of stupidity.

The 14 Int men told the UDR patrol commander to get his men out of the area ASAP, which he did. 14 Int were naturally concerned about their security from that moment on, but decided not to pull out just yet. A short time later, incredibly, another and different UDR patrol came along. The operatives could not believe it and they again waited to discover who they were. The operation was becoming a complete farce.

After this second UDR patrol was told to move out, the 14 Int men prepared to pull out themselves. This secret OP had become an exhibition booth. They radioed for a mobile pick-up and made ready to head across country to the road. But just as they were leaving, they noticed suspicious activity at the target house.

They lay on their bellies and turned their attention back towards the target. They did not notice yet another patrol, this time moving in more stealthily behind them. The leader of this latest patrol crept forward to where he could challenge the operatives. The operatives became aware of this latest intrusion and watched by the dim light what they assumed to be yet another UDR patrol, even after they heard an Irish voice call out to them. But this new patrol was PIRA, and the man who was challenging them was Simon O'Sally.

O'Sally had been patrolling the area himself at the time and had watched the UDR's movements back and forth along the same hedgerow with great interest. O'Sally deduced the presence of an OP and moved forward to investigate. He did not know it was a special forces OP or he would never have moved in so close before challenging it. Even so, O'Sally had not acted hastily and prior to moving in he had worked out that the OP was observing the house. He quickly arranged for some activity to take place to distract the OP's occupants, which gave him the diversion to move in behind them. This man was no amateur.

O'Sally and the operatives stared at each other in the darkness for a moment before realising that what each of them saw was not what it first appeared to be. O'Sally noticed the unconventional appearance of the operatives – long hair, facial hair, civilian clothes – and instantly knew he had more than just a couple of UDR on his hands.

The long weapons of the operatives were lying beside them facing the target, the wrong way to engage O'Sally. O'Sally did not hesitate a second longer. He squeezed the trigger of his M16 and emptied the magazine towards the men. Both were hit, but one managed to draw his pistol and return several rounds, hitting O'Sally in the thigh. O'Sally's men instantly scattered when the fire was returned and left him behind. Bleeding like a stuck pig and unable to stand without help, O'Sally crawled away.

The two operatives were alive but seriously wounded and could not move.

The UDR QRF were alerted, and considering they already knew where the OP was, they were not quick to arrive on the scene. It was in fact 14 Int members themselves, in the area because of the earlier 'standby', who were the first on the scene and one of them, Robbie, was a man I knew quite well. He was SBS and had been one of those who had passed my SBS selection course.

Robbie was a large, powerful, black-haired Scotsman with a mellow demeanour who had been a seasoned Royal Marine before joining the SBS. He was a close friend of one of the wounded operatives, and when he saw them both lying shot to bits something inside him snapped. Only war or a conflict of equal horror can unearth the extremes of a person's true character, and this was Robbie's first war.

He backed away from the OP as those medically trained did what they could for the two wounded men. In the distance the UDR QRF was making its way up a track towards them. Robbie surveyed the scene and spotted an M16 in the grass. He could tell immediately it was not one of their own, nor did it belong to any regular troops such as the UDR, who did not have M16s. It had to belong to one of the PIRA members involved in the incident. He quickly checked the ground around the weapon and found a trail of blood. He followed the trail to a clump of crumpled foliage in front of a bush. He carefully peered under the bush, using the barrel of his weapon to part the branches, and saw O'Sally lying there like a wounded animal, wide-eyed and vicious. O'Sally had no other weapon or he would have tried to use it. Hatred surged through Robbie. He knew O'Sally. His initial urge was to blow him away there and then. He reached in with his powerful arms and dragged O'Sally out of the bush and to his feet. O'Sally winced with pain as blood seeped from his wounded thigh, but he was a hard man and did not cry out. Robbie pulled out his pistol and shoved it into O'Sally's head.

'Do it, you bastard,' O'Sally said defiantly.

Robbie would have happily pulled the trigger, but he was aware that the UDR patrol was rapidly closing in, led by one of their officers. If Robbie pulled the trigger he would be charged with murder. The UDR officer, regardless of how he felt about O'Sally's execution, would have to arrest Robbie, as a delegated police officer, for the most serious crime. Robbie was not about to risk jail for O'Sally and he still had a card to play, if only he had enough time to play it.

O'Sally saw the UDR patrol too and realised why Robbie did not shoot. Robbie pulled O'Sally along the hedge away from the UDR.

'We're going for a little walk,' Robbie informed him.

Robbie's intention was to keep O'Sally moving until he bled to death. Robbie held him up and made him walk briskly to keep his heart pumping faster and force more blood out of the open wound. O'Sally was losing blood rapidly, but he did not complain. He accepted it. He had killed enough Brits in cold blood. He understood this was not torture. It was simply Robbie's way of getting the job done.

Robbie did not get far before he heard a voice call out behind him.

'Hey, you! What are you doing with that man?'

It was the UDR officer. He had seen something odd going on and had run over to investigate. Robbie let O'Sally drop to the ground.

'What do you think you're doing?' the officer said as he closed in with his men behind him, highly suspicious now.

Robbie stared dangerously at the officer and the men ultimately responsible for all this. It's possible the officer was not aware of that side of the story yet.

'Go fuck yourself,' Robbie said as he held the officer's gaze. The officer could see the murder in the big Scotsman's face, which had not felt a razor in several days. Robbie's wild, dark hair was long and unwashed. The officer sensed this was not the time to pull rank on this man. The fact is there would never be a time when that would be appropriate. Robbie would always blame the UDR for that day. O'Sally was given immediate first aid and taken away on a stretcher.

The two wounded operatives were also sped to hospital. By the time Robbie got back he heard that one had died on arrival.

The rest of the 14 Int Detachment retired to the bar which was the traditional response to the death of a fellow operative. Robbie calmly walked into the empty galley and made himself a wet of tea. He did not feel like company. In the solitude of the kitchen, surrounded by hanging pots and pans, whatever had snapped in him earlier now came loose and he picked up his high-velocity rifle and cocked it.

The makeshift 14 Int camp was on a piece of open ground made up mostly of thin-shelled Portakabins and caravans and it had the feel of a temporary location. Robbie aimed his rifle at the ceiling and fired. Every man in the camp hit the deck as the loud boom echoed across it. They were all aware that the flimsy buildings would not stop a high-velocity round. Many thought the camp was under attack. The word quickly spread that it was Robbie in the galley and that he had gone a little nuts. A couple of men crawled to the cook-house doors and tried to talk Robbie into calming down, but he was intent on venting his anger on pots and pans, since O'Sally had been denied him.

By now O'Sally was in a military hospital being operated on. He refused any anaesthetic, drugs or painkillers for fear he might talk while under their influence.

Throughout the camp, operators, technicians, cooks, admin staff and the unit commander lay on the ground waiting for Robbie to spend his ammunition or calm down. No one was injured and Robbie was eventually led away and kept under supervision until he could be flown back to England.

When I saw him, back in Poole a few months later, he was cheerful and seemed indifferent to all that had happened. But inwardly he had changed. It was not just the loss of a friend that caused him to lose control, it was the whole senseless bloody conflict. When you dug through the hatred and the egos, the reasons for it all started to look pathetic. But we had not joined up just for Northern Ireland. There were many other responsibilities more worthwhile. Robbie's problem as a member of special forces was that he did not experience any instinctive gratification in taking a life, no matter how deserved it was. He had no primaeval sense of the hunter-killer. Any killing revolted him. He never knew that about himself until he looked death and murder in the face. Few people get to know themselves that well.

O'Sally recovered from his wound though he always had a limp. He was given a life sentence and died in prison after starving himself to death along with Bobby Sands.

Robbie left military life as soon as he could and

got himself a job as a diver on an oil platform in the North Sea.

As for me, I was headed for the waters of Scotland to learn another part of the SBS's varied trade. The next year was going to be wet, cold and windy, and filled with laughter and tragedy, the mile markers of an SBS operative's life.

6

Within a few days of returning from Northern Ireland, before heading into the North Sea, I was sent to Brunei to attend a jungle training school run by the SAS on the Tutong Estuary. We were picking the brains of the Australian SAS, who had the most advanced jungle warfare techniques in those days, specifically small-team patrolling, instant ambush, anti-ambush and anti-pursuit techniques. The Australians learned much of their trade in Vietnam, where they achieved more kills per man than any other special forces unit in that war, and throughout their hundreds of operations they never lost a single soldier in the field due to direct action. Most of their fatalities were caused by booby-traps. The New Zealand SAS, who also saw action in Vietnam, was made up mostly of Maoris and they are still the finest military trackers in the world. They demonstrated their skills by tracking one of our patrols long enough to ascertain our direction, then moved around and ahead of us to lay an ambush which we walked into.

At the jungle training school we were joined by some older SBS members who had served in the conflicts in Aden and Borneo. During the long yomps through the jungle, bivvying up every night, these old soldiers taught us many useful tricks. Building bashers to live in, hunting, trapping, dealing with insect, plant and wildlife, and ways to make life in the jungle more comfortable. On one occasion Alan, a powerhouse of a Marine who was on my SBS selection course, slung a hammock between two trees and built an elaborate overhead shelter with attached mosquito net. Pete, one of the old and bold of the SBS, made himself an A-frame bed and shelter out of tree branches that looked like a penthouse suite compared with anything the rest of us had put together.

'What do you think of that?' Alan asked Pete as he indicated his hammock.

Pete glanced at it then looked up for a second to confirm something. 'You won't live through the night,' was his comment.

He was serious. We looked around Alan's hammock for a deadly spider-nest or snake pit or something like that but could see nothing.

'First thing you do when you make camp in primary jungle is look up,' Pete said.

We looked up, and there it was, a massive tree, a dead-fall, leaning precariously against another tree and just waiting to collapse, all several tons of it, directly on to Alan's bivvy. Alan could not dismantle his hammock

quickly enough, never taking his eyes off the dead-fall.
Every so often throughout the night you could hear the
dead trees crashing to the earth.

One afternoon off while down in the local village of
Tutong, I was enjoying a beer and a piece of *ratou*, the
local spicy taco-like pancake, with Jakers, when an Iban
walked in. Ibans are the local tribesmen who live in the
jungle. He was a proud and serious man in his forties
with jet-black straight hair in a bowl cut. Short and wiry
with lightly tanned skin, he wore a thin jacket, shorts and
leather sandals. His body was covered from head to foot
in tattoos. He recognised us as regular Royal Marines by
our berets and walked over, sat on a chair at our table
and demanded a beer in a calm, polite, mellow voice. We
looked at him, surprised by his manner, which intimated
we owed him one. He hardly looked at us, staring ahead
with his chin up and arms outstretched supported on an
ornately carved walking-stick. We bought him a beer.

We never spoke to him, and after his third or fourth
can of Tiger he suddenly started to talk about his part in
the Borneo confrontation when he was young, working
for the British against the Indonesians. He talked in the
simple English he had learned all those years ago.

He had been recruited as a tracker for the Royal
Marines. Ibans were a gentle people and used mostly
blowpipes to hunt with. His job was to lead the Marine
patrols through the jungle, tracking the enemy and
pointing out booby-traps. The Marines had always offered
him food while on patrol but he preferred to live mostly
off what he found in the jungle, adding seasonings such
as curry which he carried in a small pouch slung over

his shoulder. After demanding another beer he recalled the most memorable moment of his war.

One day he was taken out of the jungle and placed aboard an Army lorry along with several other British soldiers. It was the first time he had been in a motor vehicle. After he had been driven for a while he was taken out of the lorry and put in a long room. Many soldiers joined him in the long room and they all sat and waited. He wore nothing more than his usual bark loincloth and carried his bamboo dart quiver – his nine-foot long blowpipe was taken from him and left outside the hut.

He was given a pack and shown how to carry it on his back like the other soldiers. He had never worn a backpack before but he put it on because the British asked him to and he trusted them.

A terrible storm suddenly blew up outside and the long hut shook violently. Ibans lived in long huts themselves made from the trees that grew around them. He knew that even the white man's long huts made of metal could blow down in a monsoon and he felt safer outside. But when he tried to leave they would not let him and he became ill at ease because he thought he was now a prisoner.

No one in the room spoke to him and hardly anyone looked at him even though he was the only Iban there. He thought everyone in the hut was afraid of the storm outside because they hardly spoke and looked very serious and uncomfortable. Then after a time a door to an adjoining room opened and a man came in talking loudly.

Everyone stood up as if the man was important. Then the Iban said he was suddenly grabbed by two men on either side and walked down through the room. He was worried but they told him that it was all right and he could leave now. The storm continued to rage outside and the hut was shaken and buffeted. Everyone else was getting ready to leave. He was taken to a door at the back of the room which opened as he got to it. He froze in horror in the doorway and refused to go. The jungle was now far, far below.

He was forced to the edge of the door but he yelled and begged for them to stop, trying to explain that he was not a bird and could not fly, but they didn't believe him. They wrenched his grip from the door-frame and hurled him out. He pulled his knees up and hugged them tightly to his chest, keeping his face tucked in between them and his eyes screwed shut. When he hit the ground his knees impacted with his face and broke his cheek-bones. Then British soldiers came and cut him out of the strings and canvas that were tangled around him.

Without medical attention he worked as a tracker for two weeks even though his cheek-bones were broken. He said he saw a lot of fighting before the battle was over and then he went back home.

At the end of the story the Iban finished his beer and would not accept another. He stood up and walked out of the bar.

I enjoyed the contrast of the jungle weather and terrain with that of Britain. And the sea was like diving in a tropical fish tank compared to the mud-pools over-populated with jellyfish where we did much of our SBS diver training. Our jungle training was a six-week introductory course in case we had to join operations that were currently brewing in Central America. After-wards, I was back in the UK to learn the meat of our main role – maritime warfare.

Much of the work the SBS does, especially in water, on or below it, is pioneering and inherently dangerous. The SBS were, and still are in most areas, the cutting edge of maritime special forces warfare, both conven-tional and anti-terrorist, involving expertise in activities from beach reconnaissance, sabotage and information-gathering to oil platform and large ship assault and recapture. The US Navy's SEALs at that time for instance did not have a counter-terrorist team to talk of, but then they had few terrorist threats in those days either. In 1982, when the US Navy SEALs decided to put together their own anti-terrorist group, the SBS advised and trained its first members – a role it still performs today.

The SBS training ethic has always been, 'If we can do it in the worst possible conditions we can do it any time.' The SEALs had their own version of the saying which was, 'There's two ways to do something – the easy way and the British way.' It was intended as a dig at us but we took it as a compliment.

Specialised maritime warfare had to be pioneered by people with experience of and dedication to the sea. It was unreasonable that the SAS wanted to move in on our role. They did not have the pedigree for such a commitment. Their own Boat Troop at that time was little more than a handful of rubber boats and canoes in mint condition due to lack of use. Many Royal Marines joined the SAS and were often placed into the Boat Troop because of their background, but the irony is that Marines who joined the SAS and not the SBS usually did so because of a dislike for our water-sports – it's not everyone's cup of tea.

The average level of fitness of an SBS operative is generally much higher than that of his SAS counterpart. This is as much out of necessity as tradition. Long dives and swims followed by strenuous climbs up the sides of ships and oil platforms require a constant high degree of physical ability. Also, for conventional operations, we must be prepared to carry canoes or/and diving equipment across country on top of our normal field equipment. There was a reason for those backbreaking portages in selection. Physical training is an integral part of every SBS operative's day no matter where in the world he is. The only time we never started a working day with a strenuous physical workout was during live operations. In my time, two SBS operatives have represented England in the Olympics and many more have taken part in world-class running, triathlon and mountain-climbing events. The high physical standards are a duty. You don't need to be super-fit to charge into a building or aboard an aircraft, but if you only have a few hours' notice to scale a massive oil platform carrying heavy equipment in horrendous weather having swum miles, or to climb up the side of a supertanker while other members of your team put their lives in your hands, you had better always be in more than just 'good shape'.

When the SBS resisted letting the SAS train with them in submarines – where they hoped to learn the mysteries of exiting and re-entering them whilst submerged (E&RE) – the SAS made some arrangement with the Norwegian Navy and the German Kampschwimmers who were dabbling in the art at the time. But the Norwegians and the Germans were way behind us in the technique and were still firing themselves out of torpedo tubes. The SAS tried it for a while before deciding it was a tad dodgy and gave it a pass.

Pioneering guarantees that mistakes will be made and the SBS did not get off lightly when paying for their sea lessons. Exiting from and then re-entering a submerged submarine is the most clandestine method for coastal insertion and the infiltration of water-borne targets, and developing the skill has been costly in SBS lives.

E&RE is a process by which a team of SBS operatives 'exit' out of a slowly moving submarine while submerged at periscope depth, swim to the surface and head for their objective. On completion of the operation, the team return to the water, rendezvous with the submerged sub, swim down and 're-enter' it. It may sound straightforward but the procedure is fraught with danger.

When I returned from the jungle I travelled to Scotland to take part in my first E&RE exercise. Many of the basic technical problems had been solved by then, but there were always dangers.

I arrived in HMS Faslane, the Navy's submarine base on a sea loch in the west of Scotland, to join in rehearsals that were already underway several miles away. I

hopped on to a fleet tender, a squat Nav
set off towards Loch Long where a team
Orpheus (an O-class submarine) were op

It was a typically grey, wintry Scottish
looked black and bottomless and the mour
lost in mist. It was not raining but the air was moist
enough to wet you within minutes out on deck.

In detail, in E&RE the submarine, with its team of
SBS on board, slows to no faster than a couple of knots
and no deeper than periscope depth, which is thirty
feet. The first man out of the submarine, through the
escape-hatch, half an hour or so before the team, is
the casing diver. His work can sometimes take hours
and so he wears long-endurance mixed-gas breathing
apparatus. His job is to make sure the large air-bottles,
distributed at various points around the outside of the
sub, that the team will use to breathe once they have
exited, are all in working order. He also prepares the
team's larger operational equipment for release, which
is stowed outside the submarine in special watertight
bins under the outer casing, or skin, in readiness to be
floated to the surface on nylon lines along with the team
when they surface. Finally, he supervises the divers as
they exit the sub until they have all left for the surface,
then 'cleans up' before re-entering himself and the sub
departs.

E&RE is carried out at night and the casing diver
works in darkness, moving around the sub mostly by
feel and memory – a light could give him away to a
passing reconnaissance aircraft, boat or a watcher on a
distant hilltop. In the absence of through-water-comms

communicates with the sub by tapping the hull with a three-pound brass hammer he keeps in a leg pocket. The submarine crew are urged to stay silent when a diver is outside, giving the procedure an eerie feeling, his clangs echoing throughout the sub, telling of his progress and that he is in fact still with the sub.

The SBS team muster under the forward escape-hatch in the ceiling of the torpedo storage and firing compartment. Every submarine has escape-hatches in case the sub sinks and the crew have to abandon it. Using the hatch is most submariners' nightmare and they must all attend a training school where they learn the procedure. They rarely practise it once training is complete, mainly because of the extreme danger. When the SBS exit the sub they use virtually the same procedure.

The inside or lower hatch is opened first and a man crawls up into the tube. He breathes off a breathing umbilical (BU), a mouthpiece connected by a rubber tube to the sub, utilising the sub's air. The lower hatch is closed and the tube is flooded. When the pressure in the escape-hatch equalises with the outside, the top hatch opens and the man exits. When he is free, the upper hatch is closed again, the water is pumped out, and the lower hatch can then be opened and the cycle repeated. This is the basic concept for the SBS exit, but with a few variations.

Depending on the task, such as a maritime anti-terrorist assault, the SBS man wears a lightweight nylon dry-bag over which he straps a multi-pouched vest containing everything he needs for the assault – spare

weapon magazines, explosive entry devices and grenades, climbing equipment, personal waterproof radio,
knife, pistol, any 'special devices' and a climbing harness. The primary weapon, the MP5, is strapped down
one side or across the front of his body on a quick-release
hook and his pistol is fixed into a holster on his lower
thigh or hip. On top of all of this he carries his diving
equipment, which includes fins, mask and a small air-
bottle of only ten minutes' duration at surface pressure
called a RABA (rechargeable air breathing apparatus)
which has a male connection that plugs into the large
air-reservoir bottles outside the sub for recharging. The
bottle is small simply because a larger one would not
fit into the escape-hatch along with the diver.

The first SBS operative climbs up through the lower
hatch, which can be a tight squeeze with all the equipment, and if he's a big lad he may have to be pushed
up from below. Instead of using the escape-hatch and
releasing only one man at a time, the SBS adapted
many RN subs (all O-class, electric/diesel silent types)
by having the one-man tubes replaced with 'five-man
chambers' (it was a tight fit for four men) which looked
something like an external Calor-gas storage tank of a
diameter just large enough for a man to sit inside in the
foetal position. The team climb up through the escape-
hatch and then manoeuvre into the chamber one by one
and sit alternately opposite each other with their knees
curled up in front of them. When the last man is inside
he crunches up over the others while the lower hatch is
clanged shut. He can then sit back on the hatch giving
the others a little more room to breathe and remove

equipment from uncomfortable places like colleagues' gun-barrels and radio antennae from out of noses.

A dim light in the ceiling of the chamber is all there is to see by and a push-button intercom positioned at the waterline is the only communication, other than a small signal hammer in the event the intercom should fail. Six breathing umbilicals hang from the walls at intervals – one is spare. Each diver tests his BU and gives a thumbs-up when happy. The diver near the intercom informs the sub when they are ready to flood. Then the sea-water gushes in.

A combination of pressure and clashing temperatures creates a mist which decreases visibility. As the water comes up your body you breathe normally through your BU. You keep a mental note of where the spare BU is in case yours fails, and you watch the man opposite in case he has a problem.

The water floods the chamber to about four inches from the top of the tightly curved steel roof (waterline) leaving a small air-space. An instinct is to keep your face out of the water in this narrow air-pocket, but it's easier just to sit there, like a sardine, head under the water, in the cramped blackness, and wait. You might be out in five minutes, or you could be stuck there for half an hour. Although it's crowded, you're in your own world in the watery darkness. It's like being in a coffin after the lid has been nailed firmly shut, the coffin has been lowered into the ground and six foot of earth has been piled on top while you stay calm inside. And you have about as much chance of getting out quickly if something goes wrong. Your life is entirely in the hands of the captain.

This is not a good time to succumb to claustrophobia. The trick is to clear your mind, keep still, and think pleasant thoughts while you wait for a signal from the casing diver that he's ready to open the outer hatch and let you out.

On one occasion, during the flooding of a chamber I was in, it was the first 'run' of the day and the pipes had just been flushed with hibitain, a pipe-cleaning chemical. The pipes are supposed to be flushed clean with water after the hibitain, but on this particular day this had been overlooked. As the chamber flooded it started to foam up until the air-space was nothing but dense soap suds. I now know what it would be like to sit inside a crowded washing machine.

Before the first operative exits the flooded chamber he removes his BU and replaces it with the mouthpiece of his RABA and turns it on. He is then guided out of the chamber by the casing diver and directed along the top of the submarine casing to the 'lurking area', where he plugs his RABA into one of the larger air-bottles and waits for the others. If there is a problem now he has hours of air to breathe. Each member of the team goes through the same process.

When the entire team is out of the chamber and assembled in the lurking area, the signal is given and they follow guidelines along the casing, up the fin to where the periscope is, where they can 'let go' of the sub to continue to the surface. If this is a conventional operation such as an assault on a coastal target, the casing diver would have already released the team's stores, such as inflatable boats and their engines, from the special bins under the casing. On the surface the team pull cables connected to gas-bottles that automatically inflate the boats. By the time the SBS team is in their boat or boats and ready to head for the shore ten or twenty miles away, the casing diver has 'tidied up', re-entered the sub and it has left the area.

Many years into my career in the SBS, during a day of E&RE with my own team, one of the sub's crew, a young submariner, was so impressed with the process he could not do enough for us. In fact we were so godlike to him that he elected to be our manservant. We didn't mind.

When it was time to exit the sub he would be there, in the torpedo compartment, to assist with our equipment. On re-entering he would take our wet gear away as we undressed to hang it up and would have a hot mug of tea waiting. He insisted if there was anything we wanted to make our stay more comfortable we need only ask and he would gladly oblige.

'Dig-out, pal,' we told him.

The second day, after we re-entered, he could not hold back the reason for his awe any longer and emotionally declared, 'You blokes are amazin'. I don't know how you do that. You couldn't pay me enough. I can barely swim a width of a swimming pool under water.'

We felt he was being a little over the top, but we accepted the adoration nobly.

''Ow you can 'old your bref in that tiny li'l chamber while it floods an' nen climb out 'en swim to the surface is fuckin' staggerin'.'

We looked at him oddly. 'What do you mean, hold our breath?' I asked.

'What sort a trainin' you do to 'old your bref for so long is beyon' me.'

'We don't,' I said. 'We breathe off the sub when we're in the chamber.'

His brow furrowed and he leant forward as if not hearing me quite right.

'Wha'?' he said.

'We breathe off the sub. And before we exit the chamber we breathe off these miniature air-bottles,' I said, showing him one of the RABAs.

He looked shocked. 'You wha'?' he said. 'You mean you don't 'old your bref?'

'No.' I laughed. 'What the fuck do you think we are, sea lions?'

He looked really disappointed. 'You mean you don't do it all in one bref?'

'Sorry, mate,' I said.

'Wankers,' he exclaimed. 'Wha' a bunch a fuckin' tossers. My grandmuvver could do 'at.' And he stormed off and we didn't see him again for the rest of the operational cycles.

Much of the pioneering work for E&RE is carried out by the SBS in the sea lochs of Scotland. The lochs are calmer than the open sea but they have their own dangers and one in particular is most unpredictable, and was the cause of a fatal accident the day I approached the submarine rehearsal area in the fleet tender.

Inland lochs are fresh-water and the sea lochs, as their name suggests, are sea-water, but not always precisely so. Freshwater streams flow down from the mountains and into the sea lochs in many places and sometimes the fresh water holds together as a large body, not immediately mixing with the sea-water. Fresh water is less dense than sea-water and therefore does not support or float an object, such as a submarine, quite as well. When a submarine suddenly plummets due to hitting a less dense patch of fresh water it is called a 'depth excursion'. It's a bit like suddenly going over a waterfall you didn't know was there in the dark. A depth excursion is only a momentary inconvenience for a submarine, but for a diver, outside on the casing, it can be lethal.

There are two points of buoyancy that most affect a diver: positive and negative. A diver in an air-filled suit rising to the surface without power is lighter than the water he displaces, and is positively buoyant. If he is pulled down under the water towards the bottom of the ocean, as he descends, the pressure acting on him increases until he reaches a point beyond which he will no longer have to be pulled down and will sink of his own accord. At this point he is described as being negatively buoyant. The point between positive and negative buoyancy is called neutral buoyancy.

A diver, in a dry-suit, wearing a lot of equipment, such as weapons and climbing gear, will need to release some air into his suit from a small suit-inflation bottle attached to his waist in order to maintain his neutral buoyancy, otherwise he'll sink.

When a diver is on the casing of a submarine for E&RE he can be anywhere between thirty to sixty feet below the surface (sometimes the subs lose finite control of their depth and sink below periscope depth). He will release enough air into his suit from the small suit-inflation bottle to make sure he is neutrally buoyant at that depth. If he's too positively buoyant he'll have to hang on and pull himself along the casing of the sub in the hand-stand position which looks and feels stupid, and if he should lose his grip he'll float away and 'lose' the submarine. With the correct buoyancy, when he's ready to surface, he releases the submarine and gently fins his way up, growing more positively buoyant as he rises due to the reduction in pressure and therefore the expansion of the air in his dry-suit.

On this particular day, there were three divers getting ready to exit the chamber of HMS *Orpheus*, which was cruising at periscope depth below the surface of Loch Long – a sea loch. Of the three SBS divers using the chamber that day I knew only one, Chris, the operative who first welcomed me to the squadron. Another was an officer called Jim and the third was an NCO named Huk.

As I approached the area in the tender, although the submarine was unseen below the surface, I knew where it was because of the Zodiac safety boat, a giant-sized rubber inflatable boat used just for this purpose. It contained the dive supervisor, standby diver and safety diver, and moved silently along without its outboard engine running because it was tied by a line to the sub's periscope, the tip of which was only just visible on the surface several metres ahead of the Zodiac. A second inflatable was circling the area half a mile away to ward off any local boat traffic. My tender slowed and came alongside the safety tender which shadowed the party several hundred yards aft. I would have to wait until this serial was over before I could join the sub.

A diver can comfortably move about the outer casing of a sub if its speed does not exceed half a knot. Any faster and he has to concentrate on holding on. Faster than two knots and he cannot hold on at all because of the force of the water pushing against him. The initial danger if he lets go is that he will pass through the props. When a sub hits a fresh-water patch and takes an 'excursion' it uncontrollably increases in speed and loses depth until the commander either blows its ballast tanks or steers back up. There are many dangers for a diver during an excursion, perhaps the greatest one being that, when the sub 'drops' suddenly, it takes him below his point of neutral buoyancy making him negatively buoyant. Communications between divers and sub are difficult and therefore it is often impossible for the commander to know precisely where the men are outside.

As the serial progressed, those of us on the surface were initially unaware that the sub had cruised into a fresh-water patch and begun to dive uncontrollably – the periscope suddenly dipping out of sight for a moment was not unusual. Huk was the lead diver and was coming out of the chamber at that exact moment. He had removed the sub's BU from his mouth and was breathing off his RABA set. The sub takes a moment to build speed and the initial moment of an excursion is not always obvious to the diver. But as Huk cleared the hatch he felt his ears pop. The same team had taken an excursion to eighty-five feet a few days earlier without incident, so the experience was not new to them. The casing diver, aware himself by now of the excursion, signalled Huk to make his way to the lurking area, where he could plug into the large air-bottles and recharge his RABA. It was dark, but Huk could make out the light-coloured jackstay rope that led along the casing to the lurking area. Chris and Jim continued to exit the chamber and were preparing to transfer from the sub's air to their RABA sets. There was no immediate concern as they expected the sub to ascend back to its cruising depth eventually as it had done the previous day, but this was a much more serious excursion than anyone could tell at that initial moment. The first people to realise how potentially dangerous it was were those on the surface.

The safety boat, attached to the periscope, suddenly plunged nose-down into the water like a giant fishing float attached to a 1,000-ton fish. The diving supervisor, standby and safety diver were literally catapulted out of the boat like rag dolls as it went near vertical to follow the submarine down. But before the huge rubber safety boat disappeared below the surface the line ripped from its nose under the tremendous strain and it shot backwards almost completely out of the water. Its heavy engine, attached to the back, almost came down and hit one of the safety crew in the water. The second inflatable sped to help the standby crew, but there was nothing anyone could do to help those below. They were on their own.

The submarine continued to plummet in the less

dense fresh water. Huk was halfway along the casing towards the lurking area when his small RABA set ran out of air due to the sudden increase of depth and pressure. It was at that point that he realised the excursion was a serious one and so instead of continuing on to the lurking area and the large reserve air-bottles, he held his breath, turned around and headed back to warn the others. Huk was every bit the team player and would not have hesitated to risk his life to help an oppo in trouble.

He pulled himself back along the jackstay, now against the heavy water flow, towards the chamber. When he got there Chris and Jim were still in the process of exiting. The casing diver, breathing off his twin-tank mixed-gas long-endurance breathing set and in no immediate danger of running out of air, was receiving loud, explicit orders from the surface via his DUCS, a safety radio connected by a long cable to the surface craft. The diving supervisor, struggling in the water with his own sinking rubber safety boat, was ordering him to get the team up pronto. The casing diver signalled to Chris and Jim to ascend, but in the near darkness the signals were confusing. When Huk arrived he also tried to communicate with hand signals, warning Jim and Chris that they should not change to RABA and to stay on the sub's BUs in the chamber. Their diving suits, compressed by the depth, were tight on their bodies by now, but Chris and Jim obviously had no idea just how serious the excursion was at that point, nor could they understand the gestures in the black water. Huk could not hold his breath any longer, and since Chris was halfway out of the chamber, blocking it, he could neither climb back inside nor get back to the reserve air-bottles and connect on to them in time, so he kicked off in a bid to reach the surface. Huk had left his ascent dangerously late. His last sight of the sub was the red glow from the chamber below him where Jim and Chris still continued to exit.

Huk had no idea the sub had dropped beyond the eighty-five-foot excursion of the previous day, but he soon realised he was well below his point of neutral buoyancy and was not going up fast enough. He started to ditch equipment. It was decided later that the divers were wearing far too much. After this incident a special life-jacket was designed for SBS divers that, when pulled, inflated a massive air-bag capable of pulling up a man in full operational equipment from a hundred feet. Unfortunately, for now, the only way Huk was going to reach the surface was to fin like mad. He was still operating on the lungful of air he had when he went back to help the others, and he was going into serious oxygen debt. He was exhaling slowly as he ascended to prevent his lungs from exploding as the air expanded in them, but he could feel the world slowly crushing in on his head.

Back on the sub Jim and Chris had transferred to their RABA sets, not knowing they were practically empty now due to the depth. The casing diver was still trying to get them to ascend, but his communications cord suddenly went taut as it reached its limit and he was yanked off the casing from above like a puppet. He was pulled to the surface as he watched Chris and Jim on the black cigar shape of the sub merge into the blackness of the water.

When the sub reached 110 feet the commander ordered an emergency ascent and the ballasts were blown. Everyone hoped that the divers had either managed to get into the lurking area, up into the fin, or back inside the chamber. There was no way of knowing for sure. They listened for any sound on the casing that might indicate where the divers were, but there was only silence. The helpless SBS operatives on the surface waited anxiously.

When the ballasts were blown at 110 feet, Chris and Jim were free of the chamber and on the casing breathing off their RABA sets when they were swept off by the sudden acceleration as the submarine made its way to the surface. They were negatively buoyant and their RABA sets were soon out of air.

They opened up their suit-inflations fully, but at that depth there was little more than a cupful of air. Without ballast they would have needed engine-powered propellers on their feet to move up.

Huk had had a head start but he was still negatively buoyant, and when he emptied his suit-inflation bottle into his dry-bag he could tell by the unchanged tightness of his suit that he was deep. He finned for his life as his lungs and face felt like they were going to explode. He could not tell how close he was to the surface, or if in fact he was going up at all. When you can't tell where the surface is, in poor visibility or at night, the thing to do is watch for air bubbles. If they stay level with you or go below you, you're going up. If they overtake you,

you're not going anywhere, or you're going down. But Huk couldn't see any bubbles in these conditions, his eyes were too bulged to see anything. When he broke the surface it was a surprise to him. He choked and gulped in air. He had been so close to unconsciousness that everything was out of focus. As the oxygen surged back into his brain and his mind began to recover, he turned in the water looking for the others. The safety boat sped towards him. The submarine suddenly crashed to the surface not far away, and as the water cascaded off its deck submariners were already leaping from the hatches to search every nook and cranny in the hope of finding the divers.

The following day, Chris and Jim were found in 221 feet of water at the bottom of the loch directly under the point where the sub had began its emergency surface. Jim had managed to ditch some of his gear, but in his frantic effort to swim he had lost a fin.

I watched Huk that evening as we travelled back in the tender. He sat in the galley nursing a cup of tea, staring out of the window as the drizzle ran down the glass. I wondered if, along with everything else, he was thinking of the last time he had been caught outside a submarine as it suddenly dived without warning.

That time was in Gibraltar. The sub hadn't run into a fresh-water patch – not in the Mediterranean – it had had to do an emergency crash dive to avoid a collision with another boat.

Huk was the only diver out on the casing that day. The sub was practising E&RE drills for training a batch of new submarine captains when suddenly its sonar picked up a frigate bearing down on them at high speed. The periscope confirmed it. There were warning buoys dotted all around that part of the ocean indicating the training area boundaries. The frigate was Iranian and the crew either had no clue of international navigation signals or chose to ignore them. The submarine commander had no choice but to order an emergency dive. Huk, on the outside, had no warning and when the sub nosed down he could not hold on and was ripped away. The props missed him by feet and he spun in their vortex. He was left floating in watery space as the sub disappeared below. It was during daylight hours and visibility was good. He finned for all he was worth, and although he had run out of air, in the clear, blue waters he could see he was nearing the surface. When he burst through and gulped in the air his problems were not over. He was facing the bows of the frigate as it cut through the water towards him. He swam out of its way and it passed him by yards. A couple of Iranian crew, leaning on the rails, watched him, no doubt wondering what on earth someone was doing all alone floating in the sea twenty miles from the nearest piece of land. They didn't bother to help him.

Huk was legendary in the squadron for his near misses. His success in avoiding so many close calls was greatly due to his powerful limbs. He held the record for the fastest run up the Rock of Gibraltar, which stood for fifteen years and was only then lost to a professional racing-snake.

In Oman, with the SAS during the war there in the early seventies, Huk had been carrying out a beach reconnaissance. This consists of taking soundings of the sea-bed by dropping a plunger to measure the depth at intervals while swimming out from the beach on a line. A shark fin passed between him and the beach and then began to circle. Huk threatened the record for the hundred metres front crawl as he swam towards shore.

His last near miss was whilst climbing the famous rail bridge over the River Forth using magnets, a technique on trial for climbing oil platforms. It required three heavy magnets attached to the climber by lines and he moved them up one at a time to climb like Spiderman, always held by no fewer than two magnets at any one time. The method had its drawbacks. On this particular day, Huk was a hundred feet above the river when, after disconnecting one of the magnets whilst hanging off the other two, he stretched up and stuck it on to the metal flank of the bridge support. He could not know he had clamped on to a large flat blister – a tenuous hold on a thin patch of rust under the skin of clean paint. As he disconnected the second magnet to move it up, the high one, unable to support his weight, simply peeled off the rust. With only one magnet left to support him, which was not sufficient, he peeled off and plummeted. As if that was not bad enough, it turned out to be only the first in a sequence of problems. Sticking out of the water directly below him was a series of metal stakes six feet apart. Huk miraculously fell between two of them. Fortunately the water was deep where he hit and he was uninjured, but his next problem was how to get back to the surface while dragging three very heavy magnets with him. He felt a stack of rocks and started to climb them. The rocks made up the foundation of one of the massive pillar supports and went all the way to the surface.

I never talked to Huk, not in those early days, not even after the accident in Loch Long. I was not in his section and as a new boy I only socialised with those I knew from my selection course or my own team. Shortly after the submarine accident in Scotland Huk disappeared from the SBS.

About a year passed before I realised he was gone – operatives were always quietly disappearing for long periods. I asked if anyone knew where he was.

'He's away,' a senior operative said and gave me a look that implied I was to inquire no further.

A couple of years later I quietly went 'away' myself and, after a long journey, on arriving at my final destination, to my surprise I was met by Huk, and for a few brief weeks, while he handed over his job to me, we were friends.

7

One rainy afternoon, exactly two years after joining the SBS, I was in the squadron lines in Poole servicing my personal field equipment after a particularly horrendous two-week exercise in Scotland. The exercise was called Haggis Leap and consisted of parachuting into a loch on the west coast at night with canoes then paddling them twenty miles to a landing point. We then bagged them up and prepared to carry them, plus our field equipment (a total of 145 pounds dry), seven miles to an inland loch. But after a couple of the backpack straps, mine included, snapped under the weight where they attached to the packs behind the shoulders, the seven-mile yomp turned into a twenty-one mile relay. The portage was done in two shifts that completely ate into the following day's sleep period.

Special forces generally sleep during the day and move only in darkness, but on this exercise we were on a very tight schedule, made worse by the equipment failure. On reaching the inland loch, without any rest, we had barely enough time to paddle the fifteen miles in darkness to the lay-up point before moving on to our target. By the time we reached the target we had been going non-stop for forty-six hours, pausing only to grab a quick bite and a wet. I had never been that exhausted even on my selection course and, come dawn, after beaching the canoes and camouflaging them, I fell asleep as soon as I hit the ground, remaining as still as the boulders I was hidden between until the following dusk. I will never forget that night's paddle, because during the last few hours we all began to hallucinate.

There were six of us in three canoes and as we moved down the centre of the loch which was several hundred yards wide, one man in the front of his canoe suddenly disconnected his paddles, stowed them in the pockets in the sides of the canoe, got out his weapon, unzipped his splash-deck and began to get out of his seat. He almost capsized the canoe as he tried to put a foot in the water.

'What the hell are you doing?' his partner behind exclaimed in panic, as he used his paddle to stabilise the boat.

'Can't you see the rocks?' the front man replied. 'I'm going to pull us round them or we'll lose the bottom of the boat.'

His partner had to assure him, using their map, that it was at least half-a-mile deep where we were.

We were so exhausted we paddled like sluggish robots. We stopped at one point when one of the lads thought he could see a suspension bridge across the loch just up ahead. Once he suggested it we could all see it. We consulted our maps, but the loch was in the middle of nowhere, miles from the nearest road, never mind a major bridge. We canoed towards it but it kept its distance. We were staring at the loch where it met the horizon and the thin black line that separated it from the sky had become a bridge in our imaginations. My worst hallucinations were giant effigies of Tom and Jerry above the tall trees that lined one side of the loch, as if a Disneyland had been built there that was now empty and ghostly silent with all the lights turned off. I kept that observation to myself. The next eleven days were pretty much the same but with at least a few hours' sleep during the light hours and no more hallucinations. An Australian SAS man, a Maori and Vietnam vet attached to the SBS at the time told me I would never hallucinate like that again in my life – it was a one-off phenomenon. I never have, but then I don't think I have ever been that exhausted since. We covered 150 miles on foot whilst attacking or observing a variety of targets. Halfway we received a food and explosives resupply drop from a C130 transport aircraft. The weather varied between rain, driving snow and sunshine. Because of the weight factor we carried the minimum of everything. For instance, we calculated our minimum daily food intake for those conditions at 4,500 calories (conventional ration-packs have about 3,000 calories per day and Arctic packs 6,000) and carried no more than the exact amount. When I finally got back to Poole and took my first shower in two weeks in the squadron lines, I winced at my full-length naked figure in the mirror. My shoulders and neck muscles had developed in such a way that they seemed to join my ears, and my thighs and calves were bigger than I remember ever seeing them, but my waist had shrunk and my stomach had become inverted. I looked like an ant.

The following day in the squadron lines, the sergeant major's office wallah found me packing away the now clean and repaired canoes, and said I was to report to his boss in the headquarters building.

Young operatives were rarely called to see the sergeant major personally. I assumed I was to be reprimanded for some indiscretion. It would not be the first time I had been hauled in for a slap on the wrist. No one ever accused me of being the best-dressed soldier on camp and I had, on occasion, neglected to salute a regular (non-SBS) officer. This was not because of any disrespect. Due to the nature of the work, the relationship between officers and men in the SBS is less strict than in regular units. Where low profile is the order of the day, it would look odd if one long-haired man walked up to another in the street, saluted, remained at attention and continually addressed him as 'sir'. Officers and men often spent weeks working closely together and first names were the norm, although this familiarity was discouraged when we were back in camp and under the watchful eye of the regular officers.

By now I had my own digs in Poole and had settled into the fast-paced lifestyle of the SBS where there was no such thing as routine. Our hair was generally long because of low-profile operational requirements and we rarely wore uniforms (which irritated conventional ruperts). An operative could expect to spend more than half the year abroad, far removed from conventional forces and their influences. I had never served in a regular regiment and therefore probably found it easier than most to lose sight of uniform dress standards, and I had completely lost the habit of leaping to attention when addressed by an officer as regulars usually do.

The squadron was occasionally asked to join the rest of the camp and turn out for full blues parades (number one uniform) for visiting dignitaries, but was kept out of sight as much as possible for fear it might cause embarrassment. The commanding officer during my first few years as an SC rate (Swimmer Canoeist is our official Navy job description) was Rom. He was one of our finest field officers, well-respected and liked, innovative and far-sighted and credited with pioneering many of the maritime anti-terrorist procedures used worldwide today. He was also the main force behind getting the squadron into Northern Ireland with the SAS. He was one of those officers who put the SBS before the rest of the corps, believing they could play an even greater role in conventional and specialist operations in the future. As an officer cadet he was head of his batch, and later on achieved a high pass grade at staff college when many, if not most, officers usually failed the exam. He was tipped to make the big time, but his career undoubtedly suffered because of his passion for the SBS and he left the corps shortly after the end of his command, only having reached the rank of major. It's an indication of the nepotism that is still rife amongst senior members of the British military, where the old-boy network rather than ability gets you to the top.

On the parade ground, Rom was not at home at all. On my first blues parade, as he led the squadron on a march past a group of dignitaries on a podium, he threw one spur as he approached, and the other as he took their salute, and then he nearly lost his sword as we marched out of sight. The camp's (non-SBS) commanding officer could only roll his eyes as he took the salute. The SAS didn't have to do march-past parades for visiting dignitaries. They were so out of practice they would have been tripping over themselves worse than us.

It was the fast-paced lifestyle of the SBS and my devotion to field-craft and not parade skills that contributed to my seemingly laid-back manner. I had been away from the SBS for nearly the whole of that year and actually spent three of those months with the British bobsleigh team. I might as well have been a civvy during that period. The commanding officer at the time, the one after Rom, was a bobsleigh enthusiast and, as I was a bit of a sprinter, he asked me if I'd like to have a go as a brake-man. A brake-man is the one at the back of the bob, four- and two-man, who pushes for all he's worth then jumps in last, does little else on the run but get his head down, and is responsible for applying the brakes after the finish. On one occasion I didn't brake soon enough which resulted in us crashing through the bales of straw beyond the finishing line, causing several spectators to scramble for their lives. I was surprised that an SBS rate could be spared for such a jolly, but the corps has always shown keenness in supporting sports, and members of the SBS, even today, get involved in events such as cross-Atlantic rowing or Iron-man triathlons. Bobsleighing was a lark, but after a couple of months and several crashes as a brake-man, one memorable one with a novice driver that left me sailing through the finishing line alone on my back at 50 mph and without the bob, I decided to give driving one a shot – at least I would be master of my own destiny. After a two-week course in Igles at Berchtesgaden in Austria, I had my first race – a series of four runs down the Olympic course.

As the SBS did not have a bobsleigh and the Navy bobs had headed off for a race in Switzerland with the rest of the team, I asked an officer from the Tank Regiment, who was taking some advanced driver training lessons from the Austrian team coach, if I could borrow his for the race. Most of the ruperts I met who drove or braked for the bobsleigh team were quite hooray and snobbish. But I found them amusing. The tank officer reluctantly lent me his two-man bob along with his brake-man, who had just arrived – a captain from his regiment he had talked into coming over to give it a go. He asked me to please be careful with his bob, and not to go too fast and unnerve his new brake-man, who was completely virgin to the sport and had not even been down a run yet. I said I would be careful, but I was intent on winning the novice race and that meant pulling out all the stops. I was actually coming second overall in the competition when, on my final run, I tipped the bob on its side on the last series of bends. The brake-man got his head (helmeted of course) jammed between the bob and the ice for several yards and judging by his screams it must have hurt. I managed to throw my weight over on the last bend which put the bob upright again and we sailed through the finishing line more or less in one piece. The bob's shell was badly damaged and the new brake-man took the first train home. The tank officer was furious with me, shouting and raving that it would take days to repair the bob, and where was he going to find another brake-man? The season was coming to an end anyway, so with no bob or crew I packed up and made my way back to Poole.

Bobsleighing was OK, but I was looking forward to getting back to a job altogether more exciting and dangerous.

I entered the sergeant major's office, expecting nothing less than a bollocking, and stood there waiting for it.

He glanced up at me from his desk and handed me a piece of paper. I read it. I was not to be reprimanded. These were marching orders. A ripple of excitement ran through me. They had called for me.

'You've got ten days to sort out your affairs before you leave. That means phone, gas, electricity bills and mortgage, etcetera. I don't want to be bothered by anything civvy regarding you. Nobody will be able to contact you. You got a steady girlfriend?'

'No, sir.'

'Don't take your car. You'll be given a train pass. Take nothing other than what's on that list. Make sure you have nothing with your name or anyone else's on it – no address book, letters, bank cards – nothing that can be connected to you – don't forget to take Mummy's name tags off your socks and skiddies. You'll carry your Navy ID card only, which will be taken from you when you arrive. No one will know you're SBS. If anyone asks what your parent unit is tell 'em to fuck off and then keep your eye on 'em. Got it?'

'Sir.'

'Do you have an idea where you're going, lad?'

'I think so, sir.'

'Then keep it to yourself. The location is secret. It's volunteer only. And remember this. Not one single SBS operative has ever been anything short of exemplary in that unit. You bloody well ought to be. No one else you'll meet there will have a quarter of your skills and training.'

'Sir.'

'Good luck . . . Oh, and a bit of advice. By the time you get there have a new first name. Never tell anyone your real name, your surname, got it? Your buddy may get captured alive one day and tortured, and you'll always be having to look over your shoulder.'

That was it – short and sweet. I was on my way to begin a four-month long course that would prepare me for two years in Northern Ireland with the 14th Intelligence Detachment.

I arrived at the location known as 'Camp One' in civvies and carrying a suitcase with a change of civvy clothes, PT kit and dhobi bag. The camp was in the countryside, and I had walked from the bus stop half a mile along a deserted country lane that ran through a wood. The sign outside the dowdy, concrete entrance simply read: 'MOD PROPERTY'. The camp looked as if it had been abandoned decades ago. That was not far from the truth. It had been built during the last war and had been occupied by an American fighting unit. It was demobbed in the fifties and since then maintained on a basic level by a skeleton crew.

Inside the bramble-covered perimeter were several rows of old, single-storey barrack blocks and administration buildings. A lone cigarette-smoking sentry, standing in a fragile modern kiosk just about big enough for him, watched me walk in through the main entrance. Before I reached him he pointed towards the entrance to a brick building not far away. Apart from the sentry there was no other sign of life. The motley camp felt like a ghost town.

When I entered the building I found life, of a sort. I was met by several stone-faced members of the Army Intelligence Corps who communicated their needs to me with the bare minimum of words. They checked my papers and ID and passed me on through into the processing system. I was ushered into another room with little fuss and no conversation, where my suitcase contents were turned out and closely inspected. My dhobi bag, PT kit and spare underwear were handed back to me and the rest put back into my case, which was labelled and put to one side. I was stripped virtually naked, and after my clothes were searched they were put into a bag and placed with my case. After a cursory inspection by a doctor, I was handed a bundle of old Army fatigues, socks and boots. As soon as I was dressed I was led across the camp to a large barrack block that contained about thirty beds with a metal locker beside each one. Several other recruits were quietly making their beds. The atmosphere was solemn and filled with uncertainty, the familiar atmosphere of a selection course and one I knew so well by now. This would be my third in as many years.

I had no idea how many people would be on this course, but I had heard the pass rate was as low as the SAS selection. By now I had a solid confidence in myself when it came to this sort of thing. It was not a case of whether I could make the final cut, but how high a grade I could pass by. As I finished making my bed we were ordered to assemble outside. I put my few belongings in my cupboard and followed the others outside.

I walked out of the grot and up a narrow footpath between the buildings. It led on to a rugged parade ground that had long-established weeds and tufts of grass growing from cracks all over it. The camp had been modernised very little in fifty years and I could imagine the American regiment billeted here gathered on parade in full equipment prior to leaving it for the last time on their way to the D-Day invasions.

Mustered on the parade ground were over a hundred volunteers, dressed in fatigues like me, hoping to be selected for undercover operations in Northern Ireland. The recruits were from all walks of military life, not only the Army and Marines, but the Navy and Air Force. Fit, fat, thin, old and nerdy, confident and nervous. For this job an operative was not required to be super-fit or even svelte. In fact, the less he looked like a soldier the better.

But an operative was required to be intelligent, have a high degree of mental stamina, be able to operate technical devices, and use a pistol and MP5 to extremely high standards (after the four-month selection course, a 14 Int operative had a higher standard of semi-automatic pistol-handling than most SBS and SAS members). He had to be able to drive a car at high speeds, alone, at night, along unfamiliar country roads while reading a coded map by torchlight, give accurate, coded grid references over a concealed radio system (a hand had to be freed to press the hidden 'talk' button) and receive and decode other operatives' grid locations, all while in pursuit of an enemy vehicle – and be prepared at any time to react to an attack. None of these requirements, I was to discover, were in the least bit exaggerated.

While the senior instructor gave us a welcome talk, I glanced around at some of the others and suddenly recognised one of the faces. It was Arthur, an SBS operative who had joined the squadron a year before me, who was in the photograph I found in the grot the day I arrived in Poole, wearing the sack clothing as he boarded a landing craft after a week's survival course. We had never had a conversation before but we recognised each other. He was a similar build to me and was reputed to be a high-quality operative. He gave me a surreptitious wink. It turned out there were three of us from the SBS on the selection course, the third being Sal, who had completed the selection course after mine. We didn't talk openly to each other for the first few weeks, to disguise any prior relationship. Sal was to be the first SBS member not to complete the 14

Int selection course in our history, but for an unusual reason.

The first two weeks of the course was, as usual with special forces, devoted to a vigorous weeding-out of the no-hopers. The focus of this selection, endurance-wise, was predominantly mental. A technique for achieving acceptable results in a short time is to impose long hours of physical discomfort and little or no sleep, then, at the height of exhaustion, to apply extreme trauma, followed immediately by problem-solving under pressure. This was to be the pattern for the next two weeks. Mental stamina is dependent on physical fitness, so a swift wearing-down of both was required to kick things off.

The entire selection course was doubled off the parade ground in a column along a narrow road leading into the countryside that was part of the camp and out of bounds to civilians. No one spoke to each other. We were dropped off in pairs at fifty-foot intervals, given pencil and paper and ordered to remain in the same spot some thirty feet from the road, concealed in the bushes, and to maintain a log of any activity we saw. We were not told how long we would be there and were warned if we left the position for any reason we would immediately be returned to unit (RTUed). The instructors hinted we would be in position for at least two days, perhaps more.

My partner for this first exercise was an old, wiry man nicknamed Brock (because of his badger-like qualities) who, at forty-one years old, seemed too ancient to be doing active field duties, by modern military standards. He'd been in the mob for over twenty years and didn't look as if he had many more to do before his time was up. His hair was grey, dry and curly and started several inches back from its original start-line on his forehead. He reminded me of a Cornish fisherman, a grumpy old version, as he sat opposite, looking at me somewhat suspiciously. It was the way Brock looked at everyone. I didn't know what he was doing on this selection course and did not expect him to stay long, which was a good enough reason not to communicate with him at all. He no doubt looked upon me as some young punk and maintained his stern, silent attitude for the same reason.

With nightfall came a frost. Selection processes always overlapped the winter months when possible so the cold and rain could be taken advantage of as an added fuck-factor. The lack of clothing was deliberate. I mooched around and stuffed my jacket and trousers with as much dried grass as I could find in the limited area. Brock did the same and we competed for what little fauna there was in our patch. It itched and scratched but the duvet effect afforded us a little warmth, though not enough to allow us to sleep. The obvious thing would have been to sit close together for added warmth, but we just sat opposite each other. I would rather have been by myself than stuck with this old man. I would not have been surprised if he had been part of the test.

There was movement throughout the night, mostly the sound of a solitary person walking along the road. I was pretty sure I knew what it was.

Come morning, my suspicions were confirmed when I saw several recruits heading back along the road. They had quit and would be processed out of the camp within an hour. As on past selections, watching them made me wonder what some soldiers expected these courses to consist of when they quit at the first taste of discomfort. The Int Corps moved with clinical efficiency when a recruit quit or was 'cancelled'. Throughout the course, sometimes in the middle of the night, a recruit would be called away for no apparent reason and never seen again, his cupboard emptied, his bedding removed and the bed-frame upended literally within minutes. It was spooky in some ways, but interesting, even satisfying to watch the population of the barrack room dwindle as the days ticked away. Army Intelligence used this early phase to do a more thorough check of our individual backgrounds. There was to be no chance taken that an IRA sympathiser might infiltrate our ranks. I wondered how many of us would be left by the end. I was determined to be one of them. Brock seemed equally determined.

I learned many months later that Brock was an Army helicopter pilot and sergeant major of his squadron. He was married with two children, but one day, at forty, he was suddenly infused with the idea of being a special forces operative. He applied for the SAS and, surprisingly, was accepted to take part in a selection course. They must have missed his age on the application form, and I am sure the DS raised a few eyebrows when he arrived. It was too demanding for him physically, and although he put up a spirited effort he had to quit during one of the long load-carrying map marches. His body could no longer take the punishment. Not one to be deterred or give in easily, he immediately applied for the 14 Int selection course. He was a tough old bastard. A fine pair we made, facing each other in a bush freezing our nuts off: one of the youngest operatives in special forces teamed up with one of the oldest soldiers in the British Army.

Come mid-morning, I saw a lone instructor walking down the road carrying a small backpack. He was in field fatigues and wore a fawn beret with a winged dagger cap badge. He left the road and cut through the brush towards our position. He called out and we stood to show ourselves. As he came over he reached into his backpack and tossed us a small tin of food each. His attitude was cold and laced with contempt – typical for Directing Staff. He knew we had no tin-opener. Having food but no way to eat it was supposed to piss us off even more.

'Want some water?' he asked.

'Sure,' I said cheerfully, showing contempt for his contempt. Always take what's offered – you never know when your next chance for sustenance will come.

He tossed me a bottle and I took a gulp. I handed it to Brock. There was something familiar about this SAS trooper. He was clean-shaven and groomed compared to the last time I had seen him.

We recognised each other about the same time. He was the trooper with whom I had shared my first ambush outside O'Sally's farm a year and a half earlier. His demeanour changed subtly and he eased his harsh edge. Even if I was one of 'that other lot from Poole' I was a notch above the others, and there was nothing on this selection course that was going to crack me. He smiled slightly and nodded, the only hint he allowed that showed he recognised me.

'Cold last night?' he asked, trying to make some light conversation.

'Bit,' I said and shrugged.

He kept his voice low when he said, 'We're pulling you all out in a few hours.'

The information was simply professional courtesy. He knew I would stay in that bush if I had to until they carried me out. He paused as an afterthought before leaving to offer us a small army tin-opener – another show of courtesy.

'It's OK,' I said. 'I brought my own.' I had taped a tiny Army tin-opener, a five-pound note, a miniature button compass and a book of matches to the arches of my feet before I got off the train the day I arrived. I didn't know what to expect so I had come prepared. The wily Brock had also concealed a tin-opener on his person. Brock did not ask what all that was about between the SAS lad and me, but he gave me an even more curious look.

When Brock and I were eventually called back on to the track at midday to join the others, the column was short by some thirty recruits. I wondered how many would have been left had it snowed or rained.

We were not allowed sleep the second night, either. They kept all of us occupied with a dusk-till-dawn cross-country map-reading exercise. It was a straightforward enough circuit, but many recruits got hopelessly lost – mostly matelots and RAF personnel who had little or no previous experience of map-reading. The next day we were given initiative tests such as bridge-and raft-building using ropes, logs and oil drums, etc. The instructors wanted to assess how we worked and cooperated with each other. Late on the third night they finally let us into our beds for the first time since we'd arrived. After grabbing a quick shower, I entered the grot and slumped on my bed. Many recruits were already asleep having skipped their personal hygiene. I pulled on a clean T-shirt, shorts and socks, crawled under the crisp sheets and fell into a deep sleep the minute my head hit the pillow.

I don't know if it was ten minutes or two hours later but suddenly all hell broke loose. Explosions went off all around – thunder-flashes erupted on or under beds while men charged through the room firing guns and yelling for us to evacuate or we'd be killed. I had woken up in the middle of a pitched battle. I was in such a deep REM-sleep, I had no idea where on earth I was and what I was doing there. I could have been in another life. I leapt from my bed and tripped and stumbled barefoot in the darkness as blinding explosions went off all around. Someone fired a magazine of blank rounds straight at me from feet away. I scrambled for the door where I crashed into other dazed and stunned men desperately trying to get away. A boot slammed into my side. Something like a rubber truncheon hit me on the head repeatedly. I burst outside into the night and, in the grip of fear and total confusion, ran full-pelt. I didn't know or care where I was headed, I just had to get away. As I ran hard in my bare feet across the parade ground my brain started to make sense of the confusion. Once I recognised my surroundings, things quickly fell back into place. I paused between some old buildings to gather myself and get my bearings. I looked down at my bare feet and decided from then on I would sleep wearing trainers. The other grots had also been attacked and I could see and hear silhouettes running. It was several years before I fully appreciated the lesson learned that night. The experience seemed to loosen a compartment in my brain. Perhaps a similar compartment to the one a baby opens when it touches a flame for the first time. I believe it has given me an edge in similar experiences ever since. A voice boomed over loudspeakers ordering an end to the attack and for all course members to close in.

Once the course was assembled on the parade ground, we were given a minute to run back to our grots to dress, and then herded into a warm classroom, seated in comfortable seats and told to wait. It was nearly impossible not to fall asleep, even so soon after the traumatic awakening. We were told we were to be shown a film documentary and to watch it carefully. The lights went out and a 16mm black and white film flickered on a screen at the front of the room. It was an incredibly boring documentary on flower-pressing that lasted some forty minutes. Many fell asleep. I kept pinching and slapping myself in the face in an effort to stay awake. I punched my cheeks so hard I could feel the bruises the next day. When the film ended, we were handed questionnaires on its content. The point was, could you control yourself and stay alert?

Throughout the course we were secretly monitored.

Having been given a task to complete, we would sometimes find ourselves alone and unsupervised. I had
spotted new co-axial cable running into many of the
old buildings that had no television sets and suspected
they might be attached to hidden video cameras. The
aim was to see how we conducted ourselves when not
putting on a front in the presence of the Directing Staff.
Naturally I put on a good show, just in case I was right
about the cameras.

An important quality the instructors were looking
for was aggression. Undercover operatives in Northern
Ireland work mostly alone and far from any support.
Cornered in a desperate situation, savage, controlled
aggression might save our lives.

To assess each recruit's aggression, the entire course,
about sixty by the beginning of the second week, was
marched into the gymnasium and ordered to strip down
to shorts and trainers. A basket of well-worn boxing
gloves was brought in, about ten pairs between us.
We were lined up in two rows facing each other and
arranged in alternating order of size. The largest recruit,
named Jack, a Guardsman, I later learned, was a powerfully built man who at one time had made the Army
boxing team. He had a chiselled jaw and forehead and
looked like he had seen more than just a few fights. He
stood at the end of one row. I was placed at the end
of the other row opposite him as I was considered the
next in size. We were going to mill in pairs and I was
not looking forward to fighting with Jack one bit.

Milling is like boxing but without tactics or strategy
which means no ducking, weaving, aiming, slacking

or pausing for breath. Opponents stand toe-to-toe and at the bell slam it out like windmills until one is left standing. If someone goes down and is not unconscious he is expected to drag himself back up and continue. A referee stands close to both opponents to keep the pace going and, should either fighter attempt any of the 'no's above, he punches them mercilessly himself.

An overweight, gregarious Army officer beside me named John, who was suspected of lacking commitment, was ordered to swap places with me. John went pale as he took in Jack's build and the hams that hung from the ends of his hairy, muscle-bound arms.

I studied my new opponent, Mike, another Army officer. He was a gangly, affable, public schoolboy type whose aggression the instructors also wanted to test. Mike had scar tissue around his eyes and forehead from a windscreen he had crashed through a few years earlier. It was obvious what I had to do.

The boxing ring was no more than several gym mats pushed together to form a square. The ring was made up of benches which the rest of us sat on, facing inwards. There were no ropes. If anyone was being punched out of the ring we were to push them back in for more punishment.

Jack and John's fight was first and, as expected, lasted less than a minute. John lacked the reach and the power to take on Jack, but he did display spirit and determination, picking himself up off the floor more than once before eventually going down half-unconscious with a smashed nose. Jack gave him no quarter.

Years later, John had a near miss while he was walking

the Armagh countryside acting as a regular gravel-belly troop officer. His troop was ambushed late one night and, as John led the pursuit towards the terrorists, his webbing became entangled as he tried to push through a thicket. One of the terrorists about to flee on a bicycle noticed John snared like a rabbit. He paused long enough to unload a full magazine of M16 high-velocity bullets at John from twenty feet away. John flew backwards through the hedge and the terrorist cycled away. John's ears were ringing from the gunfire. He sat up in the bottom of a ditch and to his amazement was not dead. He felt his body for holes, certain he had been hit. He had been hit, but the only hole in his flesh was through the centre of one of his ears.

Mike and I were the next pair to mill and we stepped on to the mat and stood opposite each other as the rules were reiterated by the referee. My plan was to aim my blows at the paper-thin scar tissue on his face and rip it open.

From the instant the bell went, everything became a frenzy. I leant in and slammed ferociously at his head. I remember him hitting me in the face several times, but as in most fights, blows go unnoticed until it's over. Within seconds, blood was splashing everywhere, sprinkling the referee and those on the benches. None of it was mine. I swung blow after haymaker at Mike, relentlessly. I was much fitter and stronger than him and making a real mess of his scar tissue. Blood flowed into Mike's eyes, blinding him. He paused to wipe it away. I paused to let him. We were both shouted at and punched by the referee. I resumed the onslaught as Mike grew weaker and less effective. As long as Mike kept standing I kept slamming my punches home. Those were the bitter rules. I would not be doing him or myself any favours by stopping. If he wanted to do this job, he would have to show his mettle. If he was concerned about his looks he could quit. But Mike was not about to give up and the heartless referee let the fight continue. I had to show the killer instinct. It was expected of me. The instructors knew who I was by now. But being special forces had nothing to do with my enthusiasm. As I punched Mike to destruction and the blood sprayed over me it began to excite some primaeval part of me. There was something seductive about it. I'm not proud to say it but I was relishing it when Mike started to weaken. I felt in total control and was going in for the kill.

When Mike finally went down he stayed down. There was blood everywhere. It was a fucking mess. Applause went up from a dozen intelligence ruperts who had brought chairs and drinks into the gym to watch the show. A medical orderly hurried to inspect Mike – there was always a medic just in case. Someone was untying my bloody gloves for the next pair as I looked down at Mike lying with his eyes closed. I did not feel glorious. The medic checked his breathing passage was clear and wiped the blood from his eyes then gave the referee a thumbs-up. It looked worse than it was. I understood the necessity of aggression training, but I was not convinced this particular technique was a positive one. I certainly did not see it as entertainment for the ten nobbers sitting applauding behind me. I plonked down on to the survivors' bench while Mike was taken away on a stretcher and the next pair was brought into the ring. I looked around at other members of the camp staff crowded in the main entrance – cooks, drivers, clerks, storemen – all trying to get a good look at the blood-sport. We're all savages at bottom.

Mike was stitched back up and recovered enough to stay on the course. He made it through to the end and eventually became a 14 Int operations officer.

Camp One lasted two weeks and by the end of it less than fifty per cent of the recruits remained. The heaviest culling phase was over. From here on a gradual attrition would reduce the numbers. Recruits would fail if they could not master all of the many essential skills.

Wearing our own clothes and carrying the suitcases we arrived with, we climbed aboard a coach and drove out through the gates of Camp One. We were headed for a secret training base in Wales where those who completed the course would spend the next three and a half months.

Apart from runs every morning before breakfast and the occasional visit to the assault course, there were no demanding physical hardships at Camp Two – not compared to SBS selection, anyway. A stress-free environment was required for learning the skills needed to operate undercover in Northern Ireland – there was stress enough in that. The skills included fast driving, pistol- and sub-machine-gun-handling, map-reading, field-craft for placing and managing OPs, operating cameras and other technical equipment, and surveillance techniques by car and on foot. It was unlike SBS or SAS selection in many ways, the most important difference being that once a recruit passed through the gruelling process to test toughness and aptitude in the SBS, he then joined a team and settled in to learn specific skills as and when required. However, a 14 Int operative, on completion of the selection course, went directly into operational service. A new operator had to learn the tricks of the trade whilst involved in live operations on the ground. It is impossible to teach all the realities of the job in a classroom. This meant the early days in Northern Ireland for a new operative were the most dangerous. Our selection course learned that lesson the hard way.

The surveillance phase of the course was of an exceptionally high standard. Northern Ireland was one of the most difficult and dangerous places in the world to carry out surveillance, especially when working alone. The American CIA regularly send their operatives over (to Germany usually) to be trained by British special forces in the art of urban and rural surveillance.

The reasons for the difficulty are straightforward. A British undercover operative could not arrive as a stranger in an Irish community sympathetic to the cause and expect to go unnoticed, let alone be accepted. The IRA's vigilance was extreme. Operatives could not do something as simple as hang around in bars for instance, not in 'hard' areas. Depending on how hostile the area was, passing through even once would alert suspicion. Twice in the same day could be suicidal. An operative could not take a room or apartment or get a job, as some novelists have suggested, not if he was English, anyway.

The risks were too great. Anyone who came under the IRA's gaze in suspicious circumstances was lifted and questioned. That person remained a prisoner until the IRA were positive of their claimed identity, and even then, mistakes were made and innocents were executed as spies. The IRA were quite capable of setting traps for undercover operatives. If a member of the IRA suspected he was being watched, any subversive activity he was associated with was normally cancelled. However, there were times when the IRA pretended to maintain an operation in the hope of luring operatives into a trap.

The IRA, inevitably, caught on to many of the surveillance techniques used against them. We had to keep finding new ways of doing the same job. As in all aspects of warfare, if you don't constantly change and improve you will be defeated by those who do. The IRA are the world's most effective and intelligent terrorist group, and this is due in no small way to the quality of their enemy. In the early days, operatives worked in teams for safety. When the IRA warned its sympathisers to look out for groups of strangers, more experienced operatives were sent out on their own. Soon it became difficult for anyone to work in pairs in cars and on foot and so every operative, including new inexperienced ones straight from the farm, were expected to go solo. It was not long before the IRA began to warn their people not to ignore lone males passing through their areas, either.

If the Intelligence Detachments were to maintain the initiative they had to become more hi-tech, rely more on electronic surveillance, and improve their methods of blending in. Better technology was always arriving.

To assist with the blending in a request was put into London for female operatives.

The Military Reaction Force (MRF), the precursor to 14 Int, had used females in undercover operations in Northern Ireland in the sixties and early seventies, but it was a different game now. Not that it was less dangerous then. More than one MRF woman came close to losing her life. These days the players are wiser and the strategies more complex. MRF's females were trained only in fast driving and weapon handling. If undercover women were to be brought into the current conflict they would have to have the same intense training as the men.

It was at Camp Two during my course that we were joined by the first women ever to be trained for the 14 Int undercover detachment.

I had personally experienced the need for undercover women on my combined SBS/SAS Northern Ireland tour a couple of years earlier. I spent a night parked in a dark side-street in a small town with an SBS buddy, Bonzo, who thought we would draw little or no attention if he wore a long, dark wig in the hope we would be taken for a couple engaged in the national pastime. We were waiting to pick up a team conducting a recce not far away. We sat shoulder to shoulder, Bonzo scratching his head now and then because the wig made him itch. There was a row of houses opposite us and the lights went out, one by one, as the night drew on and people went to bed.

We had been there a couple of hours when Bonzo suddenly became alert and, without moving anything other than a finger to indicate said, 'Someone's watching us.'

'Where?' I asked, moving only my eyes.

'Straight ahead – first floor – face in the window.'

Sure enough there was the face looking right at us. We surreptitiously gave a 360-degree scan to see if anyone was creeping up on us. It was clear.

'What shall we do?' Bonzo asked.

'Let's stick it out a little longer. They can't see any details.'

'Yeah, but they can see we've been doing fuck all.'

'There's nothing I can do about that, Bonzo, old pal.'

'Put your arm around me,' Bonzo said.

I did. We snuggled closer. The face continued to watch us. Bonzo rested his head gently on my shoulder and we sat there cuddled up for what seemed an age. The face was relentless.

'This is fuckin' ridiculous,' Bonzo said finally.

'We're going to have to play it out,' I said.

'Yeah, well you might be all nice an' comfortable but I ain't spendin' the rest of the fuckin' night sat like this.'

I didn't want to move location because we were perfectly situated for the pick-up and our other options were unattractive.

Bonzo sat up. 'Right. That's it.'

'What are you gonna do?'

'I'm gonna get out and take a piss and get a closer look. It's probably a fuckin' cat.' At that, Bonzo climbed out.

'Bonzo?' I whispered after him.

He stuck his head back in. 'What?'

'You'll really get 'em wondering if you stand there

with your shlong out and take a piss. You're the babe, remember?'

Bonzo realised and got back in. I climbed out and took a piss while I craned to see who was watching us. I got back in and put my arm around Bonzo and rested his head back against my shoulder.

'We're OK,' I said.

'Why's that?'

'It's a vase.'

The problems preparing women for this kind of work were physical, political, emotional and male. Men behave differently, worse still, unpredictably, around women.

The problem for Army Intelligence was to find enough women who could qualify to begin the selection course. Bear in mind Army Intelligence was limited to recruiting solely from within the armed forces. Women with the qualities suited for undercover work against ruthless terrorists in potentially lethal situations, where they are expected to kill if need be, do not generally share the more mundane ambitions of those who join a military that at the time offered them exclusively administrative careers. Another concern was, would the kind of women who could make it through the tough selection process resemble the gender enough, which was, after all, the whole point (Hollywood film studios were not running selection). And then there was the monthly emotional cycle from which some women suffer more than others. Special forces, an all-male organisation at that time, was going to have to invent a sensitivity to the female psyche in preparing them for a front-line role. The selection process was going to have to be considerate to women until it found its feet, which would not happen until it got feedback from the fruits of its efforts and when experienced female operatives returned from the field to become instructors. The political implications of women in the front line are obvious, but won't be closely scrutinised until we lose one in combat.

The powers-that-be decided to spare the women the rigours of the men's Camp One and give them a lighter version of their own. When the genders were introduced to each other for the first week of Camp Two, one problem became glaringly obvious. There were twenty of them, and a couple of them were quite cute. We were going to spend over three months working closely together with little time off, not even weekends. Under these conditions it was likely that romantic attachments would form. In an effort to control this, we were warned in no uncertain terms that if anyone was caught in a compromising situation with any of the girls it would result in both parties being immediately RTUed. That was enough to cause most to adhere to the warning as law. But some saw it as something of a challenge. One couple ignored the warning entirely. Romance, or more accurately lust, bloomed immediately they met and they started a sexual relationship virtually the first day they went out alone together on an orientation drive. The DS were slow to pick up on the relationship at first and those who eventually did suspect kept it quiet from the command staff in the hope that the couple would have the sense to be more discreet. As far as the DS were concerned, they were there to prepare us for an important job and not to run a boarding school. If we wanted to take the risk, it was up to us. I don't doubt the temptation whiffed past one or two of the DS themselves. Another probable reason the DS were not bothered about the non-fraternisation decree was because it came from the unit sergeant major, who was non-SAS and a bit of a wanker. If a couple was going to get kicked off the course for bonking, he was going to have to catch them himself, which was what eventually happened.

We were allowed the use of a recreation room during the few evenings we did not work. It had a simple bar consisting of soft drinks and a keg of beer. Naturally, it was noted how much individuals consumed. Most of us took advantage of the rare evenings off. Some watched the crackly television, others caught up with the newspapers or sat around chatting. The love-birds were always there, usually sitting apart so as not to arouse suspicion, but they would always leave within a minute or so of each other, stretching and yawning with the excuse that they were tired and heading off to hit the hay. The pantomime was so obvious to those of us on the course we would roll our eyes at each other. Their favourite rendezvous was in the field behind the bashers, where they would indulge in carnal activities against a large oak tree in shadows beyond the security lights.

The sergeant major rarely mixed with us – as he had never been an operative, his job being purely administrative. He was a narcissistic Tom Jones look-alike who styled his hair and sideburns like the famous singer (he was Welsh to boot) and wore gold necklaces, rings and bracelets (dress regulations were civilian for everyone in the unit). Unlike many of the DS, he had no idea about the couple's tryst and just happened to be taking his dopey black Labrador for an evening stroll. It was the dog who drew his attention to the couple behind the tree. Shocked and disgusted, he immediately ordered the couple to be RTUed.

The sergeant major's non-fraternisation edict came under suspicion when the woman later accused him of jealousy because he had fancied her himself from the beginning. He denied it, but admitted she had suggested, during a formal meeting in his office when she first arrived, that he was in with a chance. Her RTUed lover was Sal from the SBS. I later learned she was an Army major and the daughter of a prominent politician.

I was one of those who saw ensnaring one of the girls as a challenge. Being an SBS operative I was advanced in many of the skills required of the course, having gained experience working undercover on my previous special forces tour, and because of that I was chosen as senior operations officer for the final week-long exercise, a surveillance operation against an IRA ASU (all SAS troopers) who were planning a bombing campaign. This role required that I remain in the control room to plan and coordinate the operation as it developed.

One of the senior instructors was a tough, unsmiling, heartless SAS sergeant named Longshank. He only had one eye and one hand, lost years earlier when he tried to beat the record for getting the greatest number of two-inch mortars in the air at one time before the first hit the ground and exploded. In his eagerness he had double-fed the mortar pipe, shoving a shell in before the previous one had left the pipe, and they exploded in his face. Fortunately they were not high explosive, which would have killed him.

Longshank was playing the role of lead IRA terrorist. In the final days our operation went slightly awry while Longshank was driving to make a vital meeting we had to cover. The team, in their cars, stopped following him when he reportedly carried out anti-surveillance drills. While driving at speed with the team in tow, he began swerving violently from one side of the road to the other. The general rule is, if the enemy shows any signs of suspecting they are being followed, the team is to pull off. It turned out that Longshank had been using his good hand to operate a radio when his ball-and-socket jointed hand fell off the steering wheel and he lost control of the vehicle, almost crashing it.

To enable us to finish the operation we received a 'hot tip' that Longshank was going to make his contact in a pub late that evening. It had been a long, tiring week for the operatives and, being a considerate operations officer, I decided to give them a break and cover the meeting myself. I would need one other operative, and as it was a pub meet, naturally one of the girls would be ideal. It was the most effective way to cover the meet and a proper use of my resources. The plan was to sit and chat like a normal couple while I photographed the meeting using hidden devices. I chose Janet, not necessarily because she was the prettiest and sexiest girl on the course, but I wanted to make it look convincing (yeah, right). As we sat in the moderately crowded country pub I did all I could to charm her, while at the same time covering the meeting. It was not too difficult, as she was in as much need of being charmed as I was of charming her. When Longshank and his contact finally left, I told her I wanted to check if the film had rolled on in the camera properly. I explained I was concerned that if we went outside to do it in the car we might be seen and therefore suggested that the most convenient place, indeed the only place, would be the toilets. She didn't argue that there was no point in checking the camera as the targets had gone anyway. She wasn't stupid and as it turned out she was just as frustrated as I was. We didn't get as far as checking the film and were at each other, kissing and pulling each other's pants down before I had locked the door. I'd never done it in a toilet cubicle before and nor have I since, but due to the unusual situation, the risk of discovery and the intense release of passion after months of temptation, it remains a memorable experience. In the debrief Longshank noted, with a suspicious eye, how realistically the couple in the pub had acted.

Driving was the most hair-raising part of the course. Everyone's driving ability had to be improved by the time we went over the water, which is why several weeks were dedicated purely to this end. Army rally-driving instructors were brought in for a few days to give a little advice, but for the most part we were simply encouraged to drive as fast as we dared. This phase was also used to practise map-reading under pressure. Course members would usually go out in pairs and take turns navigating and at the wheel. One would drive as fast as he could along the narrow country lanes and through the villages – and I mean as fast as he could – while the other did his best to map-read at speed, which meant knowing exactly where one was at all times, down to a few metres, so as to warn of direction changes, bends in the roads, humpback bridges, etc., and in enough time for the driver to prepare. My very first partner put us in a hedge the first week of the course because he could not hear my instructions. It turned out he was deaf in his left ear. I have no idea how he ever got on the course to start with.

It was all quite insane really, the driving phase, highly dangerous for both us and the locals. But this was war, and in wartime safety margins during training are stretched to their limits. The person I felt most sorry for was the DS member who had to sit in the back behind each pair throughout this entire phase. Getting into a powerful car behind two complete novices who had everything to prove – one driving beyond his abilities and the other stressed to the limit keeping track of where they were – was a nerve-racking job. As the phase progressed, the navigator not only had to keep track of his location but also report it to the control room, in code, over the radio.

The same DS member remained with each pair throughout this fast-driving phase so he could advise and assess improvement. We had a short, dark, soft-spoken intellectual type named Joe who had recently returned from a tour of duty in Northern Ireland to take up his first stint as an instructor. I think he was ex-Int Corps.

Joe began the first day as we set off, seated back in a corner with his legs crossed offering snippets of advice. Within a few miles, he was perched on the edge of the back seat with both legs and arms stretched out, his palms pressed firmly against the door-frames for stability, while frantically screaming warnings of obstacles up ahead that we were already well aware of. Towards the end of the day, when we took it a little easier on the return home, he sat back and chain-smoked mostly in silence. As a back-seat driver he actually became a pain in the arse, since we did not feel as out of control all of the time as he obviously thought we were.

At the end of each day he left us without much of a word. We decided he went directly to either a church or a pub.

The evening meals during that phase were often entertaining as everyone shared the day's events. Arthur, who was a natural driver and drove faster than all of us, had a partner, a young officer named Brien, who wore thick glasses due to poor eyesight and was undoubtedbly the worst map-reader on the course. This was not a healthy combination for all concerned, and one that the DS kept complaining about to his superiors. But it was standard practice to pair up the worst in a subject with the best in the hope that the slower person might catch up.

It's a sound practice normally, but in this case the wisdom of it was questionable. Arthur's car did not arrive back at camp on time one evening, and when it eventually did, it was lying in the back of a flatbed truck with its front end destroyed and its wheels buckled, a couple of which were rammed up into the body. The occupants were shaken up but no one was badly injured. Brien had apparently made a small but vital error while map-reading, thinking they were a hundred yards further along a winding road than they actually were.

Arthur had been driving at his usual lunatic speed while Brien, bouncing around in the seat next to him and holding on to his map book, navigated them through a village and then along a winding, hilly, country road. After taking a gentle right-hand bend at about 60 mph Brien confidently announced, 'It's clear and straight for a mile.'

Arthur took his cue and accelerated to top speed while climbing a gentle slope. As they made the crest doing almost 100 mph, a hedgerow with a gate in it appeared, running directly across their path.

'Which way?' shouted Arthur who was not known for losing his cool in any situation, but he had to make himself heard above the scream from the DS in the back who, along with Brien, was staring ahead with eyes like carrots. Further information had ceased to come from Brien, so Arthur simply aimed for the point of least resistance, which in this case was the gate, and went right through and into a ploughed field past a farmer in his tractor.

Another pair had taken out two signposts in the same day, with no idea what the signs had warned of until they walked back to pick them up and stick them back into the ground, notably shorter than their original height. On approaching one of the signs at breakneck speed, the driver yelled the phrase that became most feared by the DS in the back – 'WHICH WAY?' The driver had suddenly been confronted with what he thought was a 'Y' junction, but none was indicated on the map. It was actually a dual carriageway divider that at speed looked like a 'Y'. When no answer came from the frantically confused navigator the driver took neither of the tarmacked options and hit the central grass divider, flattening the sign in the process. It turned out to be a large arrow stating, 'Keep Left'.

The same day that same pair were driving down a narrow country lane bordered on both sides by such high hedgerows it was like driving in a tight gully. But they could see it was straight and clear for a mile and so the driver accelerated to top speed. Suddenly, just up ahead, a farmer in his car slowly pulled out of his, until then, invisible driveway. He turned his head and instantly freaked as he saw the car screaming towards him. The expressions on the faces of the two operatives and the DS could not have been any different. A collision, and a serious one, appeared unavoidable. The farmer, obviously a swift-thinking man, did the only thing he could. He floored the accelerator and punched his car right through the opposite hedge and then nosed down into a ditch as the operatives' car rocketed past his rear. After that incident, the DS member, ashen by then, insisted they drive no faster than 20 mph until they got back to camp.

Several of us were stopped by the police more than once for reckless driving, but we had a secret codeword to use in such cases. When the constable, upon our insistence, radioed the codeword to his desk, much to his consternation he was told to let us go. This codeword was also used if one of the recruits inadvertently exposed his gun in public and the police were alerted.

Although the driving phase was great fun most of the time, we never lost sight of the seriousness of it all. Trainees had died in car accidents in the past. We got off lightly on my course, the worst injury being a broken arm. Janet held the record for the number of times a driver was towed home in a wrecked vehicle – four. One more and she would have been RTUed, but she pulled it together in the last few weeks.

It's amazing that only a handful of operatives have been killed or seriously wounded throughout the history of 14 Int training. And only about half a dozen have been killed in the last twenty years in road accidents while on operation in Northern Ireland. One of them was the first female operative, who died in a motorbike crash there recently. During my first two years as an undercover operator in Northern Ireland I rolled two cars completely, both ending up on their roofs on the side of the road, both during high-speed chases along the border. One was pilot error and the second was mechanical failure. Each time I crawled out without a scratch.

On the first occasion I was trying to 'back' (support) the lead car that 'had' (could see) the target while the rest of the team were stretched out behind me having been held up by an Army vehicle checkpoint (VCP). It was a good country road along this part of the southern border and it had just started to rain. I lost control on a sharp left-hand bend, fish-tailed around the corner, went up the right-hand verge, hit an oak tree that had been there several hundred years and was not about to give an inch, bounced off it and proceeded to roll along the wide, grassy verge side over side about four times. When the car finally came to a stop on its roof I lay there for a moment checking my body for broken bones. To my surprise, I was in one piece. We did not wear safety-belts as the practice was tactically unsound – you wanted to get out of a car quickly if you came under attack.

I then saw a pair of upside-down feet running towards me along the verge and quickly grabbed my maps and SMG and stuffed them into my bag. As I crawled out of the passenger window ready to pull my holstered gun if needed, I saw that the feet belonged to an old farmer who had seen the crash from his field. I got to my feet as he came up to me and he looked relieved to see I was OK. Steam issued from the engine and the wheels were still slowly turning. He asked me if I was all right. I brushed myself down as I told him I was fine. He didn't seem to be fazed when I answered him in my English accent.

'Shall I phone for help?' he asked.

My car radio still worked and I still had my hidden ear-piece jammed into my ear. I could hear the chase in progress and knew my oppos behind me would be along shortly.

'Thanks, but that's OK. A friend of mine is not far behind.'

It was a quiet road and no one else was on it but us. A

few seconds later, the next Det car in line came around the corner at high speed and almost lost control too. It straightened up after a little fish-tail and accelerated towards us – we were standing about eighty yards from the bend.

The operative saw me beside my upside-down car and could see I was fine. I heard him report over the radio that I was 'out of it' but OK. He was naturally intent on trying to 'back' the lead car since I couldn't, and he gave me a quick thumbs-up as he sped by. I waved back slightly.

The farmer, standing at my side, watched him disappear then gave me a glance.

'Your friend, was it?' he asked.

I felt a bit stupid, but explained I had another friend behind that one.

Sure enough, a few seconds later the next operative came screaming around the corner like a bat out of hell and then headed towards us. He'd received the message about me and was also anxious to back the leader, and so he too waved as he sped past and out of sight. The farmer gave me another look. There's really nothing one can say in a situation like that.

By the time the fourth and final car zoomed by with a wave I was beginning to feel pretty foolish, standing between my upside-down wrecked car and the farmer, waving to my friends as they drove by at top speed like everything was normal.

Fortunately the last car stopped up the road after it passed and reversed back to pick me up. The operative opened the door in a hurry, I jumped in, and we sped off. I waved goodbye to the farmer, who just stared at me.

The ballet of the second crash, only six weeks after, was almost identical to the first, except it was down the left verge, this time after a tyre had blown on a tight corner, to hit an ancient oak-tree stump then spin side over side about four times and end up on the roof again. It was a Ford Capri that time and I had a passenger, another bootneck operative who'd been in the Det a good year longer than I. As we lay there upside-down he started banging his passenger window repeatedly with his elbow. I stopped him and said, 'Been there, done that, try this,' and coolly wound down the window – the experienced hand that I was.

'I'm panicking because there's petrol running down the side of your window,' he said.

I instantly looked, and he was quite right. It was gushing down.

'Holy shit!' was the general exclamation as we both scrambled out of his window as fast as we could. The car never caught alight though.

On completion of the four-month selection course, nine males and three women remained. The women, Janet amongst them, were sent to Belfast along with three of the men. Three men went to Londonderry: Mike as second-in-command, Jack the pugilistic Guardsman, and Arthur from the SBS. I was headed for South Det on the southern border along with fat John, and Brock the badger, who had worked hard to achieve his ambition to make it into special forces before he retired, and by doing so became the oldest front-line operative in the organisation.

Within two weeks, one of the men was shot dead on his first assignment.

8

Before going over the water we were given two days' leave. I went home to Poole to see some squadron friends and also to do some judo. I was a first-dan black belt by then and four months off the mat had left me rusty. I met up with a friend, Harvey, a Marine whose family lived in Dublin. He had ambitions to join the SBS one day and also to represent Britain in the Olympics at judo. He eventually achieved both. He later distinguished himself in the Falklands with the SBS by shooting a Mig fighter out of the skies with his GPMG. I believe it was the only jet fighter shot down by a hand-held bullet-firing weapon in the conflict. Jet fighters fly at an incredible speed during battle, and when low to the ground have usually passed overhead by the time they are heard. There are no simple rules to shooting one down with a machine-gun other than give it plenty of lead while trying to estimate its speed and distance in the few seconds available, and hope for the best.

Duncan Falconer

Harvey was part of the SBS team that cleared an Argentinian detachment on Fanning Head, a hilltop that overlooked San Carlos, where the main invasion was taking place. They killed several soldiers and took the rest prisoner. After taking the position, Harvey was checking the Argentinian dead (thanks for the bayonet, Harv) when a shout went up that Migs were coming up the sound and heading directly towards them. There were two jets flying one behind the other at full attack speed. They climbed out of the sound and screamed over the hilltop directly above the SBS detachment. The team had just seconds to react. Those who were quick enough opened fire with their M16s, but Harvey grabbed his heavy 7.62 mm belt-fed machine-gun and let rip skyward. Every fifth round in the belt is a tracer – a bullet that leaves a glowing red tail allowing the gunman to see precisely where his rounds are going. Harvey's tracers were seen hitting the Mig before it exploded. I later asked Harvey how he did it.

'To tell you the truth, I was aiming for the first Mig but I shot down the second,' he admitted.

The luck of the Irish.

There were several Irish operatives in the SBS. For obvious reasons, they were given the option of not going over the water. I never asked Harvey how he felt about the conflict, considering his family was Catholic. I don't think his family had any idea he was in British special forces or he would not have been able to go home and visit his many brothers and sisters. He never asked me for my thoughts either. He knew my involvement, as most others, was unemotional.

214

I went with Harvey to visit my old civilian judo club where the members were only too happy to welcome me (from where, they had no idea, of course) by giving me a serious round-robin workout. The club had twelve other black belts, and four months off the mat meant a stiff and painful following morning climbing out of bed. Before returning to Camp Two and embarkation I decided to pass through London and visit my father.

It was a strange meeting after such a long time. Now I was taller than him, broader, and, as was no doubt somewhat confusing for him, scruffy, long-haired, unshaven and loutish in preparation for the circles I was about to move in. His first thought was that I had already left the Marines. When I told him I had not, he didn't ask any questions and I never offered an explanation. He still worked as a wine waiter in a London hotel, did the football pools, met his old cronies for drinks once or twice a week and spent the rest of his time alone at home stripping down vacuum cleaners, radios and televisions – anything mechanical or electrical that still had valves – so he could fix them up and sell them at second-hand auctions. Every surface in the apartment was strewn with bits and pieces. My world was a million miles from his and he was sufficiently aware of it not to even begin to want to know. We shared a meal and a bottle of fine wine from his job on a dining-table surrounded by the parts of several typewriters. As I left that evening he hugged me as awkwardly as ever and told me to be careful.

When I arrived back at Camp Two, all the operatives

looked as scruffy as I did except Jack, the powerful Guardsman. He had a fresh Army haircut and wore a cheap, formal, grey-flannel suit that looked a size too small for him. Throughout the training he had never quite got out of the habit of walking, standing or sitting straight-backed like a Guardsman. He was recognisable as a soldier in much the same way as many plain-clothes police officers are recognisable as cops. Jack had learned all the skills of undercover work but had failed to take on the slovenly demeanour of the cast we would mingle with most. I had my ear pierced for my SBS tour and put in a new gold ear-ring to complete the look.

Before we flew out, one of the SAS DS asked Arthur and me what we thought about Jack as an operative – he respected our opinion as members of the SBS. He admitted that he had concerns. Jack's shortcomings were obvious to those of us on the course, but it was not our place to point that out to the DS, even if those shortcomings signalled a danger. However, since he asked, we were frank. We wondered why Jack had been selected for the job if they thought, as we did, he was a risk to himself and also to his fellow operatives. The answer was age-old. It was the numbers game and there was a shortage of operatives. The manpower accountants hoped that borderline cases such as Jack would improve under the pressure of live operational involvement. That had been true of many borderline cases in the past, but Jack was never to get the chance.

As Jack was arriving at North Det I arrived at South Det and was greeted by a long-haired, bearded operative in the final weeks of his tour whose job it was to 'show me around'. It was Huk, the SBS operative who disappeared shortly after surviving the submarine disaster in Scotland.

Huk was from the north-west Highlands, a farm-boy originally, a quiet man who spoke with a tender lilt and had a manner that was gentle and unassuming. In the two weeks we spent together, mostly driving around the operational area to familiarise me with the many locations of importance and learning the spots (the codes for known locations), I got to learn a little about him.

He was in his late twenties and, I assumed, headed back to the squadron to build on his already illustrious career, hoping of course he would be spared any more death-defying situations as close as those he had experienced. On our last outing, a couple of days before he left, he told me he was in something of a quandary about his future. I felt somewhat honoured because not only did Huk never talk about himself, but this exceptional soldier whom every young member of the SBS, including myself, wished to emulate, actually wanted my humble advice.

His father had died several years earlier and had left the family farm to him. It was situated miles from civilisation in the Highlands. As Huk was a serving soldier his uncle took over the responsibilities of the farm until Huk was ready. A few months earlier, Huk's uncle, who was getting too old to run such a large farm, had sent him an ultimatum. Huk had to decide whether to leave the SBS and take over the land, or give it up for good. But that was not the only problem nagging at Huk. There was a girl, his childhood sweetheart, and if he gave up the farm and did not move back to the Highlands it would mean giving her up too.

Huk had gone to school in a small town that serviced his own and the other outlying farms. He had known the girl for as long as he could remember. They always felt that they would be together one day, all the locals did too, even when he packed his bags at the age of sixteen and left to head down south and join the Royal Marines. He expected to be gone just a few years, long enough to see something of the outside world before returning. The few years turned into many and contact between them had petered out to virtually nothing. The last time he had seen her had been during a brief visit to bury his father. He knew she was still unmarried from letters he occasionally received from his uncle. She was also waiting to learn of his decision before giving up hope entirely. She had never left the small town and had no idea about his life and little of the outside world.

Huk was torn. He believed she was the woman for him, however . . .

It's hard to think of two lives so different. He wasn't sure if he could live that life of solitude again, and if he attempted to, how long he would last. He enjoyed the fast-paced existence of special forces even though he had come close to being killed so many times. The life of a farmer, in the remote Highlands, virtually cut off from civilisation, would be a radical change, to say the least.

I wasn't much help to him. There are some decisions a person has to make alone. I don't think he really wanted my advice anyway. I suppose everyone needs to talk to someone sometimes, even men like Huk. When I said goodbye to him he was deeply troubled and had not made up his mind.

Several months later Huk left the SBS and I never heard from him again.

Many years later, when I was part of the SBS training team and running phases of the SBS selection course myself, I overheard a group of young SBS members who had just returned from a field exercise in northern Scotland. They had been heading across country towards a final rendezvous in the early hours of the morning. As they crossed a stretch of rugged, treeless, boulder-strewn land, a farmer and his sheepdog popped out of nowhere to greet them. He had seen them approaching from miles away and had waited for them in a hollow. He was a mild, pleasant and genuine man and offered them a cup of tea in his farmhouse not far away. The men, always keen to maintain local relations, accepted, though they were surprised by this exceptional show of hospitality from a Highlands farmer.

The farm could not have been more isolated. According to their maps the nearest main road was some twenty miles away. The SBS operatives were fully equipped and armed as they would have been for a real operation, but the farmer did not appear curious about their get-up. When they told him they were simply regular Marines on exercise he smiled and nodded. He led them through the back door of his farm and into the kitchen. He introduced his wife, a darling they said, with the same calm mannerisms as him. She insisted they have breakfast to go along with their cup of tea. When it was time to leave, he led them through the house to the front door. In the hallway there were several plaques on the wall. One was the regular Royal Marines emblem, another was from a Royal Navy submarine, and the last was from the SBS. Beside the SBS plaque were several medals which included an unofficial campaign medal from the Sultan of Oman, a Northern Ireland campaign medal and the Queen's Gallantry Medal. The lads agreed that, although none of them could live a life as isolated at that, the farmer, who never mentioned his past nor that his nickname was Huk, seemed content.

When Jack and Arthur arrived at North Det, an operation was taking place in the city of Londonderry. The PIRA was planning to assassinate a senior member of the RUC and the Det had been asked by the RUC's Special Branch to take over the operation. The Det knew where the weapons earmarked for the hit were hidden, and planted a bug. It was standard procedure for the IRA to hide weapons in safe houses or in special hides such as the cemetery described earlier. The Det didn't want the courier who picked up the weapons but the men who were going to use them.

Arthur and Jack spent the first few weeks doing ground orientation, as I was doing with Huk, and as soon as that was complete they were given their own cars. Since Jack was such a large man he was given the biggest car the Det had, a pale blue boat that no one else wanted because it stood out like a sore thumb. Jack was eager to get out on the ground and so he accepted it. Arthur was concerned about Jack and decided to advise the commanding officer. Arthur suggested Jack should be given more time to 'get into character'. Jack had not been the first borderline case to arrive at the Det, and others before him had managed to find their feet and learn to become effective operatives. Every man was needed for the weapon-following operation, but the commanding officer gave Jack the least important job and would make a decision based on his performance. That was fair enough, and so Arthur left it alone.

That day, Jack left the secret Det headquarters with the rest of the team and parked up in a moderately busy street on the edge of the Bogside. He sat in his car listening to the radio through his hidden ear-piece as the operation kicked off. The weapons had been picked up and were on the move, being transported in a blue pick-up truck in the hands of the ASU that was going to use them. The operation had become hot.

The Det was close on the gunmen's tail in several cars while a helicopter tracked the bug from high. The IRA were aware of the use of helicopters as spies in the sky, so it flew as high as it could. The plan was to follow the weapons to the target, confirm beyond doubt the deadly intent, then step in. It came like a bolt out of the blue when suddenly the truck changed direction in the middle of the city and veered away from its expected track. The operation took a giant swerve in an effort to try and work out where the ASU were now headed. The immediate assumption was that the gunmen had discovered the tail and cancelled the hit. For a few precious minutes the Det lost visual contact with the weapons.

The blue pick-up with its open flatbed turned the corner of the street that Jack was parked in and headed towards his car. As it drew alongside, it stopped, a tarpaulin was thrown back and four men stood up in the back holding M16s. They opened fire, blasting through the roof and front windscreen at point-blank range. Several operatives were close enough to hear the firing streets away. Jack was hit thirty-six times and died instantly. The pick-up sped away and as usual the weapons were quickly handed over to couriers who hid them. The weapons were located, but the killers got away.

Days later, we learned from a tout why the IRA had changed targets so abruptly. A PIRA member had seen Jack arrive in his car, park up on the street and simply sit there. Suspicious of any new face in the neighbourhood, the PIRA member moved to where he could get a closer look. He watched as Jack fiddled with something in his ear – the one-size-fits-all radio ear-pieces never did quite fit inside Jack's large ears. The PIRA member walked past Jack's car to get a closer look and saw Jack flicking through a map book of the city. The Dets made their own map books by cutting up maps into pages, marking them with coded grids and coding obvious landmarks, and placing them into the plastic sleeves of ordinary folders. Jack's most damning mistake came when, having dropped his ear-piece on the floor, he switched on the internal car speaker to his radio to hear what was going on. The speaker is intended for emergency use only. The radio must have been set too loud and before Jack could turn it down the PIRA member heard the English voices and the slick radio procedure of the other operatives. This confirmed that Jack was either a cop or, better still, a highly prized undercover man. The PIRA member quickly reported what he saw to his commander. The target was verified and the order went out to the ASU in the pick-up to change direction. An undercover man was a much greater scalp than any police officer.

Journalists received the official Army report of a soldier's death in Londonderry giving Jack's name but not his confidential duties. After investigating the circumstances of his death, including details such as that he was in an unmarked car and in civilian clothing, the newspapers assumed he was in the SAS and reported that much along with his full name, where his family lived and where he was to be buried. For months after, Jack's family received hate mail from IRA sympathisers, and his grave was defiled.

My own first operation was a set-up, for me that is, and by my own people.

A year or so before I arrived at the Det an operation had been activated to sow the first seeds of a 'technical attack' against an up-and-coming IRA intelligence officer (IO). The new IO was visited by IRA security personnel whose job it was to advise him regarding British undercover procedures and how to guard against them. One of the best deterrents, he was advised, was a big dog, and the meaner the better. To ensure its viciousness, he was advised to rear it himself from a puppy and never be friendly with it or allow anyone else to be. Also, while it was growing up, to have someone climb over his security fence now and then and beat it. This would ensure the dog was exceptionally aggressive towards anyone trying to enter the property.

The IRA man bought himself a Rottweiler puppy and immediately started treating it badly. About the time that he bought the puppy, the Det began its long-term operation against him, starting with a preliminary late-night recce of his property.

When the team first encountered the puppy crouched in a filthy corner of the yard, they knew from experience it would grow to become a problem on future visits. If they took the puppy away it would simply be replaced, and if they did anything to incapacitate it, such as dose it with drugs, suspicion would be aroused. Therefore it was decided that as the puppy was growing up, a couple of operatives would travel at least once a week to the property at night, pick the lock to the gate and make friends with the dog by feeding it luscious chunks of meat and petting it. Most operatives were encouraged to take part in this task so that the dog would get to know them all.

As the dog grew up it came to look forward to the only care and attention it ever received. Sometimes the operatives would take it out of its ugly surroundings to a nearby field where they would play with it for hours. One night, when they saw it had been severely beaten, they took care of its wounds to protect it against infection and treated it every night until it was out of danger.

Many operatives had dogs in the Det – the place sometimes resembled a zoo more than an intelligence detachment. Some were characters. One of the dogs had a bizarre ongoing sexual relationship with an armchair in the television room.

It all started one evening when the dog, a cocker spaniel, came in to have a seat while we were watching TV. It was a lazy hound and did everything at a slow, easy pace. This particular evening, when it raised one of its hind legs to climb on the armchair, it caught its penis between the frame and the main cushion. As it pushed off with its hind legs, its penis was jammed in further but the sensation was obviously a pleasant one and so it eased back and repeated the push. It did this repeatedly, getting faster, fully screwing the armchair until it stopped. We knew it was achieving orgasm because after several months an investigation revealed that the cushion was solidly adhered to the frame. It became a daily ritual for the dog, one that we eventually grew to ignore. Since the dog always used the same seat, this rancid, disgusting piece of furniture was avoided by the operatives. Visitors were never informed and as it was at the front of the room many naturally chose to sit in it. In that event the dog waited patiently in front of the guest until the seat was vacated.

North Det had an unusual and highly popular pet of their own. As they were based close to open sheep-grazing land, it was their fancy to barbecue one now and then, during celebrations or farewell parties. Of course they did not buy them, and a stretch of lonely road through the mountains called the Glenshane Pass was the best area to poach. It was a bleak and desolate place that reminded me of Dartmoor whenever I drove across it, day or night. It was damp and misty more often than not and the traffic was always light. But acquiring a sheep exactly when it was needed was always hit and miss. It was only possible to catch one if it got itself trapped behind the fence that ran along part of the road, otherwise they would gather miles away up on the moor. The operatives would never shoot the sheep, that was far too overt. They had to corner one and grab it, then wrestle it into the trunk of a car, and smartly too, in case a farmer happened by. After several failures at getting a sheep in time for a particular barbecue, it was decided to capture one the very next time the opportunity presented itself and keep it in the camp, fattening it up until it was needed.

It wasn't long before a spry young sheep was caught and brought back and released into the compound. Within a few days, with ample food and petting, it settled in to its new friends and surroundings, including the dogs. The sheep was cordial, well-mannered and a good listener to troubled operatives who'd had one too many, but was appreciated mainly because it developed a taste for beer, which ultimately broke the barrier to full and complete acceptance. It soon took part in all camp activities and piss-ups, along with the dogs, and was even allowed to attend the occasional operational briefing – an honour bestowed only on animals that could keep quiet for long periods and not fidget. On one particular boozy night, it was announced that the sheep was to be made an honorary operative, given the non-substantial rank of lance corporal (the stripe was shaved and coloured into its front legs) and a *nom de guerre* of Harry, even though Harry was a she. (There were no women in 14 Int North at that time, so Harry was its first female operative.)

The day before the next official barbecue, the chef, who was not privy to the goings-on of the operatives, came looking for Harry to prepare her for her leading role in the feast. He found Harry sharing a couple of pints and a packet of crisps with some operatives who'd been on the ground all the previous night. The chef walked in wearing his apron and a leather belt from which hung his butcher's tools and explained he'd come to take the sheep away. The lads were a little slow in understanding quite where the chef wanted to take Harry, who still had a couple of pints in the wood. When the penny dropped, the chef was lucky to get out of the bar with his own life. That evening one of the operatives was back up on the pass looking for another sheep for the barbecue. Harry was still there when I left and to my knowledge lived a full life in the Det and died of natural causes many years later.

The Rottweiler, on the other hand, was confused when the occasional visitor arrived, not to pet or feed it, but to beat it senseless. It soon learned to tell the difference and was indeed mean and vicious to everyone except its pals in the Det. By the time I arrived the dog was fully grown. At the end of my orientation phase a recce of the IRA intelligence officer's home was planned. I was brought in on the briefing, but was not informed of the relationship between the Det and the dog. I was simply told it was a vicious man-eater that hated every living thing. My orders were to be the first man in, let the dog out and wrestle it to the ground and hold it down until the team had completed their task. I thought this was a bit much and asked why we couldn't just drug it. I was told this might cause suspicion. The Det commander explained that other operatives had done what I had been asked to do in the past and that he had every confidence I was up to the task. If that was the case, I thought, so be it. The dog was obviously not as vicious as I had imagined.

The storeman gave me a heavy padded wrangler's arm and instructions on how to use it against a savage dog – this training had not been covered on the course. For practice I was shown one of the Det dogs, a fifty-pound boxer, a playful thing and the only one willing to play the stupid game of pulling on the padded arm and growling. By the time we left that evening I was quite blasé about the whole thing.

We arrived at the house a few hours before dawn. I was to lure the dog around to the side of the compound while the lock-picker did his work on the gate. I set off and the dog slowly walked up to me from the other side of the fence, looked me straight in the eye and started to growl gently.

'Fuck me,' I said to myself. It must have weighed 150 pounds easily. Its head was as big as a pumpkin and great globs of mucous and saliva hung from its huge, fleshy mouth. The lock-picker signalled he was done and moved back into the shadows. I walked around to the gate. The dog followed me inside the fence. The others stayed out of sight. As I prepared to open the gate I stopped myself. This was utterly insane. No amount of padding was going to save me from that thing. A net and trident was what I needed. I gripped the gate and planted my legs ready for the attack. As I flung it open and stepped back I braced myself to the take the charge.

At that moment, one of the operatives called out, 'Here boy. Come on, Paddy. Scran time. There's a good boy.'

The dog's ears and eyebrows instantly pricked up as it recognised the voice and it ran right past me, wagging its rump excitedly, and started to play and rough-house with the others.

Bastards!

Within a few weeks of the girls arriving in Belfast one of them, Helen, was selected for their first operation, which was to take place inside a church. Her task was to witness a meeting between two members of PIRA and act as a trigger so that operatives outside could follow the targets away. A trigger allows the other operatives to remain out of sight until needed. As it was inside a church it was regarded as a 'safe' operation; however, a couple of operatives stayed close by just in case. The Det was not prepared to take any risks with the women operatives until they had proven themselves. The reverberations caused by the loss of a female operative, especially on her first operation, would be damaging to the organisation.

While Helen waited in a car with an operative, the targets were 'housed' inside the church. The Det commander in the operations room the other side of the city gave the 'go'. Helen was armed with a pistol, wore the standard communications system under her clothes, and was thoroughly briefed for every eventuality. She seemed OK when she left the car – a little nervous, but workable. She carried out a radio check as she mounted the steps and entered the church.

Helen confirmed the meet over her radio and everyone waited.

Half an hour later the church started to empty. The operatives outside stood by for Helen's trigger. But it never came. The last of the congregation left the church. Helen was not amongst them. Something was wrong. Helen was given a radio check but she did not respond. Concern rocketed. The Det commander ordered a team to move in.

Two operatives hurried into the church and saw the back of Helen, sitting alone in a pew, still as a statue. One of them walked up to her and saw she was alive. Her hands and legs were shaking. She was uninjured. He touched her gently and whispered her name. She nodded, but couldn't talk. She was catatonic. He talked her into letting him help her to her feet. Her jeans were soaked where she'd had an uncontrollable bladder movement. He guided her down the aisle and out of the entrance.

Nothing had happened inside the church. No one had suspected her or communicated with her. All the exercises and simulations during selection had not prepared her mentally for the real thing. That was Helen's first and last operation. She fully recovered within a few days and served out her term with the Det, but doing administrative work. The lesson learned that day was that where London might get away with playing the numbers game with men, they were going to have to reconsider the selection process for women.

Since that first women's selection course, several notable female operatives have emerged, though few have been permitted to go out alone, 'one up', if for no other reason than a woman alone in a car attracts attention, especially at night. This was demonstrated recently by the shooting of an RUC member who gave chase to what he thought was a suspicious female alone in a car at night. It all got out of hand when she mistook the men, who were in plain clothes and following her in their unmarked car, for IRA. The woman, an inexperienced operator, crashed during the high-speed pursuit and as the plain-clothes officer ran to her she shot him through the window. He died.

9

South Armagh, near the border, was part of my patch. It is considered the most dangerous operational area in the province, and known as 'bandit country' because the IRA are more aggressive here than anywhere else. They are capable of mounting mortar or RPG7 (rocket-propelled grenade) attacks, then hopping across the border into Southern Ireland to avoid pursuit by Army or police, knowing they cannot be legally followed. They are most notorious for their ability to muster a dozen or more armed men at short notice and even mount military-style border patrols. They place road-blocks on quiet country lanes to stop cars and question the occupants. This is intended as a demonstration of strength for the locals. I saw an air photograph of one such road-block showing sixteen heavily armed, hooded men copying the tactical procedures the British Army uses when manning its vehicle control points. These heavily armed road-blocks are the one thing that undercover operators, out driving alone, fear most.

If suspicious activity, such as one or two strangers wandering the countryside, is reported to the local PIRA commander, by a farmer for instance, a heavily armed PIRA response team can be quickly assembled, especially close to the border. 14 Int, who often operate along the border, usually in pairs when on foot in rural areas, have the highest respect for bandit country.

By the end of my first year with the Det, I was running several operations on my own, under the overall command of the Det CO. Some operations last years, and the manpower for each was rotated, which meant that operatives were involved in more than one at any time. It was left to the individual if he wanted to run his own operation or not. On average, given a detachment of twenty operatives, only a handful liked to run their own ops. The others remained on call as ready manpower and were always kept busy. They were either 'on the ground', servicing for an operation, or de-servicing from the previous job. On the occasional nights off some operatives visited pubs in safe areas, but generally they were content to stay in the Det and have a few beers, read a book or watch television. An operative usually waited until he had accumulated eight or nine days before flying home for R&R. This leave was calculated at one day off per week which meant we got out of there every couple of months, unless there was an operation running that required all of the manpower.

Crossmaglen, a notorious border town in South Armagh, was ominous to me because of its dark history. I had many experiences in and around that town over the years, prior to 14 Int and after. The Army camp in the middle of the isolated market town was like a Wild West US cavalry outpost under constant threat of attack. It was a magnet for trouble. The actual border was a skip and a jump from the outskirts, making it an attractive target for the IRA. Many soldiers had been killed over the years, in the camp as a result of mortar attacks, in the town from hidden bombs, and in the surrounding countryside from booby-traps or snipers. The first time I visited the camp I stayed there for a couple of nights, and the night after I left it was hit by mortars. The Army was wise to that form of attack by then and suspended nets several feet above all the structures to prevent the mortars from penetrating before exploding – this cut down the damage and danger to life considerably. Nobody was killed in that particular attack, but one young regular Army lad of eighteen lost an arm. He'd arrived that morning from England having just completed basic recruit training the week before. He was on the next flight back to his mum, minus the arm and was a civvy again a few months later.

For undercover operatives, Crossmaglen was a town you might drive through once in a day. Try it a second time in a short period and you could expect to be followed out of it, and if you were not careful, to run into a road-block several miles down the road.

Early one morning I was on the border, on foot, not far from Crossmaglen. It had been snowing during the night and now that it had stopped the land was frozen and as still as a black and white photograph. The operation was the observation of a lone farmhouse suspected of being used as a staging area for arms coming over the border. I was with my regular and most preferred partner when on foot, Max, a large Dorset country boy who played prop for the Royal Marines, his parent unit.

Max was the perfect partner. He was experienced and highly professional, quick to react in dangerous situations and relentless in any physical task. He was cold and dangerous to anyone he didn't like, and in my experience you had to be a pretty bad person for Max not to find something likeable about you. Max would beat down a brick wall with his head and fists to help a friend in trouble and would do the same to get to anyone who threatened his friends. He had missed out on much of his schooling, having spent his youth working on his father's farm. He had a Dorset-cum-Cockney accent and was aware of his academic shortfalls, but you put your life in your hands if you pointed that out to him less than diplomatically. However, determined to improve his mind, or to be precise, his eloquence, he decided to make use of the two years with the Det by adding to his vocabulary. His plan was to learn one new word every week. He figured that in two years, if he stuck with it and could remember them all, that would give him about a hundred new words.

His method was to open his dictionary at random, stab his finger at the page and choose the nearest word he liked the sound of. Once he was satisfied he fully understood its meaning he would fit it into his conversation during the week as often as possible. If the word didn't come up in everyday chat he would start a conversation that included it.

'The chef 'as 'is kitchen much more *ergonomic* these

days, don't you fink?' was a comment he came up with over breakfast one morning.

Few of us knew the meanings of most of the words he chose. Even the Det commander, a highly educated university graduate, was lost on one or two that Max came out with. His pronunciation didn't help. And many of Max's sentences – lots of little words with the one, huge, unheard-of word in the middle – were therefore followed by long, thoughtful silences from the rest of us. I learned quite a few words myself during our partnership, though I could use few of them in everyday conversation.

As dawn broke, I emerged from the snow-covered bushes in my grubby clothes – a donkey jacket over a thick woolly polo-neck and jeans with thermals and longjohns underneath. My long hair was matted and my beard still had bits of food in it from the previous night's meal, which had been eaten cold in a frozen ditch. Max had suggested a good time to break down the OP would be at *crepuscular* light. He'd used the word about eight times during the four-day OP and I was well acquainted with its meaning by now.

We were moving out at early light as opposed to dark because a booby-trap had been triggered by an animal a few days earlier and the area was suspected of harbouring others. We wanted to be able to see where we were walking. I picked up my M16 and backpack filled with field equipment and headed off by myself to do a recce of the pick-up point on the road a hundred yards away. Max would catch up after he had packed away the optical equipment and brought in our own explosive devices that we always placed around our position to cover from blind attack routes (a lesson learned from the O'Sally incident). The devices were miniature claymore mines – shaped charges that fired hundreds of tiny shards of metal outwards, fired by pressing a small hand generator. If anyone was going to sneak up on us, good luck to them.

I trudged along the hedgerow to a thicket and placed my M16 and backpack in a ditch where we could wait out of sight for the pick-up car. I gingerly climbed through the prickly thicket – soldiers who wanted to live longer in this part of the world avoided gates, stiles or any easy paths through hedges as they were favourite places to plant mines – and stepped on to a narrow, rarely used road that followed the northern side of the border at this point.

The border was defined by a rickety, sagging, rusty, three-strand barbed-wire fence a few feet the other side of the road. There were no signs indicating that this was the international border between two countries. If you could not read a map you would not know. The surrounding countryside was divided into small fields, some of them no wider than fifty feet by one hundred feet long, the boundaries of which had hardly changed since feudal times when the strip-farmed land was continually subdivided to be handed down from father to sons. The lack of development over the centuries in Catholic areas such as this was a reminder of the root of some of the problems.

There were no habitats in direct line of sight which is why I chose the spot on the road for the pick-up.

I looked for a suitable place to stick a signal marker, a common object placed in such a way that only our driver would recognise its significance.

As I crouched to place the marker, I caught a movement a hundred yards away in the otherwise still countryside. Two men were climbing through a hedge into a field across the border directly in front of me. They had seen me too, the road being a few feet higher than the surrounding fields. They kept their eyes fixed on me as they walked towards me, leaving footprints in the thin carpet of snow.

I scanned in search of others. There was no sign. They could have been farmers, but there was something about them, the way they were watching me. A ripple of concern passed through me, but ripples of concern were always doing that in this job. You learned to do nothing unless the skin broke and you were drowning in the stuff. I stood to face them and put both hands in my coat pockets. I did not want to go back for my M16 because it would mean turning my back on them, nor did I want to risk getting stalled by the thicket – if these were boyos they were close enough to run forward and take a shot at me. Anyhow, one of the tricks of undercover work was never to over-react. They might just nod 'good day' and pass me by. My left hand went to my hidden radio and my right was through the pocket of my jacket, which I had removed, to grip my 9mm Browning pistol in its holster underneath. I could fire it without having to draw it out of my pocket if I had to, not the most accurate, but definitely the quickest method to get off a shot, which was often all that counted. I wondered where Max was.

The two men also had their hands in their coat pockets. I didn't recognise them – if they were boyos they were none I had worked against before. They headed directly for me and stopped a few feet apart at the waist-high border fence, their eyes never leaving me. Their breath, like mine, was a thick steam. The width of the country lane was the distance that separated us – them in the Republic, me in Ulster.

They were older, in their forties I reckoned, their faces craggy and weathered. They scanned around, looking to see if I was alone. Both were cool and cordial but I could sense an arrogance and a malevolence. They were definitely suspicious of me.

'How yer doin'?' one said.

'Fine,' I replied.

'What ye doin' out here?' said the other.

'I'm waiting for some mates,' I said.

When they heard my London accent any doubts they had as to who or what I was disappeared. There was only one kind of Englishman who hangs around the Irish border in bandit country at dawn wearing civvies and looking as if he'd been out all night. I could not disguise my English accent – it was pointless trying to. A professional actor would have trouble fooling these people with a put-on accent. That's why this job was the most difficult intelligence-gathering of its type in the world. You could not ask anyone questions or strike up an innocent conversation without revealing you were not one of them. I felt certain they were boyos, if not official, then highly prejudiced sympathisers. If they did suspect I was a British undercover man – an SAS man, as they called all of us – they would also expect me to be armed. If so they were too confident not to be armed themselves.

'You're a long way from home, Englishman.'

As I answered I triggered my radio, which transmitted everything I said.

'My home goes all the way up to that fence you're standing behind.'

My voice boomed over the speaker in South Det operations room some eighty miles away and jolted out of his reverie the only occupant of the room, the duty bleep (signaller), who had been sitting back reading a book.

As it was early and my operation, which was closing down, was the only one going on that morning, everyone else in the Det was in bed or having breakfast. The duty bleep wheeled his chair over to the operations wall which was covered with a giant map and looked at the only operation marker on it, on the border, indicating my location. I never met a signaller assigned to the 14 Int Dets who wasn't as sharp as a razor. They were not trained as operatives, but knew all there was to know about our side of it. He realised I was having a conversation with a local and knew we avoided this type of contact. If I was transmitting the conversation it meant I was trying to tell the Det something.

He punched an intercom which connected him to the rooms of all relevant personnel and said, 'I think we've got a standby! I repeat, standby, standby.'

Bodies dived out of beds or from the cookhouse or TV room and rushed to the ops room. Within half a minute every member of the operations staff was there. 'Standby' was the most serious transmission you could send over the radio. Everyone else on the net automatically went silent to clear the airwaves. It meant an operative was about to unavoidably engage with the enemy. The next thing the ops room expected to hear was shooting. The ops staff always felt helpless in these situations because they could hear and talk to a lone operative in trouble, but could do little else to help. And it was not as if the man on the other end of the radio was a stranger, either. We drank, ate, worked, mourned and celebrated together, and all they could do now was listen and hope that when the shooting stopped, it was the familiar voice that came back over the speaker to say he was OK. This was not always the case.

'Who are you?' I asked.

There was no doubt in my mind now that they were boyos. The aggression was seeping from their pores. One of them was clenching his jaw, holding himself back, waiting. They had either not quite decided if I was alone, or they were carefully choosing their moment.

They had no idea they were being listened to eighty miles away, and they no doubt intended to dust me anyhow. They felt in control. As they talked, I kept my radio on 'send' and their voices were picked up by the highly sensitive microphone and transmitted to the operations room.

'Michael's the name.'

Michael, the one who was clenching his jaw, did not appear to be the leader of the two, but he looked the most eager to have a go. The other quietly stared at me, more intelligent and calculating than Michael. The comms room didn't quite catch the name and I repeated it, at the same time stepping slightly forward so the men's voices could be picked up better. I found myself repeating much of what they said.

'You shy?' I asked the other man who did not appreciate being talked to like that.

'Cassidy. Jimmy Cassidy,' he said confidently.

In the ops room our intelligence officer, still in his pyjamas, jotted down the name and hurried off to check it.

'Where's your mates?' Cassidy asked.

'They'll be along,' I said.

'Will they, now?' asked Michael.

Our pick-up car was still some twenty miles away and the driver was going like the clappers to get to me, fully aware of what was going on as he listened to the transmissions. I was feeling edgy. Whoever started the shooting would have the advantage. I was daring myself, looking for an excuse to start. My adrenaline was rising. Things were starting to seem like they were taking for ever. I decided to move first and destroy the bastards, but something was holding me back. A doubt, perhaps, that I was all wrong about what was going on. I rehearsed the move in my mind. I would hit Michael first. All I needed was a tiny excuse to start. Then the intelligence officer's voice came through my ear-piece and brought me back.

'I've got two possible Jimmy Cassidys of South Armagh. How old is he?' Then, quickly realising I couldn't talk directly to him, he said, 'Is your man in his twenties would you say?'

I kept silent.

'In his forties?'

I clicked the radio twice.

'That's a yes,' said the bleep.

Michael and Jimmy could not hear the transmissions, obviously. They said something to me, but I just stared at them, concentrating on what the intelligence officer was telling me.

'One of the Jimmy Cassidys I have is forty-seven. His hair is thinning – a high forehead.'

I clicked twice.

'He's five-ten, stocky, round-faced, about eleven stone.'

I clicked twice. Cassidy said something to me during the transmission. I heard myself say 'What?' and continued to listen to the intelligence officer and Cassidy at the same time.

'If it's our Cassidy he runs his own ASU.'

'I said what are you doing out here?' asked Cassidy, repeating his question.

'The other man is more than likely one of his team. Try Michael Doherty.'

'Are you deaf?' Cassidy asked.

'I told you. Waiting for some friends.'

Michael moved away from Jimmy, stretching the gap between them to a few yards. They were dividing up – getting closer to making their move. I decided if one of them made an attempt to climb over the fence I'd take advantage of his hands being occupied and engage the other first.

'Doherty is thirty-five. Dark curly hair. His eyebrows meet.'

I clicked twice and decided to take a different tack.

'You're Michael Doherty, aren't you?' I said.

Michael's reaction confirmed it.

'Yeah, it is Doherty, isn't it?' I was speaking to the intelligence officer in reality.

Michael was staring at me, wondering how I knew him. I'd stalled him.

The intelligence officer started to rattle off information from his file.

'What are you doing here yourself, Jimmy? Bit early for you, isn't it? Don't you live in Armagh? Hall Street, I believe . . . number seventy-seven.'

Jimmy's eyes narrowed.

'Two-twenty-four Saggart Road. That's where you live Michael, when you're this side of the border that is. Isn't that right? With your sister and her husband.'

Michael flashed a look at Jimmy. I talked to the two men as if I were recalling their details from memory, repeating what was said to me over the net.

'How's your brother doing, Jimmy? Another five years and he's out . . . perhaps.'

Both men were off balance.

'And how's the bomb-making school doing?' I continued to Jimmy. 'I understand you're specialising in mortars these days.'

'Who the fuck are you?' Michael asked.

I had nowhere else to go with this. They were no doubt stunned that I knew so much about them. Then I heard a familiar voice break over the radio.

'I'm twenty yards behind you, Duncan, on your left.'

It was Max. He had heard everything over his own radio and had run then crawled as close as he could without being detected. He would have his M16 pointed at them.

'If they show armour I'll unzip the fucker on the left,' he said.

I now felt in control. My confidence in Max was total. Their lives were in my hands. A desire to goad them into a fight flickered across my mind. Max would take out Michael. I would take out Jimmy. But that's not the way I am. I'm not a murderer, which is what it would have been had I gone for it. We could have got away with it, too. I could have said they had drawn first. We could have upped our score. I could have killed them for Jack and several other friends who had been killed by the IRA over the years. But body counts don't win wars. They are won by convincing the other side they cannot succeed.

'There's a rifle pointed directly at you,' I said. 'Either one of you takes a hand from his pocket and you'll both lose your heads.'

They took this information well and I could see by the subtle change in their faces that they had no doubt I was telling the truth. Perhaps they read the booming confidence in my threat.

'I'm gonna do you a favour today. Now fuck off the way you came.'

They communicated to each other with silent looks. Jimmy nodded to me then they stepped back and walked away.

On certain levels relationships between 14 Int and the SAS were deteriorating with each passing year. This was mainly due to the SAS's heavy-handedness and the cock-ups they were continuing to make. Apart from its contributions to 14 Int, the SBS had by now virtually pulled out of Northern Ireland (they sent the occasional small team over with the SAS). The SAS hung on to its role, which 14 Int battled to redefine and absorb into its own. Initially designed purely for intelligence-gathering in Northern Ireland, 14 Int was technically a wing of the SAS, though none of the members were badged. It was decided in the early days of 14 Int that, as the operatives were essentially intelligence-gathers, regardless of their intense weapon training, they were not qualified (trusted, to be precise) to handle ambushes or any kind of direct action. Therefore, whenever an operation developed to the stage where a lethal conflict was inevitable, 14 Int operatives literally swapped places with SAS troopers. There was a lot of justification for this, especially in the early days, but by now many 14 Int operatives felt that their training and level of experience in the Intelligence Detachments was higher. Although many operatives were more suited to surveillance alone, each Det had a sufficient number of able operatives to do many of the direct action jobs (every Det had at least one SBS rate if not more, several Royal Marines and Paras, as well as members of other capable army units such as the Green Jackets). Many operatives felt they could handle all aspects of the job, including deadly ambushes. I was never wholly convinced of that, simply because when forming a hasty ambush or assault there is not always time to assess each member's skills and background. I would have confidence in the man behind me, even if I didn't know him, if he was SBS or SAS. But I could not say the same about a 14 Int operative I didn't know. To be sure, there were several I did know who I would not want running into a room behind me with a cocked weapon in their hands.

Operatives were understandably pissed off when, after spending sometimes years on an operation, they had to hand it over to the SAS for what was arguably the best bit. The climax of an operation is usually the most sensitive part and key to wrapping up the case. If it got screwed up, many thousands of man hours could be washed down the drain. It was a bit like building a house of cards, and with one card left, a crowd of SAS troopers walking in, shoving us out of the way, surrounding the delicate structure with heavy breath and ham-fistedly proceeding to lay the last card on top. This happened to me personally on two operations and both times I sat with Max, out of the area, and listened to all our work go up in smoke.

The first time was in Lurgan after we had housed a cache of weapons in an old terraced house in the centre of town. We knew the weapons were to be picked up by a notoriously aggressive ASU any day. The SAS liaison officer monitoring our operation reported to the headquarters group in Lisburn that we had reached the contact phase. The SAS storm-troopers moved in.

They were briefed on the situation and given as much detail as possible, but it was impossible for them to assimilate it all and get the feel of the town in the short space of time they had. They left the briefing clutching maps and photographs of places and players, lists of cars and characters and their descriptions, and reams of notes on the operation, but with hardly any time to go over it thoroughly. We never carried any of that stuff. It was mostly all stacked into our memories. Except for updated lists of new cars and number-plates there was nothing we didn't know about the operation. But as long as the SAS kept it to a clean ambush and things did not develop into anything more complicated, they would get the job done. But Murphy's Law clearly states things rarely go as planned, and to counter-react soundly to unexpected and sudden developments, it takes knowledge and experience of the situation which the SAS troopers, arriving at such short notice, could never have had.

This particular ambush in Lurgan required someone to trigger the bad guys moving into the house and their departure. One of the Det operatives who knew all the players was wisely chosen for this task and he remained in our hide across the road. Due to the geography, the narrow streets, and the awareness of the ASU, the boyos were to be allowed to place the weapons in their car and drive out on to the main street unmolested. A two-man SAS team in a car would then move in behind and, remaining a sensible distance back, follow them to a crossroads where an RUC road-block would halt the ASU and arrest them. If the ASU surrendered that would be that, but we knew it was doubtful with this particular crowd. If the ASU reacted with gunfire they would be caught from the flanks of the crossroads and cut off from behind. Other SAS teams were stationed in various side-streets as cut-offs in case any of the ASU made it out of the corral.

The only part that went to plan was the initial 14 Int trigger.

As the four members of the ASU left the house in their vehicle with the weapons, the 14 Int operative reported it over the net. The rest of us sat back in our operations room miles away, listening to the radio exchanges. The ASU drove to the end of the narrow side-street and paused at the T-junction with the main road. They turned left and headed along the virtually empty road towards a junction with traffic lights several hundred yards away, where the RUC lay in wait. The SAS car, acting as rear cut-off, immediately pulled away from its holding position on the main road and closed on the ASU car. The move was sloppy, they were too eager and got too close too soon. The ASU, who were naturally in their most paranoid state, were on the lookout for any suspicious signs. Seeing two thugs in a car pull out from where they were parked and close in behind them was enough to send them on to the offensive.

Before the PIRA car reached the crossroads it suddenly halted. One of the men in the back climbed out holding an M16 and without hesitation opened up on the SAS car. It might as well have had a winged dagger painted on its bonnet. The windscreen was shattered and the lights shot out but somehow the two SAS troopers were unharmed. The boyo climbed back into the car and it took off towards the crossroads. The two SAS troopers pulled themselves together and immediately gave chase. The RUC were thrown into confusion by the shooting, which they could not see and did not expect so soon, and so they didn't react immediately when the first car tore through the crossroads. By the time the SAS car came through at speed, the RUC had recovered and, mistaking the shot-up SAS car for the ASU, presumably assuming it was the SAS who had done the damage, opened up on them. The car was peppered with bullets and, again miraculously, neither of the troopers was hit. To avoid further fire, the SAS troopers sped down a side-street at random, no longer in pursuit of the ASU and just trying to stay alive. The street they turned into was occupied by one of their own SAS cut-offs. This was not good news because the SAS cut-off did not recognise the car at first and made the same mistake as the RUC. Fortunately they only released a few shots before recognising their colleagues. Once again, neither of the SAS in the car was hit. Meanwhile, the ASU had dumped their car after several blocks and had charged into a house. The SAS reacted by quickly gathering to mount an assault. This took precious minutes and would allow the ASU time to regroup and prepare. When the SAS eventually assaulted, with teams charging into the house from the street and then through room after room, the only occupants found were a petrified family. The ASU had not paused on bursting in through the front door. They had gone straight out the back and into the city. They were not caught.

After listening to our thousands of man hours go up in smoke we adjourned to the bar to have several beers and dull our senses.

The second cock-up on my watch was in the area of

Cookstown. We had uncovered weapons in excellent condition in a short-term hide in an overgrown patch of ground surrounded by fields. We watched the weapons knowing they were due to be moved any day soon, and Max and I set up an ambush for the ASU we suspected would soon return to uncover them. The following morning we were relieved by another Det team who were going to watch the site for that daytime only – it was highly unlikely the weapons would be picked up in daylight. We felt the ASU would turn up that night or the next and Max and I would be there as one of the cut-off teams, waiting for them. But the operatives had some bad news for us during the exchange. The SAS had arrived in Cookstown and were taking over the op that night.

When I arrived at the garrison, I was given the job of briefing the SAS troopers on the layout of the ground immediately surrounding the hide and how we thought the ASU might pick up the weapons. The Cookstown garrison was a squalid outpost with the atmosphere of a place on the edge of the world. It was one of those pre-fab camps hastily constructed out of concrete breeze-blocks, corrugated metal and anti-mortar nets strung over dozens of Portakabins spread about the compound. A constant drizzle sprinkled on to the garrison and mud was tracked everywhere, as much inside the structures as outside – there were few concrete pathways connecting the buildings and the soldiers had given up wiping their feet. The resident soldiers had provided us with damp, cramped, well-worn cabins to rest in and wait in out of the weather until it was time to leave. Nothing would happen until nightfall and so, my briefing over, I sat back on one of the metal bunk-beds, put my feet up and read the dog-eared pages of a book I had found amongst the Det collection. I always carried a book around with me for moments such as this. There were half a dozen SAS troopers in the cabin checking over their M15 Colt commandos – a short version of the M16. I noticed how young several of them were – my age, I decided. I must have looked a lot older to them. Unlike them, my hair was long and dirty and my face unshaven. With their preparations complete they sat around waiting for nightfall.

The young ones looked bored and had obviously not been in the job long enough to adapt to the waiting hours. I figured they were newly badged. It took a few years in this business to learn how to relax and deal with inactivity.

'What time's scoff around here?' one of them asked me.

We even had a different language from the SAS. For scoff we said scran. We had a wet, they had a brew. We went for a yomp, they a tab. We went to the head, they the shitter. I checked my watch, deciding whether or not I was hungry.

'We can eat now if you want. I'll show you where the cookhouse is.' I used their terminology. I wasn't about to hint I was even a Marine, let alone SBS.

Three of the young warriors followed me across the camp to the cookhouse and, after filling our plates from the self-service counter that provided food virtually twenty-four hours a day because of the constant in-and-out of patrols, we sat around a table together and ate. I didn't speak, but they, surprisingly for SAS around non-badged types, were quite chatty. This was further proof of their short time in the unit. I decided they could not have been in the SAS more than six months and probably less. This might well have been their first tour with the regiment. Much of their chat was about life in special forces, and mostly for my benefit. They were proud of the fact they had got into the SAS, and why not? As the meal progressed they grew more comfortable with me. I showed interest. I was indeed interested. I always regarded the SAS as an organisation I might like to have joined had my life been different and had I ended up in the Army. They might never have talked with a regular soldier in the same relaxed way, but in their eyes I was somewhat special forces, if only in a limited way. I got the impression they were trying to recruit me.

One of them asked if I had given any thought to joining the SAS after my tour with 14 Int. They suggested my experience would be an advantage. All I had to do was get through a gruelling selection course, they explained.

I soon began to relish my position and played on it a little. I could not resist it. They were just young and full of it. As they went on about the unique opportunities the SAS enjoyed over every other branch of the armed forces, one of them mentioned HALO jumping. That surprised me as I did not think any of them had been in long enough to do the high-altitude parachute course.

'You've done HALO then, have you?' I asked.

'Well, no, not yet. But we're on a course as soon as we get back.'

We had finished eating and I would have to leave the camp soon so I decided it was time to burst the bubble.

'You'll love it,' I said. 'It's a great crack.'

They looked at me questioningly.

'How would you know?' one of them asked.

'I did one a couple of years ago,' I replied. I had over a hundred jumps under my belt by then.

That threw them.

'You RAF then?' another ventured. RAF parachute instructors and path-finders were the only others who did HALO apart from the SBS.

'No. SBS.'

There was a moment of silence.

'How long?' another asked.

'Four years.'

They knew that little they had said about their job was news to me. I remained sitting for a moment longer to enjoy their discomfort before finally wishing them luck that night and leaving.

Any embarrassment they felt was nothing compared to how they would feel several hours later.

A narrow country road ran alongside the length of the field where the weapons were hidden. The SAS plan was to catch the ASU in a pincer movement. The ambushers would allow the ASU to park up on the road, walk into the overgrown area, unload the cache and bring the weapons back to their car. When the ASU moved off the SAS would drive at them from both directions and trap them. If the ASU went on the offensive, the SAS would cut them down. I am not entirely clear as to what happened on that dark road that night, and not surprisingly the SAS were reluctant to discuss it in detail. Everything appeared to go as planned until the ASU car pulled away from the cache with the weapons.

I believe the tailing SAS car closed in too early once again. When the blood is up, the fear of losing the prey is often greater than the fear of losing one's life. This country road had a vehicle pass along it once an hour or so. When the ASU saw the headlights of a car move in behind them as soon as they left the hide they were not for a second going to put it down to coincidence. They abruptly stopped and climbed out with their guns at the ready. The SAS stopped some thirty yards from them and clambered out likewise. The ASU opened fire for only a few seconds before taking flight into the fields. The second SAS car, the other side of the pincer, arrived and its troopers spilled out. A shoot-out took place but it appears to have been only between the two SAS groups. Fortunately, once again, none were killed, although this time one of the sergeants was shot in the arm before a halt was called. The ASU escaped.

Max and I sat in my car in a quiet layby a mile away listening to the débâcle over the radio.

'Another home goal,' I said.

Max took a moment to form a sentence he'd been trying to fit into a conversation all day.

'Insouciant sods, in 'ey,' he said.

I might have agreed but I didn't know what it meant.

*   *   *

It was the RUC who eventually intervened on 14 Int's side regarding the issue of SAS takeovers. After several more incidents on other operations with similar results, they began withholding information from the Det if the SAS were going to take over at the climax. As a result, the situation changed in favour of 14 Int. The SAS were still to be involved in ambushes, but only at the request of the Det commanders, and then usually alongside 14 Int operatives.

10

Mr Tallyho came back on to the scene early in my second
year with the Det. I had not seen him since the O'Sally
ambush. He looked exactly the same. His drab, grey
raincoat and patent-leather shoes were probably the
same ones. He had segs in his shoes now – the curved
metal pieces you can buy to hammer into the heels and
tips of worn shoes. I noticed them because my father
always used them on our shoes. The tips, sides and
heels of my school shoes were always liberally dotted
with them. I sounded like a tap-dancer when I walked.
They were lethal on hard surfaces, especially when
jumping off the platforms of the old-style open-backed
double-decker buses. I would skid for several yards, and
if I went back too far on to my heels I would end up on
my backside.

I wondered why Tallyho was wearing them as they
were tactically unsound. But then, Tallyho was not a
soldier. He never thought in those terms. I wondered

if he had ever used his gun apart from a brief training period on the range. And what had he done for work before this job? Perhaps they had taken him straight out of college many years ago. I could not imagine him doing anything else, not now, anyway. If this conflict ever truly ended I expect he would move on to the next one, or back to diplomatic spying for MI5 or 6. Perhaps he already worked in other parts of the world doing similar tasks for military intelligence in between jobs in Northern Ireland to give him a break. And what would he do when he retired, if he lived that long? I was never likely to discover the answers to these questions. He never said anything unless it was connected to the task in hand, and then just enough to tell you what his immediate needs were.

Tallyho had been brought in because we had been working on an operation that was in danger of going tits-up. We needed his particular brand of expertise, though as it turned out, not in the way I, or anyone else in the Det for that matter, ever expected. The irony, though we never knew it at the time, was that Tallyho was the main cause of the problem in the first place.

The operation was against a man called Macaleany who was a high-ranking member of the Provisionals. Macaleany was an ASU commander who was up for promotion to brigade level, but he was having a little problem qualifying for that upgrade. We needed him to get that promotion because we were going to use it to our advantage. Therefore, the problem holding him back became our direct problem. It was his wife. He suspected her of infidelity and wanted to dump her. But if he did that it was unlikely he would get the new posting. The PIRA godfathers were good Catholics and would not look favourably upon him if he divorced her. It was also their reasoning that if a man could not manage his own household he could not be trusted with a high command.

Macaleany suspected his wife's lover was her childhood sweetheart, who lived down the street. In fact it was Mr Tallyho.

Months earlier, when military intelligence first learned that Macaleany might be up for promotion, Tallyho had been tasked with secretly 'invading' Macaleany's life to find a possible weak link that could be used to gain information from him and perhaps even 'turn' him. After researching the childless family who lived alone together in the housing estate, Tallyho decided that Macaleany himself was staunch and un-recruitable. But his wife, a quiet, dreamy, sensitive and altogether unhappy woman, might be a possible 'in' and worth taking to the next stage, which was to physically 'make contact' with her.

Macaleany's missus had been with her husband for five years but was lonely and out of love with him. Macaleany was so insensitive to his wife's feelings that it was only when she stopped having sex with him that he began to suspect she was seeing her lover, although in truth she was seeing nobody. At first Tallyho spent several weeks carefully nurturing an innocent relationship with her, one that was never intended to become in any way amorous. But to his surprise, during one of their 'chance encounters', she came on to him and, being the professional he was, looking for any way to take advantage, he encouraged this new turn in their relationship. Tallyho would do anything to get what he wanted. He was a soulless man and his only motive was gaining information.

To imagine Tallyho having sex seemed perverse to me. He just did not appear the type. As well as being totally unattractive, he was grubby, always had a cigarette in his mouth and looked constantly hungover. Had I not been forced to witness him in the act of coitus a few months later I would never have believed him capable of it. Macaleany's wife was no oil painting either, but it said little for her taste in men. Obviously my understanding of people and what makes them tick still had a lot of maturing to do, because Macaleany's wife not only found Tallyho sexually attractive, she also fell in love with him. She must have been exceptionally lonely.

It was during Tallyho's relationship with Macaleany's wife that their marriage stabilised and even improved. She was happier when she was seeing Tallyho and this was reflected in her everyday life. It appeared that, while making love to Tallyho, she could once again make love to her husband as well and therefore Macaleany ceased to be suspicious of her.

With Macaleany's upcoming promotion would come an increase in salary. Macaleany planned on using this extra cash to get out of the housing estate and get his wife away from her ex-boyfriend down the street. He borrowed money in advance of his promotion and decided to buy a new family house several miles away in the open countryside. This was exactly what we wanted him to do. It would make it much easier for us to monitor Macaleany.

Sometimes our surveillance methods verged on the bizarre. On a technical surveillance operation in Warren Point, in the holiday apartment of a high-ranking PIRA, we found that the toilet was the only place we could gain quality information. He had a wife and family in Belfast but would meet his lover at the apartment once a week. His lover was our tout. She discovered the best time to get him to talk about work was while they were making love in the toilet, which was his favourite location. He liked to wait until she was evacuating her bowels then enter the small room and get her to do things to him with her evacuated substances while he sat beneath her. Some perverted sod in MI5 wanted a video camera placed inside, but we were spared the task. The sound tapes were enough. There's nowt as queer as folk.

After several months, Tallyho decided he was not getting the quality of intelligence he wanted from Mrs Macaleany and so he pulled himself off the task and disappeared from her life without a word. Macaleany had not yet been promoted and was therefore not privy to the level of intelligence Tallyho wanted.

When Tallyho left the scene, Macaleany's wife became depressed and stopped making love to her husband once again. And once again Macaleany began to suspect she was having an affair with her childhood sweetheart.

When Macaleany's suspicions of his wife's adultery got to a stage where we thought he might do something drastic, we had to act to save the situation, and pronto. If Macaleany did not get his promotion he could not afford to buy his new house and we would lose a great opportunity to monitor a high-ranking PIRA member. The obvious remedy was to satisfy Macaleany's wife, who was pining for her lost lover. And so Tallyho was brought back in.

At least once a week Macaleany attended PIRA meetings a few miles outside of Dungannon, and it was decided to take advantage of his next one to reunite the lovers. Max and I would take Tallyho to Macaleany's house in Dungannon.

When Tallyho arrived at the Det he was his usual bland, characterless self. He climbed into the back of my car and we sat without a word, other than Max sending coded progress reports back to the ops room while I drove into the town. It was obvious Tallyho was not looking forward to the evening.

It was dark by the time we arrived in Dungannon. Over the radio I heard that Macaleany was at his meeting. An operative remained on watch in a car not far from the venue on the Dungannon road. There was a possibility that Macaleany was having his own house watched and if Tallyho was seen going in he might get a call. Macaleany was a dangerous man and we would take no chances with Tallyho – he was on loan and we didn't want to send back damaged goods. So the operative outside Macaleany's meeting had a straightforward enough job: if Macaleany left early he was to run him off the road.

I stopped the car in a quiet part of the town outside the housing estate. The three of us climbed out and we made our way through the back-streets and along a path that led through the estate towards the rear of Macaleany's house. Max split off to find a place where he could conceal himself and watch the front of the house. He reported over his radio that lights were on inside and all looked OK.

I led Tallyho down a narrow path that separated the backs of the terraced houses. It was a quiet, damp night and Tallyho's segs on the soles of his shoes were causing me some concern.

I finally stopped him. 'You're going to have to take your shoes off,' I said.

He looked down at his feet, looked at me, rolled his eyes and bent down and untied the laces. He pulled his shoes off and held them in his hands. Off we set again.

We arrived at Macaleany's back fence. It was six feet high, wooden and in good condition. I scanned around to see if there was anyone on watch. It looked clear. I pulled myself up enough to see into the back yard. The back gate was padlocked from the inside. The kitchen light was on and there was movement within.

'You ready?' I asked.

He nodded.

I cupped my hands into a stirrup. He put his shoes on the ground, placed a damp, sock-covered foot into my hands and I yanked him up. He scrambled over the fence and landed on his feet the other side. I picked up his shoes and pulled myself up on to the fence to hand them to him. He was standing in a sodden, muddy vegetable patch up to his ankles and looking down at his feet. I handed him his shoes and climbed over. He walked through the muddy yard to the back door, which had a concrete step, and then, after scraping off as much mud as he could with his fingers, he put his shoes back on. He didn't look happy.

'Stay in the kitchen where I can see you through the window,' I whispered.

'Why?' he asked.

'I don't want to let you out of my sight.'

He resented being told what to do, especially by some soldier half his age. He always worked alone. But he respected my position – no matter what your rank in special forces, if you're in charge, you're in charge of all.

I moved back into the shadows. He waited until I was hidden before knocking quietly on the door. A moment later the door opened and Macaleany's wife stood in the doorway. Years of being married to a member of the PIRA had made her an agile thinker in potentially dangerous situations and she was well aware of the possibility of prying eyes.

'Quickly. Come in,' she said.

He stepped in and she closed the door. I moved to where I could see in through the window. They both stood in the room, several feet apart, talking. I could not hear, but I could tell from the body language and their reactions that he was explaining his absence. I wondered what bullshit he was giving her. Whatever he said, it was convincing. She was softening. She moved close to him and put her arms around him. They started to kiss passionately. Tallyho didn't hang around, passed on the vol-au-vents and went straight for the main course. He reached behind her and started to pull up her skirt. He hitched it around her hips and put his hands inside her knickers to pull them down. She responded by undoing his trouser belt and pulling down his zip. Mrs Macaleany was in her late thirties and probably never once gave any consideration to exercising or the type of food she ate. Her thighs were heavy with cellulite. Tallyho grabbed great chunks of them. She pulled his trousers and underpants down and he pushed her back on to the kitchen table. His legs were skinny, hairy and white as milk. It was so obscene I could not stop myself from watching. With his raincoat still on and his pants around his muddy ankles he humped her like a Jack Russell. She was loving it.

I whispered Max's call-sign over the radio. 'One Four Romeo.'

Max answered instantly. 'Send?'

'You should see what he's doing to her on the kitchen table.'

'He's not!'

'It's revolting.'

I don't know if Mrs Macaleany climaxed, but Tallyho suddenly stopped and remained lying with his face buried in her breasts, his feet still on the floor, and panting. Then he got off her and pulled up his pants. She seemed satisfied, smiling sheepishly as she pulled up her knickers. They talked a little as she followed him to the back door. He was no doubt assuring her that he would see her again.

I moved back into the shadows. The light went out in the kitchen and the door opened. He kissed her quickly and headed across the garden to the fence. She watched him for a moment, then closed the door.

'Short and sweet,' I said as I met him at the fence.

He knew I had watched him but he showed no sign of embarrassment, or that he cared.

I helped him over the fence then joined him on the path.

'Do I have to take my shoes off again?' he asked.

'No. Let's go.' Then into my radio. 'One Three Charlie, towards the obvious.'

'Roger that,' was Max's reply.

'The things I do for Queen and country,' Tallyho muttered as we walked back through the estate.

Everything worked to plan. Macaleany's wife was happy once more and resumed shagging him. Macaleany got his promotion.

But Tallyho could not go on bonking Macaleany's wife for ever. It was rumoured that he didn't fancy her any more and couldn't get it up. And so, once again, Tallyho disappeared from her life.

It was not long before Macaleany's marriage showed signs of going on the rocks. His wife became love-sick and stopped having sex with him once again. To make matters worse, the PIRA godfathers began to grow suspicious of him. They were seeing a relationship between certain operations going wrong and his involvement in them. Instead of suspecting that his house was bugged they considered the possibility of him being a tout. If they decided that was true his days on this earth were numbered.

The image that all members of Military Intelligence

are heartless, ruthless killers is fiction. Only a lot of them are. The truth is that if there is no alternative to ending a person's life in the name of national security then so be it, but if there is, the alternative is preferred. When Macaleany's plight reached ministerial level, an order came down that he was to be saved from any attempt on his life. They felt it was unfair that he should be executed because of a situation we had created. As he was not an actual killer, even though he had been responsible for British deaths, he had also been of use, and it was considered he should receive something in return, such as his neck. Aren't we nice? But this was not an easy situation to solve.

Military Intelligence had two choices. They could lift Macaleany out of Ireland completely, tell him his life was in danger, get whatever else they could from him, then place him into a protection programme that meant relocating him somewhere else in the world. But knowing Macaleany, it was unlikely he would buy their story, believing it to be a sting, and would tell them nothing. As they had no legal right to hold him, he would go to the godfathers and report that the Brits had tried to recruit him. Suspicious of him already, the PIRA would now consider him a definite security risk and the likelihood of him being executed would be increased. MI's only other choice was to do what they could to manipulate his relationship with his bosses with misinformation, and at the same time patch up his marriage. The latter course was chosen and Mr Tallyho was ordered back in.

It was not going to be as straightforward as before getting Tallyho and Mrs Macaleany together. Since Macaleany had been promoted, his movements were less predictable. His security level had gone up a notch. He stayed home a lot since most of his meetings were held at his house. But Tallyho had his own methods, and somehow contacted Mrs Macaleany. I don't know how pleased she was to receive his message, but she agreed to meet him in a pub in Dungannon.

On the chosen night, Max and I drove Tallyho to Dungannon and parked up a few hundred yards down the street from the pub. Tallyho was armed this time. The pub was a known PIRA hangout. He could get away with a brief pint as long as he kept to himself. This was the most dangerous phase of the operation for Tallyho personally, and we were joined by another team who waited in the back of the pub in case he got into trouble. Max and I would watch the front. As in the Nairac scenario, if they were suspicious of Tallyho they would drag him outside and deal with him elsewhere. The difference was that this time we would be the ones doing the damage.

Tallyho did not seem fazed by the danger. He left us and walked down the street alone towards the pub. I watched him enter. If he was not out in fifteen minutes, Max and I would go in and look for him. Under our coats, along with our usual 9mms we carried M10 Colt Ingram sub-machine-guns, a short, rectangular box-shaped 9mm weapon with a magazine capacity of thirty rounds that fired them at a rate of 950 per minute, 300 bullets per minute faster than a standard sub-machine-gun. It was an American weapon, originally designed to fit into a briefcase and could be fired by pulling a trigger in the handle. With its incredible rate of fire it could clear a crowded room in seconds. On my 14 Int selection course I saw the briefcase version demonstrated by an SAS trooper. We were all impressed, but the demonstration was made memorable by the next SAS trooper who held the briefcase in the wrong place and blew the end of one of his fingers off.

Macaleany's wife sat alone in the pub and watched Tallyho as he walked in. They made eye contact and Tallyho indicated a beer to the barman with a grunt and threw down the correct money. He sipped some of it and caught her eye again. Then he walked out of the pub. Tallyho had the keys to my car and walked to it alone while Max and I watched from the shadows. Macaleany's wife left the pub less than a minute later and climbed into her own car. As she drove off Tallyho followed. Max and I got into the back of the standby team's car and followed at a discreet distance.

Unknown to us, Macaleany had been smouldering at home wondering where his wife was and went out to search for her. He arrived at the pub not long after his wife had left and was told she had been there alone.

Macaleany's wife drove out of the town into the countryside and pulled into a quiet layby where she killed the engine and turned off the headlights. Tallyho pulled in behind her, climbed out of his car and walked towards her.

As we drove by we saw him getting into her car. We continued until we were out of sight then pulled over. Max and I got out. We climbed through a hedge and made our way down the inside of a field to where Tallyho and Macaleany's wife had stopped. We peered through the hedge to get a look. The windows were steamed up and we could hear raised voices. Macaleany's wife was shouting. 'Bastard' was the only word we could make out, and it was one she yelled several times. It looked like a scuffle was taking place inside the car. We could not tell if he was raping her or beating her up. No matter what he was doing we could not intervene. It suddenly crossed my mind that Tallyho might have decided on one solution that would probably have put things right for all concerned, himself included, and that was to kill her. I would not have put anything past him. I remembered how casually he had requested me to kill O'Sally and his partner years before because the man had been greedy. A person could know a man like Tallyho all his life and not learn anything about him. We waited for the outcome.

After a few minutes the violence stopped. I thought to myself, that's it, he's strangled her. Then the car began to rock rhythmically. He was not killing her but making love to her, and passionately, it seemed. We settled down to wait it out. They took a long while this time. Then after they finished they talked quietly for over an hour.

Finally, Tallyho climbed out of the car and got into his own. She started her engine, turned on the headlights, pulled away and headed in the direction of her home. Max and I climbed through the hedge and joined Tallyho in the car. He never said a word as I drove back to the Det.

When Macaleany's wife arrived home, she found the

RUC waiting for her. Her husband had been arrested and was in jail.

When Macaleany had left the pub he had gone back home to wait for his wife. At midnight, an hour after the pub had closed, he took his gun from its hidden place in the garden, climbed into his car and headed for Dungannon. He drove to the housing estate and went directly to the house several doors down the street from his former home. He kicked in the door, stormed up the stairs to the bedroom, burst in and blasted several rounds into the man lying in the bed, his wife's childhood sweetheart, killing him.

11

I spent much of my time as a Det operator in Dungannon, County Tyrone. It was a fair-sized town, important enough to have the main hospital for the area. It always felt gloomy, like an industrial town in the Midlands mostly undeveloped since the war. The only locals I knew, by sight that is, were players, or related to them. I hardly went there in daylight and it was poorly lit at night. It had its gangs of youthful thugs who were to be avoided, especially after pub hours. We could not afford to get into a scrap. Before it got to that we would be forced to pull out our weapons – if they got their hands on them first they would probably shoot us with them – but any confrontation meant that the operative could not operate in the town or area again. In the backs of our minds we were aware that there was always the chance an attack could be a set-up. For that reason alone we were prepared to use our guns as a last resort to avoid any physical contact.

There was no doubt a fun side to the town, but we never had the chance to experience it.

Dungannon had a mostly Catholic population and many of the Protestants lived intermingled with the Catholics, even members of the RUC. A Protestant police officer lived in the main housing estate in the town. Every day he said goodbye to his wife and children, drew his gun, opened his front door and paused to check up and down the street. He would leave the house, gun in hand, and walk down his garden path to his car, which was parked in the street outside his house. After checking the car for bombs, he drove to the RUC station not far away. In the two years I was there he was never interfered with. His strange existence was not an uncommon one in Northern Ireland.

Dungannon and its outlying towns and villages were always good for some action. One day while I was walking through the town a 500-pound bomb exploded in the main shopping street. It took out every window for a half-mile radius and wiped out every shop within a hundred yards. The PIRA had parked a horse-box in the street packed to the roof with ampho, a low-grade explosive made from high-nitrate fertiliser and diesel fuel. The Provos telephoned the RUC to warn them and the street was cleared of people just in time. I was several streets away and was sprinkled by falling debris.

Every day seemed like the one before. The only thing that seemed to change was the weather. No one I knew, on our side, that is, was in any way passionate about the conflict. But the IRA could always be counted on to sting us once in a while and stoke our fires. Only a few months earlier, they had blown up Lord Mountbatten and members of his family, including children. I was in Warren Point when I heard the news about the bomb on his boat not all that far away. It was the first time I felt a personal, bitter anger towards the IRA. From a purely soldiering point of view, within the IRA and its many splinter groups, such as the Provos, there were a lot of men who demanded respect because of their skills, and several, mostly of the old school, had a sense of honour. But the IRA also had their fair share of bone-headed, murderous cowards, especially among the younger generation. Those were the ones we really wanted to get our sights on. But attacking civilians in their shops and pubs is not just a terrorist strategy. Unfortunately, politicians discovered by the end of the First World War that if civilians were brought into the actual physical conflict it could affect the outcome of a war.

While the Provisionals were conducting operations to make the world take notice of them, they were also planning one that would force British Military Intelligence to take them far more seriously than they ever had before. If the IRA had been successful they could have taken 14 Int out of the game for many months with the loss of many of our lives.

Military Intelligence had no idea at the time, but the IRA had done what had been thought impossible: they had completely broken our radio codes.

On my 14 Int selection, during the communications instruction phase, we were taught a basic code system. Every Det had its own codes for places and objects such as cars, or buildings, which we would have to learn as soon as we arrived. There were general codes for hospitals and police stations, for instance, but specific locations, such as the various pubs and car parks and the betting shop in Dungannon, all had their own code names. Army Intelligence were aware that the PIRA would monitor our transmissions when they could, but it was not seen as a threat. Secure comms were available. That system worked by scrambling a voice before it was transmitted. The receiver, set to the same complex coding mechanism, unscrambled the words for the listener. Even the most sophisticated monitoring systems would take months to unscramble a single transmission. But the new system's introduction was not expected for several years because, as I said, it was deemed unnecessary.

Living in Dublin at that time was a young Irish electronics genius whose hobby was communications and code-breaking. When the IRA heard about him they asked if he would like to join the cause. He was not a passionate supporter, but he was an egomaniac and keen to get recognition for his genius. With some gentle stroking he was recruited.

The IRA brought him to Belfast and gave him all the equipment and finance he needed. His target was the 14 Int Detachment that worked the city.

His first objective was to establish the frequencies the Det used. Our system was set up so that when an operative sent a transmission it never went directly to the person you were talking to, even if they were standing right beside you. It would be picked up by one of many dishes dotted all over the province and re-broadcast, but on a different frequency. It was not long before the man from Dublin had found several of the frequencies the Det used and set about monitoring them. His next task was to compile a list of all the codes they used and find their meanings.

He knew that many of the codes were for locations. The big step was to find the meaning of one location code. Once he did that it would lead to another. To achieve this he had to actually locate the source of one of the transmissions; physically track a transmission to an operative on the ground and follow him until he could identify a code used that indicated where the operator was, then mark that on the map. It would not only break a code, it would also identify an actual operative. He spent weeks cruising Belfast in search of a target. It was only a matter of time before he got one.

The operative was parked in a street watching an IRA suspect. When he gave his coded location the Dublin boy plotted the operative's location on his map and ticked that code off. When the operative moved off, the Dubliner followed him and, listening to his communications, ticked off the meanings of other codes. When other operatives gave their location as one the Dubliner knew he would race over there and identify the source. After several months the young genius had compiled detailed descriptions of most of the Det's operatives and their cars, and had deciphered most of their codes. The IRA kept the operation top secret; neither Military Intelligence nor the Dets had any idea that the code had been broken.

Fortunately, the IRA godfathers in Belfast decided not to be greedy with this advantage right away. Had they been, they might have used the information to set up a series of hits to wipe out as many of the Det's operatives as they could in one go. Perhaps they decided against that because it was more complicated than it sounded. To start off with they set up a pantomime operation to keep the Det occupied while they conducted real operations elsewhere in the city. This worked fine for a while, but obviously operatives were beginning to sense something had changed on the streets. They were seeing known targets and watching them exchange items and information, but nothing was coming of it.

While all that was going on in Belfast we were working hard in Dungannon to crack the Tyrone ASUs who were one of the most energetic in the province at that time. The head man in Dungannon was Tommy Shammy. We had found Shammy through information gained from the bug in the toilet in Warren Point. Tommy was well aware we were on to him and that we would pounce hard if he made a mistake. But he was a smart one and kept us on our toes. If we made a mistake he would jump on us just as quickly.

Tommy was high ranking enough to be privy to the code-breaking operation that was going on against the Det in Belfast, and he put in a request to utilise their new-found communications genius against us. His request was granted.

Tommy's plans for us were not as sophisticated as those of his colleagues in Belfast. He wanted some body counts, plain and simple. Dead undercover operatives on the IRA's yearly accounting sheets always looked good.

As Dungannon was a fraction of the size of Belfast it was not long before the young Dubliner had us all tagged and our codes broken. Tommy could not have been happier. All he had to do now was choose his time and his target. I had the dubious honour of being his first target, and I only have one explanation for how I survived.

We all have a sixth sense. A common example is when, for no apparent reason, you look up to see a person watching you from across the street or from a window in a house or a car beside you in traffic. In most people this is rarely developed beyond that. But if there is one job that helps develop it, it is deadly undercover work – although only if you are receptive to what your mind is trying to tell you. Some operatives refused to listen to that sense, or did not trust in it. I can't say I ever took it seriously, beyond the examples just mentioned, until one night in Dungannon when it undoubtedly saved my life.

Things had gone strangely quiet in the weeks leading up to that night. We travelled to Dungannon every evening in search of leads and came back empty-handed each time. Something was definitely not right, but no one could put a finger on it. The night in question, we had the town fully staked out using eight operatives one-up in eight cars. We were all parked up, in and around the outskirts of the town, in locations we considered secure. I was parked on a piece of waste ground in the centre of the town which was used as a car park by shoppers in the daytime. It was at the rear of the main street and at night was dimly lit and deserted but for a handful of cars. I was watching a pub fifty yards away across a street. Standing in the doorway, sipping a beer, was Sean O'Dilly, one of Tommy's lieutenants. It was unusual for O'Dilly to be standing there in the doorway and not inside with the rest of his gang. When I arrived in the car park code-named Bear Cage I reported my position over the radio. I sat in the darkness and watched O'Dilly for over an hour. He moved back into the pub every now and then for a refill, but spent most of the time in the doorway. He occasionally glanced in my direction, but that was OK. He was always suspicious and would always be on the lookout. I knew he could not see me in the car where I was parked in the shadows. My M10 was on my passenger seat under a newspaper.

Nothing else was going on in the town. The radios were silent with the inactivity. Back at the operations room the bleep and second-in-command sat back twiddling their thumbs as they had every night for the past few weeks. I poured myself a cup of coffee from my flask.

Suddenly a sensation rushed through me. I felt incredibly uneasy, in a way I had never felt before. I sat up and looked all around the outside of the car – I always kept my window wound down a few inches to prevent condensation. There were shadows everywhere, walls, garbage bins, the unlit backs of the unoccupied shops, but no sign of life. O'Dilly was still in the doorway of the pub. Then the hairs went up on the back of my neck and I felt a huge surge of what I can only describe as a kind of fear. By now fear affected me the way it affected all seasoned special forces operatives. I channelled it into aggression. I would strike out mercilessly at the first clear sign of a threat. But I couldn't see anyone. The sense was so strong in me that I did something I never thought possible for me – not based on just a feeling. I started my engine and drove out of there, taking the back way out of the car park to avoid O'Dilly.

'One Three Charlie, mobile,' I called over the radio.

A few seconds later the second-in-command came over the net. 'What's up?' he asked.

'I'm outta here. I feel a little warm,' I said which meant I felt I was being watched.

'Who can take over Bear Cage?' he asked casually.

'No,' I cut in. 'Bear Cage is hot. We should call this off.'

Whatever an operative did on the ground the desk had to back up. There was no debate. The operative knew better than the man running the ops room, no matter what his rank was. Another operator the other side of the town had a similar awkward feeling and came on to the net.

'Two Seven Bravo, I agree. Going mobile.'

Yet another operative went mobile. I had started something.

'OK,' the 2IC said, giving in, 'hard rock.' This was the code to come home. 'All call-signs check.'

Each of the operatives in turn called in and when they were all accounted for we headed back to the Det.

As soon as we got home we gathered in the TV room for prayers (brief-debrief). The Det commander was waiting for us as we came in one by one to sit in chairs facing him behind his little podium in front of the TV.

'So. What's going on, lads?' he asked, directing the question mainly at me.

I told him I could not give an explanation other than it didn't feel right. Other operatives agreed with me. Many had felt uneasy. In the last few weeks something had been different about the town. The Det commander didn't know how to deal with this. It was most unusual and he had never experienced anything like it before. He never went out on the ground with us – his job was in the Det running the operations – but he was smart enough to appreciate the difference. We suggested pulling off the ground entirely for a few days.

'I don't know what to say to you,' he replied to that. 'This is a major operation. It's what we're here for. What do I tell London? We're pulling off because it doesn't feel right?'

He had a point, but we had one too, though we could not explain it.

He looked at us for a moment while he considered the situation.

'Look,' he said, 'we can't pull off without a reason. Let's continue for a few more nights.' If we're still not getting anything, and if you still feel the same way, then we'll pull off and rethink it. OK?'

There was nothing we could say. We were here to do a job. We could not do it sitting in the Det wondering why we were uncomfortable. Perhaps the only way was to face it and flush it out. An advance to contact, so to speak. But that usually meant waiting for a soldier to take a hit before knowing where the enemy were.

I went to my little room and lay awake for hours wondering if there was anything I had seen that could have made me react the way I had. By dawn I had fallen into an uneasy sleep.

The following night, we went out to Dungannon again. One of us wasn't coming back.

We arrived in Dungannon via the motorway, which was the safest and least conspicuous route, all one-up and at intervals of several minutes. We took up positions around the town, careful not to use locations we considered over-used, shut off our engines and sat in our cars, waiting for any activity.

One of our operatives was a young man known as Noddy. He was our memory-man. Each operative carried lists of cars, number-plates, names and descriptions of players, addresses – pages of details that were always changing with new intelligence coming in every day. We were always having to check our lists against cars and characters, but Noddy seemed to be able to memorise them all. We were supposed to report over the radio whenever we saw a detail that matched one on our list. Noddy was for ever reporting listed number-plates as he drove around. His brain was a great asset to the Det, but sadly that organ let him down when he needed it most.

It was Noddy's turn to park up in Bear Cage and watch the pub as I had done the night before. When I heard him report that O'Dilly was standing outside the pub in exactly the same circumstances, I felt uneasy again.

The majority of us were parked on the edge of the town that night. There were not many places to go static in the centre and it was wise not to over-use them. In fact there was only one other car in the centre of town, three hundred yards from Noddy at the bottom of the hill from Bear Cage. In that car, with one of the Det dogs, a recovering alcoholic Labrador named Muff, was Luke. I knew Luke very well. He was the only other SBS operative in the Det at that time and had been one of the nine who passed my SBS selection course.

Luke always did himself down when it came to fears and emotions. Climbing into a chopper he could not resist reminding anyone he was with how unsafe they were and that his biggest fear was crashing. He said the same about E&RE from a submarine, climbing oil platforms, and in fact every dangerous aspect of the job. He was sincere and did not mind admitting it. But most people had fears about those activities in some way or another. They were dangerous. The thing about Luke was, if the shit ever hit the fan, for those who really knew him, he was high up on the list of men you would want by your side. He showed a seemingly uncharacteristic coolness and determination under fire. He was very bright, and even though scared, probably no less than anyone else, he could be counted on to do the right thing. In the Falklands, just a few years later, his four-man patrol was split up due to enemy activity while making their way to a helicopter pick-up. Two of his men were left behind, stuck on the ground without food for eight days in foul weather. The newspapers got hold of the story afterwards and incorrectly reported, intentionally or otherwise, that the men had lived off rats for that period. In fact each man carried twenty-four-hour emergency ration packs which we nicknamed rat-packs. Luke went back in alone to find the men. This was doubly dangerous, because not only were there heavy Argentinian patrols in that area, but the men were weak and exhausted by then and could easily have shot him as he searched for them in the darkness at the pre-arranged emergency rendezvous point. But he found them and brought them back in.

When several shots suddenly rang out, interrupting the cold stillness that had shrouded Dungannon all that week, no one knew where they had come from. A couple of operators reported it, but they were quickly told to leave the net free in case there was an emergency. A radio then opened up and we could hear the sound of gurgling mixed in with a few inaudible words. The Det commander tried to contact each of the operatives to eliminate them as sources, but whoever was gurgling on the net was holding down the send button preventing all other transmission. Luke felt certain the shots had come from the Bear Cage area and decided not to wait until the comms cleared to inform ops. He leapt out of the car and tore up the hill, gun in hand, towards the car park. The rest of us could do nothing until we found out what was going on. Some operatives suspected it might be one of ours parked up by the lake and quickly drove there, but the operative was fine. We were all unaware of Luke tearing through the town alone and in great personal danger from a number of sources.

If he encountered an Army or police patrol they would

shoot him without hesitation – a man in civvies running with a gun in his hand was a legitimate target, and they would never expect him to be a British undercover operative. Then there were the gunmen themselves – they could still be around and waiting for such a reaction. Luke felt certain it was Noddy who had been hit, but he had no idea from what direction. He saw the car at the far end of the car park in the shadows and sprinted to it. When he got there he found Noddy lying slumped in his seat. The driver's window had been shattered by bullets. Blood seeped from holes in Noddy's face, torso and legs, but he was alive, just. Luke's only option was to get Noddy to the hospital as soon as possible. He manhandled him over the handbrake and gear lever and into the passenger seat. There was no time to be gentle, he was oozing blood. The threat of gunmen was still at the forefront of Luke's mind. As he sat in the driver's seat to start the car, he could feel the pints of warm blood soaking into the arse of his trousers. He screeched out of the car park, passed the pub where O'Dilly had been standing and sped up the road.

By now the RUC had sent patrol cars to investigate the shooting and the Scots Guards, the local Army unit, were also heading towards the area. As Luke made the sharp turn out of the car park an RUC patrol car appeared in his rear. They flicked on their flashing lights and pursued him. As if matters could not get any worse the RUC assumed Luke was escaping from the shooting and was, therefore, the gunman. Suddenly Luke heard shots. The RUC were trying to shoot out his tyres. A bullet hit the car. Luke was an excellent

driver and although he was scared shitless, as he end-
lessly reminded us afterwards, he never lost control.
He was driving for his friend's life. He could not stop
to surrender and explain the situation because by the
time the RUC had got through their arrest procedure,
Noddy would probably have been dead. Luke had no
choice but to lose them. We all knew the town like the
backs of our hands, and perhaps better than the police.
The RUC could not compete with his driving skills, nor
did they have his incentive, and in less than a minute
he gave them the slip. Other police patrol cars were
reacting, but they assumed he was trying to make his
way out of the town and so coordinated themselves on
the outskirts to stop him. That was just fine by Luke
because he was headed for the hospital in the centre of
the town. Noddy rolled around in the passenger seat
while Luke continuously talked to reassure him.

Suddenly, Luke's car came under fire again, this time
from the Scots Guards, and then, a few streets later, from
the UDR. This was becoming ridiculous. Luke eventually screeched into the hospital car park and came to a
halt outside the main entrance. He dived out of the car,
gun in hand, and ran inside. He was literally covered
in blood and the few people in the foyer stopped and
stared with gaping mouths. A couple of civilian security
guards saw him from the other side of the entrance
and made their way towards him. He ignored them,
grabbed a wheelchair and pushed it outside to the car.
He dragged Noddy out of the passenger side and into
the chair. Noddy was still alive but slipping in and out
of consciousness. Luke charged up the ramp with the

wheelchair and burst in through the entrance doors once again. He was just in time, because by now the Scots Guards and the UDR were surrounding the hospital and moving in, convinced that Luke was a terrorist. He levelled his gun at the security guards in the foyer, who immediately backed off – they were unarmed.

Luke was filled with adrenaline and shaking. The hospital was not safe ground. The majority of the staff and patients were Catholics and not to be trusted.

'Where's a doctor?' Luke shouted.

A couple of nurses stepped into the foyer, but froze in horror along with everyone else at the sight of these two men covered in blood, one pushing a wheelchair, wild-eyed and pointing a gun. Luke didn't wait for an answer and charged on, pushing Noddy through swing doors and along the corridor as blood dripped from the wheelchair, leaving a trail. He paused outside every door to kick it open, gun levelled, in search of a doctor. He scared the hell out of patients and nurses as he made his way through the hospital.

He finally burst into a room where two doctors were tending to a patient. Luke could not care less about anyone else. His buddy was dying.

He pointed his shaking gun at them and yelled, 'Fix him. Fix him or I'll fucking kill you!'

A security guard burst in and Luke aimed at him like lightning.

'Move and I'll fucking kill you too.'

The guard froze in his tracks and threw his arms up.

'I'll kill all of you!' Luke left Noddy and grabbed one of the doctors and pulled him over to the chair.

'If he dies, you die! I fucking swear it!'

The doctors were initially frozen with fear themselves, but they pulled themselves together, their professionalism kicked in and they set to work on Noddy. The doors suddenly burst open once again and a tough-looking matron stepped in. Luke levelled the gun at her as she stood beside the security guard with his arms in the air. But this woman seemed fearless. She looked at Luke and said, 'Put the gun down, please.'

'I'm a British soldier!' Luke shouted.

'And this is a hospital. Put the gun down.'

There was something about her calm, assertive manner that Luke latched on to. But he kept his gun aimed as she passed him and started helping the doctors. Noddy was lifted on to a bed and they worked quickly and efficiently. Commands were given for blood: everything was now directed towards saving Noddy's life.

The matron turned to Luke and looked him over. 'Have you been shot too?' she asked.

Luke shook his head.

'Then sit down over there, please. You're in the way now.'

Luke found himself obeying her. He lowered his gun at last as the activity concentrated on saving Noddy.

After a while she came over and looked down on him. She said softly, 'They killed my husband a year ago. He was RUC.'

Noddy had been shot seven times at close range by a .38 special and a 9mm pistol. One bullet had passed through his mouth, shooting a piece of his jaw and tongue away, which is why we could not understand what he had been trying to say over the radio when he was first hit. The other bullets had entered his torso, and one went through his thigh and scrotum. But he survived. I bumped into him several years later at the Boat Show in Earl's Court, where he was running a small Army promotion stand. He seemed fine, but I could tell the experience had left mental as well as physical scars.

Luke was himself a few days later. All operations were halted while an investigation was carried out. Military Intelligence was already working on it and the young Irish communications genius was eventually captured, after which he offered to work for the British. His offer was declined. We had our own geniuses, we just hadn't known the IRA had theirs. Within a few weeks, a secure communications system was brought in and we resumed our work. All in all, we got off lightly, considering the mayhem the Provos might have caused. Our personal score was settled a few years later, long after I had left the Det, when Tommy Shammy ended up behind bars and Sean O'Dilly was killed.

When Luke retired from the SBS years later he joined the police in England. Due to his background, he was eventually placed in the armed response force and was the oldest cop in it, and a rookie to boot. He was not in the force very long before he joined a section called in to help calm demonstrators who were trying to block the building of a motorway through some woodland. The situation turned nasty and at one point Luke found himself cornered by a dozen anarchists who were responsible for the increased tension between the demonstrators and police. This group's only objective in life was to travel to demonstrations and incite trouble. By the time other police officers had arrived, the anarchists had beaten Luke to the ground, surrounded him and kicked him unconscious. It was obvious his career was over even before he went to hospital. He's OK now – his mind, that is. He's as sharp as ever, but he can only walk with the aid of a cane, and if the series of operations he has to endure over the next few years are not successful he might be confined to a wheelchair for the rest of his life.

When I last saw him, he joked, 'With the compensation I got, it might all have been worth it if I could still get my pecker up. Now that is scary.' The latest good news is that Luke *can* get his pecker up.

Luke's room-mate at the time was an old scouser named Bert, a steady operative with an emotional range from blank to melancholy. I never once saw him smile, although that did not mean he was always unhappy. Bone-dry would best describe Bert. He smoked Woodbines and was allegedly responsible for the drinking problem of the old black Labrador Luke had had in his car when Noddy was shot. Bert retrieved Luke's car after the incident. It had been there some eighteen hours before anyone thought about it, and poor Muff was still in it. She'd done a good job protecting it from curious locals and had barked and snarled furiously at Bert until she recognised her old drinking partner. Bert said she peed for ever when he let her out of the car.

Bert was only good for surveillance jobs. He had a touch of rheumatism and if he inadvertently ended up in an OP in cold weather, whoever was with him would probably have had to carry him out to the pick-up point.

Bert was very much a grey man and kept to himself, but he had one habit that pissed everyone off. When he was feeling melancholy he would come into the bar and play Slim Whitman on the bar stereo. There's nothing wrong with Slim unless you have to listen to him. American country and western ballads just did not seem to fit that environment.

We attributed Bert's low spirits to his taste in music, as the songs were always wailing on about losing a girl or getting hit by a train or a stolen pick-up truck and winding up in jail. After taking endless stick about his music, Bert announced one day that he was not going to bother us with it any more as he had purchased a cassette-player from Lisburn and would listen to Slim in private in his room. The player even came with a headset so Luke could be spared when he was in the room.

Bert took to falling asleep listening to the music with his headset on at night. The player had an auto-reverse and so Bert's music was piped into his brain continuously while he slept. Bert now hummed and sang the tunes out loud, a direct result of his brainwashing. This was particularly annoying for anyone who had to spend a day in a car with him. He'd apologise once he realised, or was asked to shut up, then without knowing it slip into another song a few minutes later.

This problem was discussed in Bert's absence one night and it was decided to try an experiment that might confuse, or even better, alter his taste in music.

While Bert was asleep, with his headphones on and listening to Slim, we crept into his cabin and changed the cassette to Ian Dury and the Blockheads. We chose Ian Dury simply because Bert detested his music and would walk out of the bar if anyone played it. Bert never woke up and spent all night listening to the tape on auto-reverse.

Bert always slept later than most of us, and walked into the galley the following morning while we sat around chatting after breakfast. It was noted that he was humming one of Ian Dury's songs. He got a few bars into it and stopped himself with a pained expression.

'Foock sake, there I go again singing that foockin' rubbish. Who put that foockin' crap on my tape deck when I was asleep? Bastards!'

The astounding thing is, Bert eventually got to like Ian Dury and the Blockheads, or so it seemed, because he borrowed the tape and would sometimes even play it in the bar. For most of us the Blockheads were not a lot better than Slim, but it was a fascinating phenomenon.

A few days later, Bert walked into the galley humming a new tune. He stopped himself when he saw us grinning at him.

'What the foock am I singin' now?'

'Prokofiev's *Romeo and Juliet*,' someone said.

'Bastards,' he said as he sat down to eat. 'Sounds more like an army marchin' than a couple of lovers.'

He hummed a few more bars over breakfast, then admitted, 'It's better than that Blockheads crap anyout.'

Bert completed three tours in Northern Ireland with 14 Int over six years before retiring to civvy street.

12

By the time I reached the end of my tour in Northern Ireland I was twenty-three years old and aware of an acute change in my attitude towards life. I had been preparing myself, mentally, to return to the SBS, but there was something nagging at me. At first, I wondered if the work had affected me in some way. I don't mean I had gone a little loopy, although 14 Int did have a history of the occasional operative being 'touched' by the job. There was a rumour of one operative some years before who had died in mysterious circumstances a few months after leaving Northern Ireland. The suggestion was that he had killed himself. A fellow operative, a former Green Jacket, threw a wobbly in the Det bar one night shortly after I left and threatened to shoot one of the women. Some said there was nothing unusual about that: it was the woman and not the job that drove him mad.

I had gained an unflattering reputation for being cold and unemotional while in 14 Int, an odd accusation to be levelled at a special forces operative, one might think, but not so. I was simply used to internalising certain things, as I had learned to do during my childhood. But something had changed in me in the previous two years, or something that had not had a chance to develop was aching for attention now.

The thought of going back to the SBS, a comparatively regimented lifestyle compared with the Det, working with larger teams than in 14 Int, and being a smaller cog in a bigger machine seemed to have lost some of its lustre. My only other options were to stay with 14 Int or go outside. But I had grown bored with Northern Ireland and there was little attractive about civvy street either. It was also true that I had not given civvy street a fair crack. I wondered if by being in the military I was missing my true calling in life, whatever that might be. I had to find out what was nagging at me, and if I needed to go back into civvy street to do that, I would. But what if I was wrong? What if civvy street was not where the answer lay? Then what would I do? Like Huk, two years earlier, I spent my last few weeks in Northern Ireland in a quandary over my future. I too needed to bounce my thoughts off someone, but someone who could give me sound advice.

During my final week at the Det, while I was taking a Marine through his orientation, the commanding officer of the SBS happened to be visiting and took the time to drop by each Det location to say hello to his lads. At that time I was the only member of the SBS in South Det, Luke having left six months previously. Over a cup of tea in the cookhouse and after some polite chit-chat about the job, I confided my concerns to him. He was an understanding man and to my surprise simply suggested I took a year off. He explained that it would mean resigning from the military, but, he assured me, with my record, I could return to the fold as long as I didn't stay outside too long.

This made me feel a whole lot better. I could go in search of myself without burning my bridges. If I found what I was looking for outside, then this would be the end of my military career.

When I caught my flight out of Aldergrove Airport I looked down on the land and wondered if I would ever be back. I had a strong sense of nostalgia even then and expected I might return when I was old and retired. I did return a few years later, but not in a way I expected.

I returned to the SBS in Poole just long enough to carry out my leaving routine and drove out through the main gate a civilian. Not many operatives noticed I had left. I had been away for so long anyway. It all felt very strange. The SBS had been the family I had never had, and now I was alone in a way I had never been before. I had left home, I was my own boss and could go where I wanted, when I wanted. I was not so naïve as to expect things to be quite that simple. To live I needed to make some money. I was thinking like a civvy already; money had never mattered before. Now it was of prime importance. The first thing I had to do was get a job. But what on earth was I going to do?

I spent the next twelve months roaming the world doing many things – from troop-training in foreign countries to deep-sea diving, living in parts of Europe and West Africa for most of that time. But I never found whatever it was I thought I was looking for. Perhaps the timing was wrong. Maybe I had just needed a break. Job offers were coming in, the result of feelers I had put out earlier. I had an opportunity to become a saturation diver in the North Sea, diving deep and earning a packet for every day under pressure. I could own a big house in the country with a new Jag in the driveway within a few years if I could put up with the unhealthy existence. Long-term security jobs in the Middle East and Asia offering twice the money the SBS paid were also cropping up. I passed on them all. I was not ready for life as a civilian.

Amongst other reasons, civvies seemed generally weak and soft to me, and I did not share their interests or their heroes, who were either sportsmen or pop stars. I am aware it is I who am in the wrong century. I was always impressed by those in history who could take great hardships without complaint. I would prefer those days when, if a man was injured, no matter how seriously, in battle or otherwise, it was self-discipline that kept him composed and in control. Today our heroes, all fictional, for we have no real ones in the classic sense, are admired more for their weaknesses and vulnerabilities, except female warriors, who appear to be adopting those classic male qualities. Another reason I wanted to return to the service was because as a civilian I was like 99.99 per cent of the population: a nobody. By that I mean I did not feel in any way different or special, nor a contributor any more. I had known what it felt like to be somewhat special or important. As a British special forces operative I was one of the few. It was not a macho thing being in special forces, not the way civvies seem to think. No one outside my immediate circle knew what I did. I felt special to myself, even if I was not to anyone else. And that was important to me and what I missed.

I telephoned my old commanding officer, the one who advised me to take the break in the first place, and he immediately invited me up to the squadron lines for a chat. Things were busier than ever, he told me, and the service was expanding to accommodate the SBS's increased worldwide responsibilities. On my way to meet the boss I bumped into Lieutenant Smith, who had just come back from a two-year stint with the SEALs in Norfolk, Virginia. Smith was the only officer on my SBS selection course. He had fully embraced the easy life in the States, even in the SEALs, and had put on about forty pounds to prove it. He told me with great enthusiasm that I was wise to come back, as life in special forces was going to get pretty exciting in the coming years. He never explained further than tapping his nose and winking. Of the ten of us who had passed selection together, he reminded me, there were only six left. We were down to five a few months later after Smith died while diving in Scotland when he pumped the wrong gas into his breathing apparatus. He entered the water for a simple jackstay swim, a quarterly requirement, and never came up.

At a short meeting with the boss, I gave a brief run-down of what I had done with myself while in civvy street.

He stood up and shook my hand. 'Welcome back to the SBS,' he said.

I walked out of his office and through the lines. There were many unfamiliar faces, but then I had been away for over three years. The way I was greeted by some operatives, I don't think they realised I had been a civvy for the past year. It just goes to show how busy we always were and how little we sometimes saw of each other. It was good to have a normal conversation once again with people who spoke my language. It was good to be home. But there was one small obstacle I had to overcome. A little bit of bureaucratic nonsense that should have been a simple formality but almost turned into a nightmare.

Prior to returning to the ranks of the SBS, I had to go back to the Commando Training Centre at Lympstone and do a refresher course on basic weapons and drill. This course was for everyone who had gone outside for over a year – I overshot by a day or two.

Our course sergeant major was a crusty, stiff, humourless, old-fashioned man of war. He was a platoon weapons instructor (PWI) by trade and had spent much of the latter part of his career dealing with raw recruits. After all those years of being treated as a god by thousands of noddies, who jumped at the sound of his voice and obeyed his every whim like lightning, it appeared he had developed a bit of the Roman Emperor syndrome not uncommon amongst certain PWs. He had just been transferred to running the rejoins and did not like the job one bit, I suspect mainly because we did not react to him in the same way noddies did. In his welcome speech he said that he did not approve of Marines being allowed back in once they had gone outside. As far as he was concerned, we had returned because we could not make it in civvy street, and that was not a good enough reason to be a Marine. There was some truth in what he said. As it turned out he disliked me more than the others, for two reasons. Firstly, I was too relaxed and had a far too familiar air about me which he described as 'verging on insubordination'. The other reason, which I did not discover till later, was that he had failed an SBS selection twenty years earlier. When he learned I had gone straight from CTC into special forces, and at just nineteen, it irked him even more. I did all I could to avoid him, but it seemed he had plans for me.

On the final day of the two-week course there was no formal passing for duty parade. The corps wanted us away without fuss, as if this sort of thing, people coming back inside and all, never went on. That suited us just fine. We each had our reasons for returning but none were because we missed parades. I could not get into my civvy clothes, bundle up my bedding and equipment and return them to the main store quick enough, so I could hit the road to Poole and the SBS.

I parked my car outside the main store and walked briskly in carrying my bedding and equipment. I plonked them on the hundred-foot long counter and drummed my fingers as I waited for the storeman on the other side of the cavernous room to move his arse out of his chair and come over and sign them off me. A door opened and closed on the far side of the room. It was the sergeant major, immaculate as always, and he was staring straight at me. He kept the other side of the room so that he could use his well-practised booming voice.

'What do you think you're doing?' he bawled.

'Leaving routine, sir,' I replied smartly. You didn't need to shout to be heard in this building. The acoustics were fine.

He was theatrical in the way he slowly walked around the counter towards me as he talked. All sergeant majors were like that, hands behind their backs, chins sticking out and looking at subordinates as if they were odious.

'What leaving routine?' he asked.

'I'm going to my unit, sir,' I replied.

'Where are your draft orders?'

I didn't have any. They had never even crossed my mind. I had not reached a rank yet where paper administration meant anything to me, apart from target and sit-reps.

'You can't go where and when you want to, laddie. You need signed pieces of paper that inform us you are moving from point A to point B. Without that paper I can't let you go.'

He knew I didn't have the papers. The SBS were in their own world and no one in our admin block probably remembered I was even here. The usual routine for Marines rejoining was to visit the PSO after the refresher course, just like noddies on completion of training, and wait for him to sort out a draft. I knew where I wanted to go, that's the only reason I returned. The SBS wanted me, were expecting me, so why wait for orders that were inevitable? But knowing the SBS and how busy it was, it might be a month before someone in the admin block asked, 'Where the hell is Falconer – didn't he rejoin?' Even if I had thought about the draft orders, I wouldn't have thought anyone here would even have noticed I was gone. How wrong I was.

'You'll stay here until you get your orders and not a minute less.'

I was already starting to feel ill at the idea.

'Don't worry. We'll keep you busy, son. I need a bedding storeman. I think a man of your experience can handle a job like that.'

He knew he was getting up my nose and was loving it. I could believe that when my orders did eventually come through, and with no help from him, he would hang on to them for as long as he could. I could be here for six months, and as a bedding storeman! I could see myself strangling him long before six months. The irony was, a few days earlier, aware of his feelings towards me, I had kidded about sneaking off without him seeing me. One of the other rejoins was surprised at the way the sergeant major had turned out. He had known him before and said he used to be a decent bloke. He was highly decorated, with a QGM for Aden and an MM for Borneo, plus a Mention in Dispatches from somewhere else.

He was not to be taken lightly. His achievements and his rank demanded respect if nothing else, no matter how bitter he had become.

'Is that understood?' he asked coldly, a few feet from me.

'Sir.'

'I can't hear you.'

'Yes, sir,' I said in the same low voice. I wasn't some nod punk to shout his head off at. Those days were long past. I would go to cells before I did that. Perhaps I was being a prima donna and sulking because I could not leave, but he was sticking pins in me for personal reasons and that was just as bad. Fortunately, he did not push me that far. He had plenty of time to enjoy getting me worked up.

'Take your bedding and equipment back to your grot. I'll see you back here tomorrow morning when your new duties will be explained to you.'

I shut my mouth, picked up my gear and walked out of the building.

I stood outside to catch my breath and absorb this latest crud. Trucks of noddies in their blue berets drove by on their way to some training exercise. The camp was a hive of activity as usual. Recruits were running about and being shouted at everywhere. Five years earlier that had been me. It didn't seem that long ago, but a lot had happened in that time. I saw the sergeant major leave the building through a far doorway and watched him march up the road. He paused to chastise a nod for some indiscretion before continuing on his way.

Six months of this, I thought to myself. I shuddered. No way. I'll go insane.

I walked back into the store and dumped my stuff on

the counter. 'Here, mate. Hello! Would you take this, please?'

The storeman eyed me from across the room.

He got off his arse and came over to me with a look of curiosity.

'I fort the sarn't major said you were to stay?'

'You must have misunderstood,' I replied. 'Sign this lot off me, would you?'

'Ar dunno if ar should. Ar mean, I 'erd 'im say you were stayin'.'

'Know what? Forget it. Don't sign it off. Keep it for yourself. It's a gift.'

I walked out of the building, climbed into my car and drove through the bustling training camp and out through the main gate. Technically I was going AWOL. But not in my eyes. I was headed for my unit. They could have locked me up for eighty days, I found out later. Had I known that, I might at least have made a few calls to the squadron first.

When I arrived in Poole it was as if I had never left and I was soon totally embroiled in my new team and its duties. Once more the gods looked down on me and decided I was to be left alone. I don't doubt the sergeant major made an official complaint and tried to have me charged for insubordination and leaving a place of duty without orders, but his paperwork must have got caught up in the same SBS admin system that forgot to send me my draft orders. I never heard another word about the incident.

However, I did hear a year later that the sergeant major's time was up and he had gone outside himself.

I tried to imagine him as a civvy, sitting in a pub some-where, staring blankly at his pint and seeing his life in flashes, as you do when you have done so many things worth remembering. It must have been even harder for him, considering he had once been a god.

Back in the SBS, I was placed into the Maritime Anti-Terrorism teams. In the three years I had been away they had advanced in the art of recapturing large ships and oil platforms. It was an exciting and innovative time. Equipment was more hi-tech and, unlike in the past, when it was bought off the shelf and adapted, much of it now was being designed and constructed for our specific needs: pressure-proof, waterproof, shock-proof, lightweight, corrosion-proof – in general, SBS proof. Weapons were more efficient – the German P11 had arrived for trials, the only truly silent weapon on the planet, electrically fired and deadly underwater at up to ten metres. Communications were smaller. Assault boats were faster and more portable and the RAF had developed better methods of dropping them into any sea in the world. Satellite technology was being integrated to improve tracking, navigation and worldwide communi-cations. Climbing techniques were speedier. All kinds of civilian technology was being adapted to our needs. A secret group of scientists, not unlike the fictional charac-ters led by 'Q' in the Bond films, was coming up with specialised weapons, explosives, knock-out gases and general gadgetry. Every member of the squadron was encouraged to find new ways to improve the skills and techniques needed to operate quickly and clandestinely in all weathers. If an operative, no matter what his level of experience, had an idea on how to improve any aspect of the job he was encouraged to submit it to our vigorous in-house research and development department, or he was given the money to go out and purchase, test and then report on it himself. There is no doubt that this unique, complex yet proficient system helped put the SBS above all others in this business.

Unlike conventional field battles, where tactics are more flexible and largely dictated by the terrain and the enemy's deployment, special forces anti-terrorist assaults are a combination of physical might and technology working in swift syncopation, pre-planned and finely choreographed. Once initiated, they move relentlessly into the heart of the problem with precision timing, not pausing until their ultimate goal is reached. An example is the Iranian Embassy siege in London, where every soldier knew precisely where they were headed, what they were going to do when they got there, and who was not going to survive the confrontation. Special forces exercises for these types of operations, which involve several different agencies, are more accurately called rehearsals.

To add reality to these rehearsals we usually employ an enemy. On one such major SBS rehearsal against an oil platform in the North Sea utilising the Navy, Air Force and MI5 (for hi-tech surveillance), the Army provided manpower to act as terrorists on board and hold the hostages we were to rescue. What the SBS teams involved in the actual assault did not know was that the enemy was in fact going to be members of the SAS. It seemed the SAS wanted to see how we were progressing in a medium we had succeeded in keeping them away from. To make matters even worse, the SAS terrorist team was led by a senior NCO named Jenson.

It was no secret how much Jenson despised us, but it was the 'why' that was so curious. He was a stocky, powerfully built man in his late thirties and every bit the lone alpha wolf. He had a humourless, dark personality and from what I understand was quite disliked within the SAS itself, while at the same time being one of their most revered members.

In this business, if a man has killed another in battle, it improves his stature in the eyes of his fellow operatives. To have had more than one kill adds to that kudos. If a man notches up an unusually high number of kills, his aura can then, understandably, take on something of a demonic hue, even to us. The majority of special forces operatives go an entire career without a kill. Jenson had eighteen, the highest of any British special forces operative, and higher than any terrorist I ever heard of for individual, separate incident kills. Most of them had been accomplished through the sights of a sniper's rifle. He was a tradesman who enjoyed his work.

I first saw the infamous Jenson on a remount exercise a few months after I first joined the SBS. This exercise was to simulate terrorists taking over a nuclear energy plant. In all there were about fifty SAS and a dozen SBS divided up into assault teams. Jenson was the overall senior NCO. The combined assault team waited in a remote section of the complex in preparation for moving forward to the contact area via underground tunnels.

We all wore the familiar black assault uniforms and sat around quietly waiting for the word to go. Jenson, dressed in black the same as us, but with a personally tailored leather weapons harness, spent most of the time slowly pacing the cavernous hall like Darth Vader. The younger members of the SAS avoided his gaze. When, after a brief communication over his radio, he grunted for us to move out, we all obeyed.

I thought he disliked the SBS for the standard SAS reason – we were that other group who arrogantly reckoned themselves special too. But I later learned the deeper reason for his obsessive animosity: Jenson had begun his military career as a Royal Marine, had attempted an SBS selection and had failed it.

The Royal Marines is where Jenson learned his sniper skills (all SAS and SBS snipers are trained at the Royal Marine Commando Training Centre).* It was during his SBS selection that Jenson discovered his fear of being underwater in zero visibility. Claustrophobia is nothing to be ashamed of – in the SBS's experience, on average one in seven people suffer from it, many without realising. But Jenson took the failure personally. Determined to make it into special forces, he set his sights on the SAS. Typically of Jenson, not about to risk failing with the only other worthwhile special forces unit, he sneaked up on to the Brecon Beacons one night and built himself a hide. The Beacons are where the SAS hold their selection courses and Jenson's plan

* The US Navy SEAL teams' current sniper training school was set up by the SBS.

was to spy on them. But his hide was discovered and he was brought in for questioning.

When he explained why he was watching them they were impressed and allowed him to join a selection course. He did well and quickly rose through the ranks. Jenson's boner for the SBS never diminished over the years and he has, no doubt, contributed to much of the SAS's negativity towards us.

Had we been told that Jenson was going to be on the oil platform as head of the enemy it would have come more as a warning. Jenson could not openly screw with the rehearsal, but he would do what he could to make us look bad. There was conflict ahead for someone. Whoever ran into him was going to have to treat him as a terrorist, as well as deal with his reputation.

Even if we had known about the SAS being on board, we had more important things to worry about. As we arrived in the North Sea, a huge storm was building nicely.

There are many ways to get a large team clandestinely aboard a huge oil platform. One method the SBS was trying was to climb up and get on to it from the water. There are disadvantages to all approaches. Certain aircraft can be spotted miles away and the hostages killed and the rig blown up before a team can land on it. Some surface boats are also impractical for similar reasons. Approaching a rig from underwater is one of the most difficult techniques. During storms and in a sea known for its fierce rip-tides it is highly dangerous for a submarine to maintain a position close to an oil platform that has a sub-surface web of ropes and cables and many other unknown hazards emanating from it. One practical method is to release the teams a distance from the platform where they can swim to the legs under cover of swell and darkness.

Twenty of us were to assault the rig that night. Our mission was to neutralise the terrorists and rescue the hostages, while at the same time securing the deck for sixty Royal Marines who would rope down from helicopters and then operate directly under our control to dominate and secure the rest of the platform.

The method of releasing several teams at a time from a submarine chamber, E&RE style, was virtually *passé* by now, and for this kind of work, too time-consuming anyway. The SBS needed the ability to release four to six times that number in one go. For security reasons I cannot describe the new methods, but the old ones were just as hair-raising.

The O-class sub, had a raised flat deck called the casing that ran the length of the sub on either side of the conning tower. Between the casing and the actual cigar-shaped skin of the sub was a gap about four to five feet deep. This hollow area was laced with all manner of pipes and bracings and large pockets of space which could be used for storage. The top of the casing deck was made up of large plates that could be unbolted and removed. For our purpose, a number of these plates were removed at the rear of the sub, between the conning tower and the props, to expose a trench long enough to accommodate several teams of squatting men. Breathing umbilicals were fitted, one for each man and a couple of spares, and a brass hammer on a line for communicating with the crew inside. It has always been my experience that no matter how technologically advanced we got, there was always a reliance on a primitive device somewhere along the line to ensure success.

We rendezvoused with the sub by helicopter beyond the range of the rig's radar and visibility. It was close to midnight. Fully armed and equipped and wearing oxygen re-breather (bubbleless) diving sets, we all leapt into the stormy sea and swam for rope-nets the crew had temporarily attached to one side of the sub for us to scramble up. Because of the experience I had gained previously, I was the special entry man, which meant I carried certain secret devices weighing over forty pounds in addition to my regular equipment. Under the watchful eye of the captain, atop his conning tower, who was considerate enough to position the sub so we could climb it on the leeward side, we made our way along the casing and into the trench. Waves were crashing up and over the side of the sub, and two of the crew almost got washed off the casing as they fled inside the conning tower.

No effort was made to make the trench area comfortable, nor were there any straps to hold on to if it got turbulent. It was up to the individual to find a nook in the cramped, black, lidless metal coffin and hold on. Because of my extra equipment, I sat at the furthest point rear, a slightly more spacious position, and looked forward at the others in two lines down either side with their backs to the outer casing and their legs facing inwards.

Once we were in position, the BUs tested and final

equipment checks carried out, the sub flooded its ballasts and dived. The sea gushed in through holes in the casing all around us and then spilled in over the top through our roofless metal trench. One moment we were in a thundering gale on the surface, the next we were under the chilly, clear, silent waters of the North Sea. Tiny salt-water lights beside each operative and the swirling, fluorescent micro-creatures made it lighter than on the surface. Everyone kept an eye on those closest to them in case they had breathing problems. I cleared my ears as the sub gently dropped to around sixty feet and increased forward speed. Any deeper and, because of the time we would spend below the surface, we would have to do stops before surfacing or we might suffer from the bends.

The sub cut smoothly through the water like a whale, but our trench, a huge gouge in the sub's smooth side, upset the hydrodynamics. The faster it got, the more violent the turbulence became as the water dipped into our recess. Where I was sitting, at the back looking forward, I was hit by the full force in the face and my BU hose oscillated wildly. I kept a tight hold of it. Losing it meant serious trouble. At this speed, anyone who needed to leave the trench to escape to the surface would be swept along the casing and through the props.

The first time this form of multiple-man release was tried, no one had any idea what speed a diver could bear inside the trench. My wig-wearing date in Northern Ireland, Bonzo, had been in a trench during trials in a Scottish loch a year earlier when the sub hit a fresh-water patch and plummeted. It lurched violently as it increased speed. Bonzo said it was like being in a washing machine during the spin cycle. After the sub surfaced and the submariners hurried out to check on him, Bonzo had been pushed far towards the tail and was jammed amongst the pipes and bracings. It took a while to extricate him. If he had lost his BU he would have been a goner.

A foil, like the spoiler on the back of a sports car, was fitted to the front of the trench on the casing to force the main power of the water up and over us. It helped. We trundled along for well over an hour before we sensed a slowing down. I was cold and shivering hard by then. Another twenty minutes of that and I might have found myself suffering from hypothermia. I was cold by my own choice. Others had worn more clothing under their dry-bags. Physically, there were two phases to this rehearsal. Half would be spent inactive, sitting around motionless in the cold water, the other half would be extremely active, climbing an oil platform, which was exhausting enough in calm weather with no equipment. I had not climbed a platform carrying this much weight before. If I had worn too many clothes I might have seriously overheated on the climb. Therefore I chose to freeze now so I wouldn't get heat exhaustion on the climb.

By the time the sub came to a stop, I was very anxious to get going and move my limbs to warm up. But I had to wait my turn. Because I was the man with heavy equipment, I was to bring up the rear. However, what happened next caused me enough excitement to forget any other concerns.

When the sub stopped completely, and was dead in the water, a series of bangs on the casing from inside was our signal to change from BU to our personal breathing apparatus. This in itself was tricky. It was not like an ordinary air-set. If any water got into the mouthpiece and soaked the carbon dioxide absorbing powder it would create an alkaline cocktail rendering it unusable and the diver would have to emergency surface. Every diver transferred from the sub's air to their pure oxygen sets without a problem. We took a few minutes to ensure all our equipment was secured to our bodies and ready for use. We were buddied up in pairs as an added safety precaution against the upcoming swim through the storm.

After an all round thumbs-up, the overall team leader signalled the sub with the hammer and, with his partner, led the ascent of team one. The four teams departed at three-minute intervals so as not to cause congestion at the foot of the oil rig. When my team came to leave, the first pair gave a thumbs-up and ascended. My partner, Steve, followed them and, clutching my equipment, I kicked off out of the now empty trench and headed for the blackness above. As soon as I left the sub I ran into a serious problem.

My special equipment, a very bulky cylinder which was a new trial item to the squadron, was wrapped in styrofoam flotation rings tested to make it just positively buoyant at thirty feet. But it had never been used in this situation before, and the hour-long submersion in the buffeting trench along with the occasional excursion to deeper waters, and therefore greater pressure, if only for a minute or two, had gradually squeezed and collapsed many of the tiny air-sacs around the surface of the rings – something I had not allowed for. To add to the problem, the sub was not at thirty feet, where it was supposed to have been when it released us, but more like sixty, making my equipment even more negatively buoyant and therefore heavier. As I pushed off from the sub I let go of the equipment, expecting it to float up beside me. Instead I felt it yank hard at my waist, where it was attached by a line. I was shocked how heavy it was. It was like swimming with an anvil tied to me. I increased my finning to full power but I had the horrible feeling I was not going up. This was confirmed when I saw the vast shadow of the black sub yards to my side seemingly moving slowly above me, for it had not changed its depth. I suddenly felt a sharp tug on my arm from above. It was Steve on the other end of my buddy line. I was pulling him down too. I finned with the desperation of someone suddenly recognising the distinct possibility of biting the big one if he did not. I was breathing rapidly as I worked furiously in an effort to gain some vertical headway. My breathing apparatus had a regulator set to dispense enough oxygen for a normal, relaxed swim, and I soon began to suck on an empty bag having used it all up. I yanked the tap of the bypass valve to put a blast more oxygen into the system. Steve was pulling hard from above but I still had no sense of ascending. The sub had disappeared from view by now and as the sky was black there was no indication of any progress north. I noticed bubbles were passing me on their way up. I was going down and pulling my buddy along with me. My only option was to ditch everything. Not to lose equipment was ingrained in us and, stupid as it sounds, it was a difficult decision to make even then. But I was at the point of desperation and so I gripped the taut equipment line attached to my belt to release it. But I could only use one hand to unclip it because my other was being pulled above me, attached to Steve who was a powerhouse of a swimmer and finning hard himself. The device was too heavy to pull up and unclip. I scrambled with my free hand to find the diving knife strapped to my calf. As I ripped it from its housing it was a complete shock to me when I broke the surface and found myself in the swirling storm. The moment Steve had kicked in, we had in fact been moving gradually upwards, not as fast as the bubbles, but up nevertheless. I pulled out my mouthpiece and shut it off so as not to let the water in. I took in great gulps of air. Steve was doing the same. He looked at me with a red-faced, knackered expression.

'Fuck's sake, Duncan. You fall asleep or what?'

Steve was not angry or vexed in the least. He rarely got mad at anything and was a steady, strong operative in any environment, especially in the Arctic, where he was most at home above the tree-line. The truth was, Steve didn't know how desperate the situation had been. He thought I was just taking my time and he wanted to get to the surface. Had he not pulled me up, I would have sunk far below my point of neutral buoyancy, which meant that even after cutting away the equipment I would have continued to the bottom of the North Sea.

When I told Steve in detail later what had happened he thought I was exaggerating. Many years afterwards, at his SBS leaving bash on his way to civvy street, I described to him again exactly what had happened that night. His reaction was the same as when I first told him. He gave me a nod and a soft smile, suggesting that I was still exaggerating, then changed the subject.

The distance between the troughs and peaks of the waves ranged between thirty to forty feet. My equipment floated beside me, where it was now only just positively buoyant. Steve was a few yards away on the other end of my buddy line and I scanned around for the rest of my team. They were several waves away, bobbing in the blackness, one moment above us, the next below or obscured from view altogether. We finned towards each other. I pulled my face-mask up on to my head, keeping it handy in case the spray got heavier, and we settled in for the ride. We would not need to fin to the rig. A raging current would take us there.

The navigation lights on the rig were visible over a mile away. It looked like a Christmas tree. There was no sign of the other three teams but I didn't expect there to be. If all went well we would soon meet up. We were riding a tidal-stream that swept through these waters at six to seven knots. It would deliver us straight to the rig in ten minutes, provided the sub had dropped us off at the correct spot and the senior NCO (whose job it was to calculate the speed and direction of the tide) had got his end right. If we were not on a precise collision course with the platform we would sail right by it, next stop Iceland.

We needed to pass directly between the legs, underneath the mass of the platform. If not we would be unable to 'grab' it. We could not estimate whether or not we were going to miss the platform until we were close. By then we would have little chance of making up more than a few yards of error.

The first team would be at the rig nine minutes ahead of us, with the other two teams equally spaced behind them, which was why we could not see them. We each carried emergency lights and SABE Tac-B emergency radio beacons in the event we did miss the rig, but in these conditions it would be a hit-and-miss business finding us. The incentive to catch hold of the rig was a big one.

This was the enjoyable part, drifting effortlessly through the night as if in space. In the SBS I often had experiences that have made this planet appear un-earthlike. Free falling between layers of clouds where mountaintops poke through like islands in a sea of cottonwool. Or on a plateau far above the tree-line in Norway in the dead of winter, skiing in the eye of a white-out when the wind has ceased and feeling as if the entire world has disappeared and there is nothing but me left in the emptiness. This was one of those moments. The sea and sky were so black it was hard to tell where one ended and the other began, and we were black specks with white bloated faces in tight, black hoods floating in a vast emptiness towards what looked like a space station. There were no other lights in sight, no land, and the only sound was the wind snipping the peaks off the swells and hurling them into the next ones.

Before long we could make out objects on the rig such as the windows of living quarters and the many catwalks and stairways illuminated by the safety lights that hung above them, flickering as the gusting wind shook them to their bolted mounts. The size of these North Sea structures never ceased to impress me. The angle that I approached them from made them look even more imposing. The structure was assaulted by wind and rain and the huge, rolling swells that thumped against the massive supporting legs – large enough to drive a freight train through their centre and down into the earth. It looked devoid of life, but there were some three hundred people on board. All knew we were coming some time tonight and only essential crew were outside. Anyone else would be terrorists and we would have to deal with them. The rig had everything you might expect to find in a small city – postman, blacksmith, bartender and surgeon, all there to support a corps of engineers and construction workers. I always felt it would take a particularly insane terrorist to actually try to capture a North Sea oil platform and then hold on to it. Many of the so-called roughnecks who work on them have military backgrounds. It would not be like taking over a cruise ship with its mostly elderly clientele and soft crew. If a terrorist turned his back for a second on one of these roughnecks, it is likely his next experience would be a wrench crashing through his skull.

Nevertheless, the taking of an oil platform by terrorists was a possibility and we would be ready to take it back if that day ever came. Besides, there was a flip-side to all this dynamic work we were doing. The British government has always made an income from selling its military's knowledge and skills, as well as using them to cement political relationships with other countries. The SBS and SAS were constantly abroad on training missions. Nearly every terrorist incident in recent years has had an SAS or SBS operative behind the scenes advising, or in some cases, disguised in that country's military uniform and leading the assault, such as in Mogadishu for the German special forces unit GSG9 several years ago. It was all part of our arms trade. Security is big business and if countries or major corporations want the best, Britain is the first place they shop. If a friendly foreign government wanted to know how to secure an oil platform, there was only one place in the world they could buy the knowledge, tried and tested and, like any good product, constantly being updated.

With four or five hundred yards to go we decided, thankfully, we were on track. The navigator had done his job perfectly. It was time to snap out of the pleasantries of the free ride and prepare for the most difficult, most strenuous and most dangerous phase.

Our speed was deceiving as we closed on the platform and we had to make ready quickly. I could not yet see any of the other teams, but I had no doubt they were there.

Each team had its own hook-on-man, whose job it was to snag one of the legs and provide a leash for the others to attach to. A fairly important job, for if he failed we were back to the missed rig scenario and sailing off into the blackness. The hook man had only a few seconds to secure the leash. The rest of the team then hooked on to it, strung out in a line like beads on a thread. Once secured each team member prepared for the climb.

I cannot give details of the techniques we used to climb the platform without compromising security, but by the time my team arrived at the platform, it was obvious all was not going well. Team one should have already had a couple of men up on the spider deck, team two should have had at least one, and team three should have been well on their way, but we could see only the first man still struggling to climb out of the water. They were being hampered by the horrendous weather. As we sailed under the platform to join the crowd my hook man found a strong point and secured the leash to it. The rest of us crabbed on to it and we held station in the rapid tidal-stream. Two teams were on one leg adjacent to us and the other was diagonally opposite. The lead climbers, attached to their leashes at a point closest to the legs, had the toughest time with the heavy swell. When the trough reached that part of the leg it left the operative dangling out of the water, banging against the leg, and when the peak arrived (there was a forty-foot difference between peak and trough), he was held several feet under for a few seconds. Needless to say, when the moment came for him to remove his diving equipment, his timing had to be spot on.

I was at the back of the long loop-line and was not being dragged out of the water or under it. Being the special entry man and the most encumbered, I was to be one of the last out of the water.

At this moment we looked like a bunch of amateurs. Perhaps we had bitten off more than we could chew in these extreme conditions. But we had nowhere else to go but up. What kept us pressing on was not any fear of the consequences of peeling off and being lost in the middle of the North Sea in a storm. It was the relentlessness inherent to our character. That was why the selection process was as demanding as it was. We would never give up.

My heavy equipment was bashing against me one moment and pulling violently at my waist the next. I was beginning to worry about the connections that held it. How much more of this could they take, I wondered. A wave shunted my team halfway around the leg of the rig and I found myself within arm's-length of the ascending link. I seized the opportunity. I had discarded my diving equipment and buddy line and made the decision to remove my fins, unhook from the leash and grab the link. I was moving out of turn, but due to my own precarious situation with my equipment and the problems we were all having getting out of the water, I felt justified.

I let go of the leash and grabbed the link. I rode a couple of swells while I pulled my equipment over my shoulder, held by its carrying-strap. I psyched myself up for the climb – the extra equipment was going to make it a tough one. This was mostly arm work. I chose my moment, rode the swell as high as it would go, reached up and gripped the link as the water dropped away. The equipment hung off my shoulder like a dead body. My feet bicycled in mid-air trying to hook on. I pulled myself upwards. A swell came and whacked me, but not my whole body, just up to my knees. A tangled operative below me who grabbed on was pummelled by the full force and lost any headway he had gained in trying to follow me. I held on and continued up and reached the spider deck. I scrambled over the rail and moved into position, crabbed on to the rail, in case a gust of wind hooked me off, unhooked my H&K and kept vigil above while the others continued to fight the elements to climb out of the water. I glanced at the equipment lying at my feet, not looking forward to the next horrendous climb, and decided I was going to have to work with the engineers to find a way to make the fucking thing smaller and lighter. I'm happy to report that I did.

It took over half an hour for everyone to make the spider deck. Amazingly we never lost anyone or any equipment. There was no time to waste. We still had seventy feet of rig to climb to get to the first working deck.

This massive oil platform had six legs in total, four outside and two inside. The two inside legs had ladders welded to them from the water-line to the spider deck and then stairways continued up to the main deck. These ladders and staircases were out of bounds to us. The SBS never use any ascending aids integral to the rig. The same goes for big ships. They are obvious approach routes and can be monitored or booby-trapped.

Again, I cannot describe our methods for security reasons, but when the first pairs eventually arrived at the main deck, they went straight into action to secure entry points for the rest of us. We could expect to encounter enemy from that point on, but they would be dealt with swiftly and silently.

The terrorists knew we would be coming some time and patrolled every conceivable entry point. They had operated a watch routine over the previous few days but had been monitored. The decks of a large oil platform are hard to defend against our techniques.

Two terrorists we had observed checking over the side every ten to fifteen minutes were now huddled together under some machinery to get out of the weather. It was the early hours of the morning by now and they were getting cold and bored. When the first members of the assault team climbed over the side and on to the main deck they quickly engaged this pair before they could react.

We could expect at least ten more terrorists. Up-to-the-second intelligence was coming to us via radio from MI5 technicians monitoring all communications on the platform. They told us that at least four terrorists were holding several hostages in the main control room. A possible four more were in the galley with several hostages, and the rest were roaming sentries.

The four assault teams quickly mustered at their respective entry points. Time was of the essence now. We had to hit them hard and decisively before they realised we were on board. If the terrorist sentries we neutralised were radio-checked and did not report in, it would be assumed they had been eliminated. The terrorists would be ruthless with us from that point on. I led my team speedily towards our pre-planned objectives.

My role now was to get through a bulkhead in a small compartment adjoining the control room to enable an assault team to gain a surprise entry. My entry device was the ultimate lock-pick. The assaults on the control room and galley were carried out simultaneously by two of the other teams. Doors were burst open, flash-crash (explosive) devices were tossed in to confuse and disorientate, immediately followed by the team, all of whom were wearing gas masks and throat communications. These entries were one hundred per cent successful and pronounced the occupying terrorists dead and the hostages rescued.

We could hear over our radios the body counts of terrorists and the securing of hostages in their locations as the teams took one location after another. Team three had moved to the main deck to secure it for the Marine helicopters that were thundering towards us in the blackness. Once my team had finished our entry, we went in search of the remaining wandering terrorist sentries. From the moment the shooting started it was a mad, controlled rush to eliminate and secure before hostages could be 'killed' and explosive devices initiated.

Steve and I saw two terrorists running into a building. We reported it over our radios as we pursued them. Two other SBS operatives across the platform headed for the other side of the building to support us. There were two doors into the single-room building where the terrorists had fled, one either side. I quickly consulted with the pair on the other side of the building by radio and we formulated a hasty plan. I opened one of the doors and Steve and I tossed in a couple of flash-crash. The terrorists fired at us as we ducked away from the opening, not charging in after the flash-crash as they might have been expecting. At that same instant the other SBS pair entered through the other door and fired on the terrorists, the intent being to hit them in the back as they faced in our direction.

When the shooting stopped, I waited for the shout, 'Clear!' from my partners inside, but instead I heard arguing. Steve and I opened the door and looked in. One of the terrorists was claiming he had killed the SBS pair. That SBS pair happened to be a couple of monsters, probably two of the largest men we had at that time, named Fleck and Chalky, both powerful, highly motivated and extremely professional. With Fleck and Chalky you could chat and joke around all you wanted before and after a job, but during it you'd better have your mind focused on just one thing – success. Fleck and Chalky would never be convinced they had not taken out the two terrorists first. Fleck grabbed the arguing terrorist and pulled his balaclava off to see who he was talking to.

'Jenson,' I said. Steve recognised him too.

It was only then that we realised the SAS were the enemy.

Fleck and Chalky did not know Jenson's face, but they knew about him, and didn't give a toss, either. Jenson pulled away and kept mouthing off about the low standard of the entry. The other SAS terrorist kept out of it. Fleck, a quick-tempered man with a bit of Turkish blood in him (his nickname was Abdul), wanted to fill in Jenson there and then, and it was all we could do to stop him. But we could not stand around arguing all night as we still had a rig to clear.

'Tie 'im up and leave him 'ere,' suggested Chalky.

'You fuckers ain't tying me up,' Jenson said with a threatening look.

It might have been a bit over the top to grab him and force him to the ground. He was, after all, Jenson, and a senior SAS NCO to boot. Fleck and Chalky could have argued that it was an exercise privilege and probably have got away with it, but they opted for the diplomatic approach.

'You stay in this fuckin' room. All right?' threatened Fleck. Then to Chalky, 'Let's get on with it.'

As Chalky and Fleck left the room, several waves of Sea King helicopters touched down on the main deck to unload their cargo of Marines dressed in black like us and armed with H&K machine-guns.

But Jenson could not let it go. He followed Fleck and Chalky outside to give them another tuppence worth. This was a grave mistake. Jenson had misjudged the two men. His continued complaints about their soldier-ing abilities were more than Fleck and Chalky's short fuses could take. Fleck spun around, marched back and grabbed Jenson viciously by the neck.

'Shut the fuck up or I'll belt you. I don't give a shit who you are,' he shouted.

All that did was anger Jenson and he tried to pull away from Fleck's grip and started swinging his fists. Now Chalky leapt in, grabbing Jenson on the other side with powerful arms, while Fleck slammed a fist into Jenson's gut, winding him and bringing him to his knees. Jenson paused to suck in air, but Fleck and Chalky had not finished. They lifted him to his feet and, as he struggled and lashed out, they forced his hands behind his back and tied them together with plasti-cuffs. Jenson couldn't believe this audacity and started to shout and twist and kick at them.

'Untie me, you bastards!' he yelled.

'I think he wants the full treatment, Fleck,' said Chalky.

'I believe he does, Chalky.'

'Untie me!'

They ignored his pleas, dragged him to the rail that ran along the edge of the main deck and pushed him over it. Jenson screamed as his gut hit the top rail and his head tipped over and down, his hands tied firmly behind his back – nothing but boiling black ocean far below him. As his feet came up to follow him over the rail, Fleck and Chalky grabbed them at the ankles and let him down as far as they could. Jenson dangled over the edge with Fleck and Chalky each holding a foot in one hand. Jenson screamed like a stuck pig as he gaped at the thrashing waves a hundred feet below. If they let him go he was a dead man.

'Don't drop me. I'll kill you, you bastards!' he screamed. His yell did not travel far over the sound of helicopters buzzing overhead.

Chalky and Fleck remained unfazed by his threats.

'Are you gonna be a good boy now or are we gonna drop you into the ogin?' Chalky asked. 'It's your choice, laddie.'

Jenson had a sudden and drastic attitude change as it dawned on him that they might be serious.

'Please,' he suddenly cried out. 'Let me up.'

'Are you going to be good?' insisted Fleck. 'My hands are gettin' tired. Are yours, Chalky?'

'Fuckin' right,' Chalky replied. 'Can't 'old on for long.'

'Please,' Jenson continued to beg.

They let him sweat it out for a few moments longer until he assured them he would play the game, then they dragged him back on board and let him fall to the deck like a sack of spuds. They walked away and left him there with his hands tied up.

'Bastards. I'll kill you, you hear me! Bastards!'

But the point had been made, and taken. Jenson never did anything about it. His image had been tarnished, but he'd get over it.

Jenson had a long career in the SAS and remained at the sharp end of many of their operations for years to come. The last I heard of him was not long ago. An older SBS operative, Bob, who had taken my place in South Det soon after I left, was passing through Gibraltar when he almost literally bumped into Jenson. Jenson had done a considerable amount of work with the SBS by then and had learned to be tolerant and even civil to us. Bob was curious as to why Jenson was in Gib, but naturally did not ask. Something was up, though: the signs were obvious to a seasoned pro. Jenson was carrying a small holdall and Bob was certain he was armed with a pistol in a shoulder holster under his coat. The following day, three members of an IRA ASU were shot and killed while preparing to plant a bomb with the intention of killing and maiming. Had the IRA succeeded they would probably have killed more locals than British. Gibraltans are a laid-back lot and I doubt half of them know or care where Northern Ireland is. It would have been difficult to get them to understand why their children had died for the IRA cause. Had the SAS not killed the ASU and the bomb gone off, it might have been even more difficult to explain to those parents why the British had not shot them when they had the chance.

The last I heard of Jenson was that he had gone outside and was looking for civvy employment. I doubt he will ever be short of work in today's world.

After the oil platform rehearsal, the animosity between the two units continued to simmer below the surface and Jenson's threat to kill an SBS operative was to become a reality not long after. Although he personally would have nothing to do with it, one of ours was destined to be shot and killed late one night by the SAS on a lonely hillside in the middle of the Falkland Islands.

Despite the animosity, respect for the SBS was on the increase, and not only from the SAS, who had by their own admission been impressed by the way we took the platform, knowing they could not have accomplished it themselves. Some of the Navy élite were also hearing positive things about what we were trying to achieve, and not just in retaking oil platforms. But many at ministerial level still had to be convinced that we could carry out these difficult assaults in real situations. It was a bit like being in a chorus line. We felt we would only ever get noticed if we got a chance to do a solo.

There are many arms of the British military and all of them vie for special attention and funding as well as a chance to prove themselves. The anonymity of the SBS sometimes worked against us in this area. There were senior ministers and even top brass who thought the SBS was little more than a boat-driving unit (the US Navy has a Special Boat Section who are exactly that). In this area the SAS had another huge advantage over us. They were well represented in London (today's commander in chief of all British forces is former SAS) as well as being the heroes of film, and mysterious celebrities in the press (even before the spate of SAS books). The SBS were going to have to do some PR work that could penetrate the bigwigs in the corridors of power.

To this end, the SBS began a campaign aimed at educating government ministers, members of GHQ, and officers who might soon rise to that position, in our skills. This campaign consisted of countless demonstrations in swimming pools, at sea and in our killing house. No member of the SBS was exempt from this advertising crusade. Royalty was not ignored by us, either. I once joined five other operatives to demonstrate climbing on board a naval frigate from the water undetected as it travelled at top speed while Prince Philip observed from a grandstand seat in a helicopter.

At one time, it seemed we were doing nothing else but these demonstrations and it was sometimes difficult not to get carried away with the unreality of it all. The temptation, after climbing on to a ship's deck, to prance around on tippy-toes like the Flying Arpeggios at Billy Smart's Circus, taking bows and waving to the audience, was great. After a demo in the camp swimming pool to show climbing techniques from out of the water using the high diving-board, an operative ran in and presented the sergeant in charge with a bouquet of flowers he had borrowed from somewhere. We were the only ones who were amused.

We often tried to put a bit of realism into the demos to give them some lift (something we learned from the Navy SEALs, who were great at putting on shows), but our special effects sometimes made the demos memorable in ways we did not intend. On one occasion, in the killing house, Mudders, an enthusiastic SBS sergeant, one of our Captain Hurricane look-and-act-alikes, personally prepared a room-entry demo for a two-star Army general.

This consisted of having the visiting dignitary inside the actual killing room while operatives burst in firing live rounds, shooting the place up around him. The dignitary was instructed to stand against a wall behind a thick, white line on the ground, and in no circumstances to move over it during the demo. The room was not much bigger than an average living-room and was furnished to simulate an office, home or ship's bridge. Life-like dummies holding weapons to represent terrorists were placed randomly about the room. The instructor stood in the centre of the room, surrounded by the dummies, while he described the scenario to the dignitary.

On a given signal at the end of his talk, the team, dressed for business in standard SBS assault gear and gas-masks, would smash open a door, dump flash-crash as they charged into the room, and unleash a barrage of live machine-gun bullets into the terrorist dummies, leaving the hostage/instructor untouched. This always impressed the visitor who, wearing ear-defenders and goggles to protect his eyes from any particles, was only inches from flying bullets. Sometimes a vase was placed close by the visitor and deliberately shot to bits to reinforce the realism.

On this occasion, Mudders, always keen to impress, decided to add a little extra. He manufactured several exploding caps taped to condoms filled with red ink which he placed under the shirts of the dummies. These were to be electrically fired from outside the room on the team's entry.

The entry, which lasts barely seconds, went off perfectly on Mudders' cue, and as soon as the terrorists were all shot, the cry 'Room clear!' went up and the assault team remained frozen in their final positions so that the general could see them when the smoke from the flash-crash cleared. Mudders remained in the centre of the room, facing the general and looking smug, but when the smoke cleared he realised with horror that he'd overdone it. The general, standing alone with his back to the wall in his dress uniform, was completely covered in red ink from head to foot. Mudders had obviously put far too much ink in the condoms. He himself had been out of the 'splash zone' where he stood alongside the terrorists. The general was unaware of his new paint job since the condoms had gone off at the same time as the flash-crash and the shock of the blasts had masked the impact of the flying liquid. When he took off his goggles as the smoke cleared, the skin around his eyes was the only part of his body not crimson. When he stepped away from the wall his silhouette was perfectly outlined on it. Mudders did not know what to say, but as the general was unaware of the situation he simply escorted him outside and into the fresh air, where the general's staff and senior members of the SBS were waiting for him to review the rest of the SBS assault teams.

The general's staff officers looked horrified at the state of him. Mudders could see his career flashing in front of his eyes. The staff decided not to tell their boss until later on. I don't know how the general reacted when he found out, but to his credit he took it no further and Mudders hung on to his stripes.

13

Chasing and then climbing aboard huge tankers or cruise liners moving at speed has never been without its anxious moments, even though the process is relatively straightforward.

The general technique was for teams to chase down a ship in high-powered speedboats, climb the sides of the vessel from all directions and storm the superstructure while helicopters came in with support teams to recapture it. As in much of our work with boats, on the surface or below it with subs, probably the biggest danger was going through the propellers. I have personally witnessed three men on different occasions peel off the side of a fast-moving ship, either due to equipment failure, or from exhaustion. Each time, it was a nerve-racking moment waiting for that person to surface after disappearing under the moving vessel. I stood helpless and watched a friend get dragged under the arse-end of a moving supertanker after one end of his climbing rope uncoiled, dropped into the water and wrapped around the prop, while the other end of the rope was hooked to a climbing device around his foot. He surfaced only after having cut himself free from the line just in time. He said he could feel the proximity of the props.

I watched from a helicopter as the bows of a rigid raiding boat (a fibreglass boat that can take a dozen men) nudge the stern of a tanker while climbers were preparing. The tanker's bow wave suddenly welled up and swamped over the front of the boat, literally sucking it down towards the props like some greedy beast as the men leapt out. There were so many near misses over the years, it was only a matter of time before an SBS operative went through a spinning propeller. The day it happened we almost lost three men.

Two SBS teams of four had just completed a parachute jump into the sea in rehearsal for an operation. A type 42 naval frigate was acting as the mother craft from which several rigid raiders and inflatables were dispatched to pick up the men and their chutes. An SAS sergeant from their boat troop, who was actually a former Royal Navy sailor, was acting as liaison between the ship's captain and the crews picking the parachutists out of the water. One of the inflatable boats, which had just picked up three SBS parachutists, was at the stern of the frigate unloading their gear. The frigate was moving ahead slowly not far from the coastline, which bowed out in front of it several miles ahead. The frigate's navigator indicated to the officer on watch that on their present course they would soon run out of sea.

It appears that, without consulting the SAS LO or any

other SBS operatives on board or on the end of a radio, someone ordered the frigate to accelerate and change direction. Perhaps if the usual number of matelots had been on deck, one of them might have warned the bridge that boats were close to the frigate, but Germany was playing England at the time and most of the crew were inside watching the game.

Modern frigates, with their high-powered turbine engines, can accelerate very quickly. In seconds, the inflatable in the stern, along with the three operatives, was sucked under by the awesome force of the props. Several SBS men on board the frigate had been looking down at the inflatable at the time, helping with the unloading. It happened so quickly they couldn't believe it. The inflatable immediately popped back up severely damaged, but there was no immediate sign of the three men. Somebody sprinted to the bridge screaming for them to stop engines while others ran along the sides of the ship and waited anxiously – there was nothing else they could do.

Although it was only seconds, it seemed an age before the first man broke the surface. Others leapt in to help him, but he was OK. A few seconds later, a second man surfaced. He was also uninjured. Both had somehow passed either side of the prop and it had missed them. It took several more seconds before the third man appeared, but it was obvious that he was in a serious condition. The sea was turning red all around him. He looked as if he'd been attacked by a shark. His legs were bent in places where there were no joints. More men immediately dived in to save him.

It is not yet clear whether he actually went through the prop or was slammed against the 'A' bracket that supports it. Some say if he had gone through the prop he would have been sliced up like a loaf of bread. Whichever it was, he broke both his femurs, his jaw, received deep lacerations to the head and required hundreds of stitches. Luckily he had been wearing a dry-bag, if not he might never have floated to the surface, at least not as soon as he did. After five months, he returned to the SBS for light duty and is expected to eventually make a full recovery and return to operational teams.

One of many delightful SBS cock-ups (there were countless of these, too numerous to mention) I had the pleasure of being present at occurred in the English Channel, and might have caused a minor international incident had we not escaped as quickly as we did.

There were twelve of us in a high-speed rib assault boat waiting for a certain Channel ferry to come by. The ribs were originally designed as sea-rescue craft but adapted for our use by adding more powerful engines – a set of 240 Mercury overboards. They were the first generation of our high-speed ship-assault craft. It had a solid fibreglass deck and inflatable sides and could do speeds of around 45 knots with twelve fully rigged operatives aboard. They were not the most comfortable of boats to travel in at speed. Men sat on the inflated sides facing inwards, sitting opposite each other. In heavy seas, the side-to-side jolting could cause kidney pains after an hour or so. But better, much, much faster boats were already in the wings.

To help practise our many techniques on a variety

of vessels, we had an arrangement with several British ferry groups to use their boats for training purposes. We had the sailing schedule for their cargo ferries and intercepted them purely to practise our clandestine boarding techniques. The crews were warned not to over-react if they came across armed men in black climbing on board.

It was a lovely summer's day and we were bobbing around on the calm waters with our engines turned off – the ferry was late. We were fully rigged in our black FRIS (fire retardant immersible suit) assault outfits, carrying weapons, and sitting on the deck with our heads resting back to catch a bit of sun. The young officer running the rehearsal kept checking the schedule and navigation aids and searching the horizon with his optics. We wondered if he had got the time and location right. It didn't matter to us. It was a nice day to lounge around – one of those days when you wondered what the poor people were doing. Then a shout went up.

We sat up and stared at the speck in the distance, waiting until we were sure. Within a few minutes, we could make out the large, red ferry heading across our path towards Southampton. We hurried to prepare ourselves, zipping up suits, tightening straps, pulling on hoods and checking that all equipment was secure while the coxswain started up the powerful engines and gunned them till they were warm.

When all was ready and secure and we were sitting down the sides of the boat holding on to our support handles, the coxswain gradually accelerated to top speed. I leant into it as the boat got faster and faster, skimming across the water and bouncing gently over the few ripples. With each gentle bounce the engines gave a short shout as the prop left the resistance of the water for a fraction of a second. When there was a heavy swell, the boat left the water entirely, jumping from wave-top to wave-trough, the engines screaming longingly with each leap as the prop searched for water.

A large seagull appeared in front of us, flying a foot above the water. The coxswain needed to adjust his angle only a little to get in behind it. The seagull never ascended or veered away, and though it kept looking back at us with irritation, it remained on our course. He was huge, with a wing-span of five or six feet. We accelerated alongside it and it stayed with us for several hundred yards. I could almost reach out and touch its wing-tip.

We quickly closed on the back of the huge ferry and approached it hard and aggressively in preparation for a stern assault.

It was some forty feet from the water up to the stern rail. As we closed on the stern, we jumped the ship's bow wave as it grew from the corner and slowed to maintain pace with the port stern quarter. We never paused to check the security of the climb, always leaping right into it. He who hesitates is lost (in anti-terrorism at least) and we applied that philosophy to every aspect of our work.

Again, I cannot give details of the climbing techniques, but the first man scurried up. Once at the rails he prepared the way for the rest of us. I was second man up behind an Australian character, Rhino. Rhino had originally visited the SBS as an exchange sergeant from the Australian SAS, but he liked it so much, on returning to Australia he resigned from the SAS and returned to England to join the SBS.

As we ascended, we passed the rusty name of the vessel, its letters embossed vertically for a length of eight or ten feet. As we had approached from the stern we had not seen it before, and besides, each man had been concentrating entirely on his responsibilities. I noticed one of the chipped and over-painted letters was a 'Z'. I seemed to recall there was no 'Z' in the name of the ferry we had been waiting for. When I reached the deck I called down to the officer and asked him to confirm the name of the boat we were supposed to be assaulting. He looked at the name on the boat and was suddenly unsure.

While he searched his schedule, we went ahead at full steam and the rest of the team climbed on board. Normally we would have continued the assault and taken over the bridge and essential control points of the ship, but this was simply a boarding rehearsal, and a good thing, too.

'Shit!' the officer exclaimed as he found what he was looking for. 'Get off! It's a bloody Frog ferry!'

At that, a door leading on to the stern deck opened and a French crewman, going about his normal duties, took one step out and froze on seeing us. He stared at the ten heavily armed men in black standing on the deck yards in front of him. One can only imagine what was going through his mind. He leapt back inside the ship, slammed the door shut and we heard the bolt being thrown across.

We were just as quick as we grabbed our gear, leapt overboard into the water, scrambled and hauled each other into the rib boat, which then turned and powered away at full speed while we hung on. By the time the crewman could have raced up to the bridge to report the boarding of terrorists we were out of sight. We never heard from the French regarding the incident and can only imagine the captain must have thought the crewman was either drunk or losing it.

Tragically, Rhino, my Aussie friend, is confined to a wheelchair now. He was abseiling with his team from a helicopter in Belize, Central America, when, as last man out, at 200 feet, he got entangled in the rope. He was being choked to death by his rifle sling which was caught on the chopper's night-sun (searchlight) when the crewman cut it away and he fell. He was clinically dead by the time the rest of his team got to him. With their medical training they revived him, but his back was broken. Rhino was a great loss to the SBS.

A few weeks later, the French were the target of another special forces gaffe, this time a combined SBS and SAS cock-up. It happened while we were HALO parachuting in the south of the country outside a town called Pau.

Special forces HALO parachute jumping takes place from around 25,000 feet, about five miles up, whilst you are breathing oxygen and carrying weapons and the bulk of your personal equipment between your legs. When a man is fully rigged and ready to jump, he has to shuffle along the cabin, looking something like a beetle walking upright on its back legs with the rifle attached vertically down one side. If extra operational equipment is needed, such as 4x4s, bikes, canoes or snowmobiles, these are placed inside large cylindrical containers six feet long and four feet wide. The containers have barometrically operated sixty-foot, heavy-duty parachutes that open automatically at around 3,000 feet. Prior to the cylinders, we used six-foot square wooden crates. The cylinders took over from the cubed crates because, due to the poor aerodynamics of the crates, they had a tendency to go wherever the hell they wanted to.

It was the jump team's job to follow the loads, but the crates would change direction without warning across the sky in one direction, then zoom off in another. The team, usually four at a time for training purposes, would try to maintain a large diamond formation a hundred yards apart above and around the crate, facing inwards to keep an eye on it, ready to move wherever it moved, or, more to the point, to get out of its way. The trick was always to stay higher than the crate, but a most important rule was not to let it get directly below you. If that happened, just as its chute opened, a free-faller would hit it like a fly on a windscreen.

There were to be only two container jumps that week in Pau and they arrived in a truck, which backed up to the tail-gate of our C130 transport aircraft which was parked on the peaceful, sun-drenched runway. There was only one cylinder available that day, and so the RAF, who always organised the jumps, had hauled out an old crate to jump with. There were six SBS operatives and about eight SAS troopers on that trip. We all gathered around the first container, the standard heavy-duty wooden crate, to lift it from the truck's tail-gate and up no more than two feet on to the rear ramp of the C130. We took the strain, and on the command 'Lift!' picked it up and nearly bust a gut getting it the short distance on to the ramp. It was ridiculously heavy. It was full of sandbags to simulate equipment. We then faced the cigar-shaped cylinder, gathered around it and braced ourselves for another gut-busting lift.

On the command 'Lift!' we heaved it up, but it was empty and we inadvertently slammed it up into the tail of the plane five feet above us. The sandbags for both containers had been stored in the wooden crate which was why it was so heavy. We laughed at ourselves, and left to fit our chutes while the air crew sorted out the containers and the irritated pilot inspected the underside of his tail for a dent.

Within an hour we were airborne and climbing to 25,000 feet. I had no stomach butterflies by now, as we had been jumping constantly for days. However, that wasn't the case for me on the first jump of the week, when I always experienced a slight nervous-ness. I don't think I was the only one, as everyone was always quiet and thoughtful in the aircraft for a first jump. By midweek, everyone was their usual self and chatting away normally right up to putting on the oxygen masks and then falling out the back without a care.

Free-falling with full equipment, with cumbersome loads between your legs, was not as straightforward. The load made it more difficult to manoeuvre and if it shifted in flight it was awkward to control, and the free-faller was often forced to adopt some strange body positions to maintain stability.

In Pau, a popular discussion while preparing to jump was deciding what the French Army had given us for lunch that day. I had learned from experience not to ask until after I had eaten it. I'm not squeamish about food, but after the first meal in the camp, where the menu often showed a choice of sheeps' brains in a white sauce or pigs' intestines in a red sauce for starters, and sheeps' testicles or some part of a horse for the main course, I decided to just eat whatever they wanted to give me, as long as I did not know what it was till afterwards.

I was in the first stick along with three SAS lads and would be jumping with the conventional wooden cube crate. The cigar would come out close behind with the second stick, another mixture of SBS and SAS.

As we were all breathing oxygen through masks and could not talk properly, the jump-master held up a card that read: ONE MINUTE (till red-on). The cubed crate was pushed by crew members to the edge of the rear ramp on rollers and stopped there, held by blocks. We shuffled alongside it, dressed in black, breathing through oxygen masks, wearing dark bug-eye goggles, weapons fixed down our sides and backpacks secured between our legs, as the jump-master gave us a final check. The Pyrenees formed one side of the horizon and below were uneven, chequered fields and woods crisscrossed by country roads and boundaries and dotted with farms and villages.

The drop zone (DZ) was several miles away and it was calculated that, although we would actually jump out over an inhabited area, after the free-fall and the wind-drift under silk we would land in the DZ. There was no single clean field to use, the DZ being a large area of farmland the French had cleared for use with the local farmers. In this part of the country many of the fields had maize growing in them and it was sometimes hard to tell from directly above if the plants were two feet tall or ten. There was a big difference when it came to trying to haul in and fold up a chute in ten-foot maize and remember where the nearest edge was. A trick I soon learned was to try to be the last to land and watch where the others touched down. If a jumper completely disappeared into the maize I would do my best to avoid that particular field.

The red lights around the door flashed on.

We shuffled right up to the edge of the tail-gate. I was front man and I leant slightly over so that I could see the land below. There was something mesmerising about it, perhaps because it was so unnatural to be seeing it from this height, or perhaps it was the obvious fact that only one small thing had to go wrong for this to be my last two minutes alive. I had already had one parachute malfunction by then and the memory was always vivid prior to a jump. The SAS had lost several men over the years, but they had been HALOing longer than us and had many more men. We eventually had our first, and so far only, casualty when one of our lads died in California while jumping with the SEALs.

An aircrewman, attached to the aircraft by a life-line in case he fell out, crouched by my side and gripped the block that held the container in position.

The green lights went on all around the door. The

block was removed and the container was pushed out by crewmen. I jumped out right behind it, almost touching it, tightly followed by the other three. Within seconds we were spread in formation around the crate. But something was wrong.

Normally, to keep up with a container, I only needed to spread my limbs out comfortably, like a spider, to maintain pace with it. For some reason this container was plummeting like an elevator with its cables cut. And it was not moving from side to side very much as usual, either. It was heading towards the earth like a screaming meteor. I pulled my arms into my sides and pointed my head towards the earth in a straight dive in an effort to catch it up. I must have been dropping at over 120 mph, which was our average terminal velocity with the equipment we carried, but it was obvious the crate was going even faster and I did not stand a chance of catching it.

A quick scan around showed me I was not alone. The rest of my team were tracking earthwards like missiles in an effort to keep up with it. Meanwhile, the cigar container was released behind us, closely followed by its team who found themselves in a completely opposite predicament. On leaving the aircraft the cigar-shaped container seemed to go up. The team had to stretch themselves out like starfish to grab as much air as they could in an effort to stay with it. They rolled over on their backs to keep an eye on it and dropped uncontrollably away from the cigar as it got smaller above them. It didn't take a genius to work out what had happened.

By some misunderstanding on the part of the RAF

crew, none of the heavy sandbags had been shifted from the wooden crate to the cigar. The wooden crate was double its recommended safe weight and the cigar was empty.

I was at 5,000 feet when the container's chute opened and then instantly shattered to bits under the awesome weight-times-velocity of the crate. It continued, unimpeded, hurtling towards the earth. A ripple of concern passed through me as I realised there were farmhouses directly below. Suddenly my body was jerked by a horrendous power.

My head whipped forward on my neck like a rag doll's and my feet whiplashed under me and swung up till they faced skywards, then lashed back down, my heavy bundle still firmly between them. I groaned as the wind was knocked out of me. My chute had been pulled at 3,500 feet by the automatic opening device we always used and my body had not been in the ideal position. I had been concentrating so much on the crate's impact point I did not notice my own height. My goggles were halfway off my face.

Seconds after my chute opened, I felt a shock wave come up from below. The crate had hit with such impact it shook the ground like an earthquake. I had not seen exactly where it had landed, but there was a cottage at the point of impact and I steered towards it.

Just before landing, I released my heavy pack from between my legs and it swung from my waist on a line. A grassy field sloped down towards the cottage and I chose a landing spot fifty feet from the building. As soon as I hit the ground, I climbed out of my chute harness, ditched my equipment and hurried towards the cottage. The SAS lads were not far behind me. We gathered at the short picket-fence that divided the field from the cottage's small vegetable garden and studied the scene.

All was quiet and peaceful. The back door was only yards away. It was an old red-brick building with a slate-tile roof. There was no sign of the crate. A tile slid from the roof to join several others freshly shaken to the ground by the tremor. Suddenly we feared the worst. We were about to move around to the front of the house, praying the crate had not fallen inside, when we saw it, or at least the top of it, in the middle of the vegetable garden not far from the back door. The top was only just visible a couple of feet below ground level in a neat, square hole. The entire crate was compressed into the earth as if it had been driven in and countersunk by a giant hammer.

The door to the cottage creaked open slightly and a man and woman poked their heads out to look around warily. They stared at us wide-eyed. They had no idea what had caused the earthquake and looked a little frightened.

There was not much we could do. We waved, bid them 'Bonjour', then 'Au revoir', and left them to figure it out.

They'd find the crate, or the top of it, the next time they went out to pick some vegetables.

Meanwhile, the other stick had landed in a field and were craning skyward watching the cigar container as it floated down. At 3,000 feet its sixty-foot parachute opened, which actually gave it some lift. They watched until it drifted out of sight over the horizon giving no sign of ever landing. It was never seen or heard of again.

To cap the day off, one of the SAS troopers, who had jumped with the stick after the containers, was missing. He was a sergeant major and, in all the drama with the crates, no one had seen him since he left the aircraft. A search was carried out by the French military and when by midnight there was no sign of him, the worst was feared.

The following morning, as a French Army search party was leaving the camp, the sergeant major arrived through the front gates carrying his bundled-up parachute. It turned out he had extremely poor eyesight and had been hiding the fact from the Regiment. Had they known, his field days would have been over and he would have been stuck behind a desk for the rest of his career. His routine was to jump as normal, then on his way down, take his glasses from his pocket, pull off his goggles, put on his glasses, then replace his goggles over them. He could then see the ground and his altimeter.

On this occasion, he had fumbled and lost his glasses in free-fall. He had not jumped with full equipment and therefore had no automatic opening device. He had no choice but to estimate his altitude generously and pull his chute, then take a guess on a direction. On landing, he packed his chute and made his way, his bearings all mixed up, to a small country lane, where he thumbed a lift off a passing farmer. When he was picked up, he either didn't explain where he wanted to go well enough in his limited French or the Frenchman had a wry sense of humour, or perhaps he was feeling a little vindictive. The farmers were compensated for any damage done by jumpers, but they still did not like it and had no choice in the matter – military training had to take place somewhere. Whatever the reason, the sergeant major was apparently dropped off even further away and was eventually picked up by the gendarmes late that night wandering through a small town with his parachute.

The SBS were often placed on standby alert for immediate operations around the world, but these nearly always fizzled to nothing more than a long, boring wait in some hangar, aboard a ship, or on an airborne aircraft. I did enough of these standbys – threatened hijackings of ships that turned out to be someone with a plastic gun, or a coup in some banana republic that ran out of steam before it got to our embassy and threatened its staff. But that was the job. Hurry up and wait.

It was with this sceptical attitude that one day, whilst on a command course back in good old CTC, I received a warning order to stand by for a move to the South Atlantic because the Argentinians had just attacked the Falklands. The Royal Marines Falkland Islands detachment trained at Poole before heading south and so I knew a couple of the Marines who had put up such a good fight, defending against all odds, killing several Argentinians without sustaining any losses themselves before sensibly surrendering. But now that all of them were on their way back to the UK after a brief confinement, I fully expected that the politicians would sort the situation out without the need for military retaliation. Most of us did. We under-estimated both the situation and Prime Minister Margaret Thatcher's toughness. The Argies obviously did the same regarding the latter.

At that time, the Guatemalans were threatening to make moves on Belize and there was a rumour that the Spanish were rattling sabres towards Gibraltar, which they wanted back. Thatcher had to send a message to the world making it clear that, although a shadow of our former might, we were not ready to let the hyenas tear us apart just yet.

I was given the choice of quitting the course and heading down into the South Atlantic or staying put. If anything did develop, I was assured I could follow on later. The choice to remain was an easy one as I fully expected the teams to be back in a few days or weeks after a long, boring sea trip. As it hotted up and war looked inevitable I was ordered back to Poole, but only to discover I was to be part of a twenty-man SBS team who would be held back in reserve.

There was one bit of news that made it even harder to be left behind. Special forces were going to the Falklands some six weeks ahead of the task force, to pave the way for the invasion. Perhaps it was because of our advertising campaign, or our vast improvement or the fact the Falklands were islands and water was our business. Whichever it was, the SBS was going in behind the enemy lines – and ahead of the SAS by some three weeks. We were going to be first in, but I was not to be part of that. It was the most bitter pill of my career.

14

It was a frustrating time for the twenty of us left behind in England while the rest of the SBS plied their trade in the South Atlantic. We weren't the only ones – the SAS also left a lot of men behind to cover their counter-terrorism responsibilities.

I was in fine company, though. Many of those in Poole with me were amongst the most respected men in the Branch. We liked to think we were some of the best as well, since the CO had ordered that the core of men who remained in reserve were to be equal to any task that might arise elsewhere in the world, related or not to the war in the South Atlantic. Of course, the part about all the best staying behind was rubbish, but we needed to find some consolation.

It was not easy being so far away from the rest of the squadron while they were at war. We prayed something would come from us being stuck back in the rear. Maybe something else would happen elsewhere. Threats to

British interests did not cease just because we were busy in the Falklands. But to our disappointment, during the conflict no significant actions took place which required our response. We were kept busy reacting to a few possibles, but all the standbys turned to nothing.

My team commander was Paul (Coke to his friends), unequivocally one of the finest SBS operatives in our history. Coke had already received a BEM for his work in the SBS. Several years earlier, when the SBS was called on to provide a team of divers to photograph the underside of an Eastern Bloc ship, Coke was selected as the primary operative. The last diver on record to have tried it, Buster Crab, was never seen again, but Coke successfully carried out the job with his usual high standard of expertise and professionalism.

I was pleased to be in Coke's team, because if any important task came up he would be most likely to be selected first. The other two members of our team were Steve, from my submarine experience, and Fleck, who had hung Jenson over the side of the oil platform. Every day Coke would go into the ops room to bug the ops staff for jobs and find out what was going on down south. The mood was sombre to say the least as we moped around the now deserted lines.

We tried to keep our minds off things by practising climbing techniques and room entries in the killing house, or on diving trips along the coast, staying close to Poole in case we were needed. But it was difficult to remain focused on an exercise when so much was going on elsewhere for real. Coke tried to distract us by turning the exercises into fun. For instance, the dives would be planned as serious compass swims but would turn into lobster- and crab-hunting expeditions, and the room entries would evolve into home-made wax-bullet shoot-outs in the dark with flashlights – a precursor to the paint-ball games civvies play. But even turning the SBS headquarters into some kind of special forces Butlin's didn't help. All we wanted to do was get stuck into the war.

An American SEAL operative, Chuck, who was attached to us at the time, had to suffer our frustrations every day. He knew what it was like. While he was stuck in England with us, many of his comrades were operating in Central America. He organised a barbecue at his house one evening and invited many of the wives of the men who had gone down south in an effort to cheer them up. Unfortunately a couple of the more dim-witted wives got drunk and started slagging us off for reasons that totally eluded me.

'So, are you lot the cowards who wouldn't go to war, then?' one stupid tanked-up bitch shouted from across the room surrounded by a few of her smirking friends.

It was all I could do to stop Fleck from grabbing her and throwing her over Chuck's garden fence.

The mood was such that I think the ops room would have invented a job just to keep us off their backs. An opportunity finally came when Coke and I were called into the ops room to receive a warning order.

On entering the ops room we were greeted by the ops officer, who briefed us on the proposed mission. My eyes lit up when I saw the map on the wall behind him with several coloured pins in it. It was not of the Falklands, but Argentina itself. We were told that Thatcher had stated that if one more battleship was hit by an Exocet missile, the mainland airfields would be bombed. Coke, myself and three others were going to be dropped off the coast of Argentina by submarine to set up a series of observation points to watch airfields and report on fighters departing towards the battle fleet. We were put on standby to go for several weeks, but as the attacks tapered off it was decided to cancel the op. That left us even more frustrated. The SAS had done a similar operation using a helicopter insertion through Chile. It was a complicated mission requiring the helicopter to be burned on landing followed by a long yomp to the targets. It would have been more clandestine for us to enter the country by sub, and would have been less of a yomp, but for some reason the SAS got to do it their way.

Our own man in GHQ in London was an SBS captain better known to us as Bluetop. I'm not sure why he was so named, but he was small and he did buzz around a lot. To his credit he worked feverishly against higher-ranking SAS officers (an example of how badly represented we were in London) to find us things to do. One day, Bluetop flew excitedly into Poole with a task he had managed to secure for us. We were to fly out to a European harbour in a top secret mission to sink a South American merchantman.

The makers of the Exocet missiles that had claimed so many British lives in the South Atlantic had assured the British government that no more of them would be sold to Argentina. Military Intelligence obviously didn't believe them, and were well aware of the route that containers of Exocets continued to take overland to the foreign harbour where they were loaded on to merchant ships bound for Argentina.

We actually got to the point of stepping into the water the other side of the harbour from one such merchant ship and, wearing our bubbleless breathing apparatus, planned to compass-swim half a mile to the ship and place high-explosive limpet mines on its hull. But literally at the last minute London decided not to extend the conflict into European waters and we were ordered to pull back and let it sail unmolested.

Instead we were to fly to Gibraltar and wait for the South American merchant ship to pass through the Pillars of Hercules and into the Atlantic, where we planned to attack it in international waters. Our task was to capture it from the air, landing on it from helicopters, take off the crew, and then plant explosives and sink it. Once again London decided to cancel the op at the last minute. Their argument was they believed the conflict would be won by the time that actual batch of missiles arrived in Argentina. Their gamble proved to be correct.

The cancellation of the ship assault from the air was a disappointment because it was a technique we had pioneered for years and had rehearsed often, but had never had a chance to try out for real. The closest we had come in the past was when an Iranian frigate, being built in Scotland for the Shah of Persia, tried to set sail having been detained by the government when Ayatollah Khomeini took over that country. Just before it planned to sail, the captain lost his nerve and decided not to risk it.

No military force in the history of the world had as yet captured a ship from the air and sunk it. The SBS naturally wanted to be the first to succeed in this complex and dangerous operation since it was we who had pioneered the modern techniques. Our chance was finally to come.

The *Narwal* was a 1,300-ton Argentinian fish-factory ship that had been shadowing the South Atlantic battle fleet as it zig-zagged around the Falklands prior to the main invasion. There was no hard evidence at the time that the *Narwal* was spying on the fleet, but it was believed that its purpose was to direct the Argentinian air force on to it.* However, it was well within the exclusion zone placed around the fleet and, after it refused to acknowledge several warnings to back off, the fleet's commander ordered that it be destroyed.

The weather was horrendous that day, as it was for most of the conflict. Two Harriers were dispatched to take out the ship, but because of the exceptionally foul weather, low cloud-base and poor visibility, it was a much more difficult task than it would otherwise have been. When the Harriers reported their difficulty in engaging in *Narwal*, an SBS team was hurriedly formed and flown off in search of it in two Sea King helicopters. Their mission was to board the ship, remove the crew, and sink it.

The team was led by an SBS sergeant named Alfie,

* After the incident, the Argentinians continued to accuse the British of attacking an innocent civilian fishing boat.

who was Rhodesian by birth. Alfie was a wiry, experienced and capable operative known for his loyalty and consideration for his men as well as his cheeky sense of humour, especially in tight situations. He demonstrated this latter quality to such a degree on this ship assault that his fame within the SBS is assured.

The team was well aware of the problems facing this operation. First of all, they knew little about the ship itself beyond a sketchy description from the Harrier pilots. Neither did they know what defences it had if any, how many crew there were, and what obstructions were on the deck and superstructure. This last factor was most important as it strongly influenced the choice of boarding point.

Another problem was the helicopter pilots the assault party would use. The SBS team were going to carry out a specialised maritime anti-terrorism (MAT) assault technique that usually required hours of rehearsals on the part of the pilots because of the precision flying it involved. But the only pilots available at such short notice had never operated with the SBS before, nor had they rehearsed roping down a team on to a pinpoint, even in calm weather conditions. This was to be a 'by the seat of your pants' operation for everyone involved.

The plan might never have been considered had it not been for a boarding technique the SBS had developed only a few years earlier for MAT. Previously, when operatives abseiled from helicopters they used devices that clipped on to the line and applied friction to control their descent. On reaching the ground the tension had to be removed from the line before it could be unclipped to allow the next man to clip on from inside the helicopter and slide down. This was far too slow for the SBS's needs, especially if the touch-down point was 'hot'.

The SAS's solution had been to dangle several lines from the chopper, one for each operative, but it still required precious seconds to unclip from the line at the bottom. It also increased the area needed to land a team – the SBS had to be able to land as many men as it could get into a chopper, up to twenty at a time, and touch them down on a single pinpoint, such as the roof of a ship's bridge or a narrow gangway. In foul weather, using several thin lines, the risk of entanglement was great (during the Iranian Embassy siege, an SAS operative got tangled up abseiling down the side of the building).

The solution was a simple one, inspired by the age-old fireman's pole. Using a single rope – two-inch-thick hemp was ideal – with one end fixed into the roof of the chopper, the operative, wearing a pair of heavy-duty leather gloves, slid down, legs wide apart, gripping only with his hands. He applied the brakes just before hitting the deck and sprinted away instantly on touch-down. This method also allowed more than one man on the rope at once. As soon as the first man left the chopper, the second was right behind him – or above, to be precise. In practice, we used thirty-foot lengths of rope with as many as four men sliding down at any one time. Men descended as fast as they could without breaking their ankles at the bottom. The incentive to get out of the way on touching down was great unless you wanted a size-twelve boot slamming on to your head.

It was decided to use a ninety-foot rope to board the

Narwal because the obstructions on the deck, such as rigging and antennae, were unknown. With the weather as bad as it was the ship would be lurching up and down, so the first operative would have to choose his moment carefully before sliding down the rope. This was another advantage over abseiling since the abseil device requires the operative to be on firm ground to disconnect from it.

A dozen men climbed aboard the two Sea Kings and left the battle fleet behind and headed towards the *Narwal*. Meanwhile, the two Harriers that had originally been sent to sink the ship remained relentless in their attempts.

They strafed the ship with cannon-fire several times and even managed to hit it with two bombs, but a 1,000-pounder they dropped failed to explode. This was because a 1,000-pound bomb needs to be released above 500 feet before it automatically arms, otherwise the resulting explosion would destroy the aircraft that dropped it. Due to the conditions and poor visibility the bomb was released just below that optimum height. It was a ballsy effort by the Harrier pilot to have hit the target at all.

When the helicopters found the *Narwal* it looked like it was riding a roller-coaster as it lunged over the endless series of mountainous waves. The pilot of the first chopper, Alfie's, did his best to manoeuvre his craft over the bouncing ship, and the ninety-foot rope was tossed out. It swung in over the bows of the ship, but the bows were not only moving up and down, they were lurching from side to side as if out of control. Something was not quite right.

The operatives were dressed in their regular assault gear and carrying their primary H&K machine-guns across their fronts ready for immediate use, secondary pistols in holsters on their hips, chest harnesses filled with spare rounds, and explosive packs on their backs. They crammed at the door ready to go, but it was quickly decided that, due to the erratic movements of the ship, instead of all piling on to the rope right away, Alfie would slide down first and hold the other end on the deck for the others. The rest of the team could then zip down in the normal way.

The pilot did his best to hold his position over the boat and though he was having difficulty there was no time to waste. Alfie grabbed the rope, swung out on to it, and slid down towards the boat.

The rope was just inboard as Alfie headed down it, but as he closed on the deck the ship suddenly lurched and dipped away. He slammed on the brakes as he found himself more or less level with the ship, but dangling out over the grey, hungry sea. The pilot tried to manoeuvre Alfie closer, but was having trouble controlling the chopper in the severe winds. Alfie could not last long where he was. There was no way he could climb back up even if that thought had crossed his mind. To add to his problems, the rope was soaking wet by now and his hands were losing friction. If he ditched into the ocean he had little hope of being rescued. As if matters were not bleak enough, Alfie then saw a figure exit from a door in the superstructure and head along the deck towards him. He gripped the rope with his feet and released a hand so he could reach for his pistol.

The pilot continued to try to swing the rope towards the boat, but could not get it closer than six feet away. Alfie would never make it if he tried to dive for the rails.

The Argentinian crewman paused at the point on the rails nearest to Alfie and studied him for a second. Alfie could not see a gun in his hand. The crewman disappeared momentarily as he ducked down to grab something. Men on the helicopter tried to get him in their weapon sights but were hindered by the erratic movements of both ship and chopper.

When the man reappeared, he was holding a long hook and pole. Alfie was swinging around a little and could only hope to get a pot shot at the man if he tried to whack him off the rope. But to Alfie's surprise, the crewman hooked the rope and, with a great effort, pulled Alfie to the rails.

Alfie scrambled on to the deck, keeping hold of the rope for the rest of the team, who quickly followed.

'Thanks mate,' he said to the man as he levelled his pistol at him. The team began storming down the rope.

Alfie grabbed the crewman and demanded, 'Take me to the captain.'

The crewman was stunned. When he had pulled Alfie in he had not known the choppers were British. For reasons that were not apparent at that moment the man was expecting an Argentinian helicopter. Even though the crewman had probably saved Alfie from disaster, this was not the time for niceties.

'Where's the captain?' Alfie repeated threateningly.

When the crewman did not answer, Alfie hit him on the head with the pistol, not to knock him senseless, but to convince him they were not there to play around.

'*Dondé el capitano?*' Alfie shouted in pidgin Spanish.

The man protected his head and burbled something about the captain but still refused to indicate where he was. Alfie had had enough.

'For the last time. Tell me where the captain is or I'll blow your fucking head off.'

He grabbed the crewman fiercely and shoved the gun into his head to remove any remaining doubts he might have that Alfie was deadly serious. The man was scared stiff, but he pointed a shaking finger at himself and slowly enunciated what he had been trying to tell Alfie all along.

'Me *capitan*,' he said.

Alfie rolled his eyes and handed the captain over to one of the lads who was fluent in Spanish.

'Tell him to muster all his crew on deck. Those who don't can go down with it, I don't give a fuck!'

As the operatives spread through the ship they found evidence of the recent Harrier attack. One crewman had been killed by machine-gun fire, and in an internal corridor they found another with one of his legs literally hanging on by a thread of flesh. Further up the corridor was the unexploded 1,000-pound bomb which, on entering the side of the ship, had passed through the crewman's leg.

Alfie caught sight of a man hurrying out of the superstructure carrying several box-files. He was heading for the side with the intention of throwing the files overboard.

Alfie gave chase and stopped the man at gunpoint, warning him that he would follow the paperwork 'either into the chopper or overboard – whichever you prefer'.

The man understood English perfectly and chose the chopper. He was an Argentinian intelligence officer and the files contained proof that the *Narwal* was indeed spying on the battle fleet.

While several of the SBS searched the ship for crew, a team prepared the charges while the rest helped captured prisoners to be winched up into the waiting choppers.

The helicopters were slowly filling with the bedraggled crew members, closely guarded by SBS operatives. As the crewman with the leg hanging off was winched screaming into the Sea King's cabin, he was inspected by Colby, a Desperate Dan look-alike but without any of that character's gentler traits. Colby decided that the leg could not be saved, took out his knife, cut through the flesh holding it on and tossed it out of the helicopter.

When every crewman was aboard the two Sea Kings, Alfie remained on board the *Narwal* with five other operatives to plant the explosives. It was decided, because the Sea Kings were so crowded with prisoners, to ferry them back to the fleet and return for Alfie and his men directly after.

As the Sea Kings departed, one of the explosives party found Alfie, who was in the bridge checking through the paperwork, and gave him some disturbing news.

'I've just come from the bilges. This tub is taking water fast. It's sinking.'

The ship had sustained more damage from the Harriers than had been thought, which is why it had been so out of control and also why the captain had been expecting an Argentinian rescue that was never coming anyway. The question was, could it stay afloat long enough for the choppers to come back and pick up the team?

Alfie stuck with the mission. Collecting the team off the *Narwal* was someone else's responsibility.

'Our job is to make sure this ship sinks. Place the charges and wait for my word to initiate them,' he ordered.

The operative hurried away while Alfie radioed a message back to the fleet to explain the situation. He looked through the window at the blackness beyond the ship's lights, hoping the Sea Kings would be back before the ship sank.

When Alfie went back downstairs he heard a loud, rhythmic thudding coming from one of the corridors. He was joined by a couple of other men to investigate the unusual booming noise. When they opened the door to the corridor they froze.

'Holy shit!' was the general exclamation.

The ship had drifted on its axis and was rolling heavily. With each lurching action the 1,000-pound bomb had started to roll along the corridor until it slammed into a bulkhead, then it rolled back to the opposite bulkhead with the next lurch.

They quickly grabbed what they could and, jumping

over the bomb as it rolled at them, placed objects in its path until they could stabilise it. Their situation was beginning to look a bit serious, to say the least.

When the SBS on the Sea Kings heard the *Narwal* was sinking they unloaded the Argentinian crew in double-quick time and sped back to pick up their team-mates.

Alfie saw them arrive with some relief, then ordered the fuses to be ignited. The rest of his team were winched up to the Sea Kings as fast as possible. The seconds were ticking away as the fuses burned and, as the winch was lowered to pick up Alfie, who was the last man aboard, he had disappeared. He had been on deck seconds earlier, and now he was gone.

'There he is,' one of the men shouted as he saw Alfie running from the bridge. In his hands he was carrying the ship's wheel and two bottles of fine red wine.

The SBS are part of the Navy, and there are some naval traditions that cannot be ignored, no matter what the circumstances. There is an old Navy saying that states, 'If it moves salute it, if it doesn't, paint it, And if it isn't bolted down, requisition it,' to which the SBS added; 'If it is, unbolt it.' This refers to memorabilia. An intricate part of every SBS operative's first-line equipment was an adjustable wrench. Its unofficial use was for unbolting gizits. We spent a lot of time rehearsing live firing and explosives techniques on old Navy ships destined for the breaker's yard, and most operatives had a brass porthole or two hanging in his home.

There were anxious moments as Alfie fumbled with his prizes and fixed himself into the winch.

'Quick. Winch him up!' shouted one of the explosives

team to the chopper crewman as he anxiously checked his watch.

In true movie fashion, literally as Alfie left the deck, the explosive charges went off and rocked the ship. A cheer went up as the ship listed and was swallowed up by the Atlantic to join the many others that have ended up there throughout history. A grinning Alfie was pulled inside clutching his wine and wheel.

The SBS's first ship attack from the air in the history of warfare had been a success, but perhaps not without a little help from the enemy. Such is war. The fine wine was consumed by all ranks of the assault team that evening as toasts were made, and the ship's wheel was wrapped up and secured as booty. It hangs to this day in the Frog Inn, the SBS's unofficial bar in the Poole camp.

The SBS felt good about their small victory and morale was high. But the smiles were soon wiped away when the news reached us that one of ours had been killed. Kiwi was the only SBS man to die in the Falklands, but what made the news even more disturbing was he had been shot by the SAS.

One problem that hamstrung the SBS throughout the Falklands conflict was the lack of communication between the SBS and the SAS. There was no joint special forces command at that time and they had separate headquarters. Having two special forces units operating behind enemy lines and not always in strict syncopation could only lead to problems. The SBS did not have satellite communications at that time and the SAS did. Neither did the SBS have an adequate HF radio system.

This made it impossible at times for them to coordinate operations with the SAS.

The invasion of the Falklands was in full swing when Kiwi's patrol of four SBS operatives, along with four Royal Marine mountain leaders (MLs), was dropped off by a rigid raider on a beach miles ahead of the advancing British troops. They were headed across the barren, treeless land for a rocky hilltop from which they would observe and report Argentine troop movements. Both teams were following the same route for several miles prior to eventually splitting up and heading towards their objectives.

Navigating at night was difficult on the Falklands because of the lack of easily recognisable landmarks. Also the compasses used were designed for the northern hemisphere and were problematic, but all the patrols had that trouble and were making do well enough, relying more on contours and features. The craggy, rolling hills were hard to distinguish from each other, and in the darkness, distances between the looming silhouettes were hard to determine.

Kiwi was a powerhouse of a man. He was not tall, but when I first met him he had twenty-two-inch biceps, having taken a fancy to bodybuilding for a few years. When he realised that having large Schwarzenegger-type muscles meant he had to carry and feed this extra bulk, which was completely useless for this kind of work anyway, he slimmed down to train himself for triathlons, a much more suitable conditioning for special forces work.

Shortly before the Falklands, he trained for several

months to have a crack at the sit-ups world record, which was held at that time by a sixteen-year-old boy, I believe. A light frame was needed to even hope to equal the boy's record of several thousand. Kiwi was far from light, but he was never interested in hearing about what could not be done. He was extremely fit, courageous and had a great sense of humour, especially when it came to his own antics.

We gathered in a local pub and surrounded him as he began his sit-ups on the pub floor. I can't remember how many he did, but it was into the thousands, although he failed to reach the record. But as Kiwi would say, 'Winnin' wouldn't mean much if no one else 'ad a go.'

When he could finally do no more, he was helped to his feet and handed a beer, which he poured into his grinning mouth. The flesh on the small of his back had been worn away, but he never gave it a second thought. He hugged his new wife from whom he was inseparable and said, 'I think I'll 'ave a go at press-ups next time.'

The two patrols had been yomping together for several miles when the MLs paused to query their location. There was some dispute as to where they actually were. The ground had been covered by another SBS patrol a few days before and Kiwi was sure of where he was. After some disagreement, the two patrols eventually parted and went their separate ways. Kiwi's number two was Colby, the self-appointed leg surgeon from the *Narwal* adventure.

Kiwi and his team pressed on for several more miles and arrived in the area of their final position. But they were not a hundred per cent clear as to their exact location with regard to the map. This was a dangerous situation to be in. For every patrol's operating area there was an outer ring, a buffer zone, that was out of bounds to that patrol and all others. This was intended to prevent patrols on the outer boundaries of their own areas from coming into contact with each other. As long as everyone stuck exactly to their route they should never come into contact with another patrol. If another one was seen in your area it was presumed enemy. That night, the area adjacent to Kiwi's was owned by an eight-man SAS fighting patrol, armed to the teeth and dug in waiting for bear. Argentinian special forces patrols were reported to be moving in groups of four in the area looking for British special forces, and the SAS wanted to bag one.

Kiwi's patrol was in fact just outside their area and inside their buffer zone. It appears the SAS patrol had also misjudged its position and were not within the boundaries of their area. They were dug in inside their own no-go buffer zone that overlapped with Kiwi's.

As Kiwi's patrol arrived on the barren hillside, the SAS saw them, brought all weapons to bear, and waited for them to move closer into range.

Kiwi, unaware they were being scoped, actually paused the patrol to study the ground. He knew something was not right and that it was highly dangerous being misplaced in this locale. Before he took the patrol another step he had to figure out his exact location. They were inside the SAS's killing zone as it was, but the SAS wanted them even closer, and so they waited.

Kiwi decided to leave two of the team there and he

went forward with Colby, who was several yards behind him, to recce the hill crest – the spot where the SAS were hidden – to confirm their exact location.

Kiwi was a dark-skinned, squat figure with a slender, wiry moustache. To suggest his features could have been mistaken for Latin would be fair, especially in the dim light. Probably more damning was the chest harness he was wearing, which was very similar to the ones Argentinian special forces wore. All the SBS team had these. At that time, the Argentinians had a better chest harness design for the terrain and conditions than the one the SBS were using and, in the usual style of learning even from one's enemies, the men had the ship's tailor make copies of them. It's likely these two factors helped to seal Kiwi's fate.

As Kiwi closed in with Colby, who was well spaced out behind him, an SAS trooper called out, 'HALT!'

Kiwi stopped immediately and started to raise his hands. He was only yards from the SAS patrol. What happened next took only seconds. Kiwi never had a chance to even open his mouth. The instigating moment probably came, although it is unclear, when the two SBS operatives in the rear reacted to what they thought was a contact with Argentinians, and went to ground. The SAS opened fire. Kiwi was hit from point-blank range. The second round that struck him in the chest ignited his spare ammunition, which exploded, ensuring his instant death.

Colby could do nothing but dive and roll about the bare ground in an extreme effort to avoid the hail of fire. The two SBS operatives in the rear also came under heavy fire. In a fire-fight, verbal communication between soldiers is imperative to establish fire control. But the SAS firepower was loud and heavy. The most astounding thing about the whole incident was that only Kiwi was hit. The SAS fired everything they had at the other three, including grenade-launchers. Hardly a shot was returned by Kiwi's patrol simply because they had little cover more than a few inches high to get behind and they were doing all they could to avoid being hit. It must have been like a frenzied duck shoot from the SAS point of view, but none of the remaining ducks would go down. They kept rolling and zig-zagging all over the show. It then appears that, since the SAS had all started to fire together, they ran out of rounds at about the same time, and as they hurried to change magazines, in the sudden pause in the noise, they recognised the English voices of the men they were shooting at.

The SAS patrol leader called an immediate halt to the fire.

After some verbal exchanges, nationalities were confirmed and weapons were lowered. Colby's first thought was of Kiwi and he ran to his friend and held him in his arms. He could not believe Kiwi was dead at first but it soon became obvious as the others closed in.

There was a strained silence between the two patrols. No one argued that the other was in the wrong place – this would only truly be confirmed later. It was pointless anyway. The incident was reported to both sets of headquarters and Colby was eventually ordered to bring in the patrol while the SAS remained in position. Colby and the other two SBS operatives placed Kiwi in a sleeping bag and buried him under a pile of stones while the SAS watched silently from their position a few yards away. The two patrols sat apart for a while without exchanging a word, then the SBS team gathered their gear and headed off towards a helicopter pick-up several miles away.

Several days later, Kiwi's body was retrieved and brought back home to England.

It was not the end of the matter.

When the Falklands conflict was over and the victorious troops headed home to England, most of the SBS and a handful of SAS went back on the RFA (Royal Fleet Auxiliary) *Resource*, which was headed for the Ascension Islands, where the men would then take a VC10 home.

The cloud that hovered over the SBS operatives after Kiwi's death still remained and not all members were celebrating the end of the war with as much gusto as the rest of the task force. To pass the time on board, most men hung out in the bar and played board games or read. Colby and the other two from his patrol were on board the *Resource* along with – an oversight, on reflection – the SAS patrol that killed Kiwi.

The SAS troopers might well have been ignored by the SBS on board had one of the patrol, known as Ging, not begun to discuss the shooting incident with a couple of his SAS colleagues. He did not realise that the man sitting next to him nursing a beer was Colby.

Colby had been deeply affected by Kiwi's death. Not only had he been a close friend, but he felt he shared the responsibility for them being misplaced.

The precise words Ging used to describe the incident have been argued over, but there seems to be no doubt that his tone was that of a braggart. He was accused by those close by of saying, 'We should've killed the lot of 'em.' Whether he meant that the others were lucky not to have been hit, or that he would have been content to have shot them all, only he truly knows, and perhaps Colby, who remains in no doubt.

Colby snapped.

Colby was a brute of a man and another corps rugby player. He was not to be trifled with at the best of times, but especially when he'd had a beer. He stood up, grabbed Ging by the throat and started to pummel him. Ging's SAS colleagues leapt in to stop him, and might have had difficulty getting Ging out of Colby's powerful grip had it not been for half-a-dozen SBS men who rushed over to help separate them. Unfortunately for Ging, another SBS man, a particularly hard, squat Scotsman and former member of the Foreign Legion who had a reputation for taking on entire pubs when the mood took him, had also heard, or misheard, the comment. He took over from Colby, who was being held down by the others, and proceeded to take Ging apart. On Ging's best day he was not even a close match for the Scotsman, and it was not until his face had been smashed and a chunk of his hair had been ripped out of his skull that the Scot was pulled off.

The SBS CO was immediately informed of the incident and he quickly contacted the CO of the SAS by radio to ask him to remove his men ASAP. (Apparently the gist of his request was that he could not otherwise guarantee that a certain SAS trooper would not go missing before the journey's end.) A chopper was flown over a few hours later and Ging and the rest of the SAS section were extracted to another ship.

The SBS performed well throughout the conflict and, despite the usual routine of having many of our successes being credited to the SAS, the powers that be knew we had done well. When all the troops were back home, Thatcher took a helicopter ride to Poole to personally review the SBS and praise them for their outstanding work. She did not go to Hereford. There was a reason for this snub.

Thatcher had come to distrust the SAS because they had used their satellite communications system throughout the conflict to report directly to their headquarters in Hereford, circumventing the overall headquarters in London. This was a severe breach of procedure.

It seems that what at one time appeared to be the SAS's advantage, their self-assuredness and relative autonomy, and the SBS's disadvantage, their traditional ties to the Marines and therefore their strict adherence to protocol, created a reversal of fortune for both units.

In the eyes of London, the SBS, having proved their worth and that they were every bit as good as the SAS (if not better in many areas), suddenly became the unit of choice. This was borne out on many occasions and quite demonstrably several months after the Falklands, when the SBS were chosen, without the SAS, to conduct a sudden and important operation against Eastern Bloc special forces which, for reasons of national security, cannot be described in this book.

* * *

When the squadron returned from the Falklands it was quickly back to business as normal. But a few months later, tragedy struck again with the loss of the SBS's most highly decorated and respected operative – Coke, my team commander.

15

I was still in MAT and part of Coke's team when, a few days before Christmas in the Poole headquarters, he came into our team office holding a new experimental American limpet mine and asked me if I wanted to join him on the range to try it out. The SBS were looking for a new mine at the time and this device appeared more sophisticated than others we had tested. It had a new type of electronic timer built in, but the anti-lift device had been removed as the Americans did not want to divulge its full intricacies unless we committed ourselves to buying it.

I was busy at the time, up to my ears preparing a report after a MAT reconnaissance we had just completed on a new class of supertanker. I declined to go, and said I would catch up with him later that evening. Coke was a handsome man and, though he had been quite the lad in his younger days, he was now happily married to a lovely girl he had met in Hereford while working there with the SAS – the one that got away, some SAS used to call her.

Early that evening, as it grew dark, I closed up the office for the night and headed into the HQ building to change into my civvies before going home. As I stepped into the corridor the sergeant major walked out of his office looking ashen, having just received a phone call.

'My God,' he said, 'Coke has just been killed.'

As I have said before, Coke was the most highly respected man in the squadron and the news of his death rocked the entire organisation. The man probably most affected by his death was the sergeant in charge of the explosives range that day and the last person to speak to him. It was Colby.

Coke had arrived at the range with the limpet mine, and a large plate of steel was laid out in 'the pit' and the limpet magnetically stuck to it. Once the limpet was in place everyone else cleared the range and went back to the safety of the bunker while Coke set the timer. He set it to give himself time to walk back casually to Colby and the others with a minute to spare.

When he got back to the bunker he checked his watch and counted down the last few seconds to the explosion. But nothing happened. After a few more minutes it was declared a misfire. The procedure at that time was to wait thirty minutes, and if by then the device had not blown, it was the range supervisor's job to go back to the unexploded charge and, using a lump of plastic explosive, to detonate it. Nowadays, mainly due to this incident, when dealing with electronically initiated devices, ATO is brought in and the device is blown using a robot. On a range, a piece of plastic explosive is placed beside any electronically timed device so that no one need go back to it in the event of a misfire. The charge is blown electrically from the bunker.

At that time, going back to detonate unexploded devices was not uncommon, especially in training, where novices occasionally cocked up the initiation. As long as the correct amount of time was given for a possible 'slow fuse' it was a safe procedure, if a little nerve-racking.

Whilst training an anti-terrorist unit in Europe, teaching them how to throw hand-grenades one day, I had a string of misfires. The grenades were of poor quality, and after three in a row failed I had to go out alone each time, find them and blow them up. After the third time, feeling a bit frayed, I cancelled the exercise.

Coke went back to the charge while the others remained in the bunker. A minute later there was a shattering explosion.

When the others came charging out of the bunker and into the pit, Coke was lying beside the buckled sheet of steel. Both his legs were gone and so was one arm. His head and torso were severely scorched, but to their amazement he was still alive. The trained SBS medics immediately went to work to try to save him.

They rushed him to the nearest hospital, Blandford Military Hospital, but the doctors and nurses were so horrified by Coke's injuries that they panicked and were useless. The SBS medics pushed them aside and took over. One of them found a vein in his arm and inserted a drip into it. They then transferred him to an ambulance and he was rushed to Poole General. But

Coke died shortly after arriving there, surrounded by his colleagues who had worked so hard to keep their friend alive.

We will never know exactly what happened in those last few seconds before the blast.

The following day, most of the men could be found in the rugby club on camp, which we used for piss-ups. As is the tradition, a keg was opened and everyone gathered for a drink. As I came into the camp that morning I was called into the sergeant major's office.

'I'm afraid I have a rather unsavoury job for you,' he said. 'Someone has to go out to the range and clear it up, if you know what I mean.'

At first, I thought they had chosen me because I was Coke's second-in-command and they did not want just anybody picking up his body parts and putting them into a bag. I was wrong.

When I arrived on the range I took a moment to look at the place where my friend had been killed. I walked slowly around, searching the ground. There were small pieces of his body everywhere and I set about picking them up and putting them into the plastic bag I carried. I did not use gloves. I was not disgusted by the lumps of bone and tissue in my hands. They were part of my friend.

I took them to Poole General, where I asked if I could lay them with Coke's body, but the old man who ran the mortuary held his hand out for the bag. He was a gentle old soul who'd had some experience in dealing with the friends and relatives of those who had just died.

'I wouldn't see him if I were you,' he said. 'Take my

advice, son. Let your memories of him be those of when he was alive, not as he is now.'

I took his advice, gave him the bag and left.

When I arrived back at the camp I went to the rugby club to join the rest of the men. As I entered, I noticed a few people glance at me then look away, as if they had been talking about me. There was an odd atmosphere. I got a pint of beer and while I sipped it I looked around. Several sat alone, some with tears in their eyes. Others talked quietly in small groups. The problem with being such a small, tightly knit unit, working closely together and often with the same few people for many years, is that the pain of losing one is so much greater, like losing a close member of one's family.

One of the men in a group at the bar turned to me and said, 'Job done then, Duncan?'

His tone was, if anything, aggressive.

'You know why you were sent out to the range, don't you?' another said.

I didn't understand.

'Because you're a cold, heartless bastard, that's why.'

The comment hit me like a slap in the face. I looked around at the many faces, all of whom seemed in agreement with the comment. I saw Colby across the room finish his pint and head for the door. I left the bar and followed him outside.

'Colby?' I said.

He stopped and looked at me with sad eyes.

'What did they mean?' I asked.

'Don't you know?'

'I don't think I do,' I said, wondering if he would

confirm something that I had first heard from a drunken operative while with 14 Int.

He was calm and spoke softly. There was no anger in his voice, just sadness.

'It's just how they said it. They don't dislike you or feel bad towards you. You're just cold and emotionless. Soon as someone asked who was going to pick up the bits, you were the obvious choice.'

I had never considered myself emotionless. As I said before, I just kept it hidden better than most. You could not be as nostalgic as I was and not have feelings. I thought the reputation I'd gained in Northern Ireland for cracking right on with the job after we lost some-one, as if nothing had happened, was an asset in this job. It was, but that didn't mean people would like you for it.

Colby, however, had no time for my problems. He was lost in his own memories. As he stood in front of me, his shoulders began to shake as he started to cry. He could not hold it in any longer. Tears rolled down his face as he let it all out. Witnessing the deaths of two of his closest friends and in such a short space of time was a lot to hold on to, and now was a good time to let it out. It affected me deeply. Suddenly, all the control I had exerted so easily all my life was brushed aside. It was as if watching this powerful, accomplished soldier crying like a child had opened the flood gates. I could not help myself. Everything welled up and gushed out of me. The tears filled my own eyes and spilled down my face. I could not stop them, nor did I want to. I was in fine company.

'I miss him as much as everyone else,' I stammered.

Colby patted my shoulder then walked away and left me there alone.

I walked back to the club, opened the door and stepped inside. Men looked at me and were surprised to see the tears in my eyes and on my cheeks. I had not come back in to show I could cry, I just wanted to be with them. I made my way to the bar and to my pint, but I could not drink. As I stood there I felt an arm on my shoulder, then another old friend came over. Soon, several of those I had always considered my friends came over to share their grief. Before long the singing started and it turned into the good old piss-up Coke would have wanted us to have.

The following day faxes and signals came in from military units all over the world which Coke had worked with or trained with over the years, offering their condolences.

My thoughts went out to his wife, who remained strong throughout the ordeal. For days afterwards, there was always at least a couple of the men and their wives at Coke's home to comfort her. She never showed signs of weakness and kept a brave face whenever she was with them, but sometimes she could be heard crying softly in her room alone.

Five years later, she married another man from the SBS, Lou, a quiet, private man who had been a friend of Coke's. He had loved her from afar all those years after the incident and had respectfully been there for her whenever she needed help. He made her happy once again and we were all pleased when they married.

She'd had no children with Coke, but a few years later she and Lou had a son.

A few weeks after the boy's birth my father died and I went to London to bury him. He'd had a heart attack in his council flat in Battersea and immediately walked three miles, alone, to St Thomas's Hospital, where he had another one and died. It demonstrated his toughness but also his loneliness. The next day, before I left my father's flat for the last time, I telephoned Lou and his wife to tell them I was coming down to Poole that evening and I would pop round to see them – I had been away for some time. A stranger answered the phone, a friend of Lou's wife, and said she could not talk to me at the moment. Lou had just been killed while on combined operations training in Germany with GSG9, German special forces.

16

A year after the Falklands conflict, I became part of the SBS training teams. I had come full circle in the squadron, now renamed the Special Boat Service, a title somewhat indicative of its promotion, and was instructing newcomers and passing on the knowledge and experiences I had gained.

As I left my office one pleasant afternoon, I bumped into the colonel of the camp, a non-SBS officer, but a great fan of the Branch. He was a tall, greying character, yet another former corps rugby player, and a practically minded and fair man. He knew me through my reputation as a hard but fair instructor – I was usually Mister Nasty on the selection courses. A few months earlier, the colonel had asked me to deal with a batch of young officers in training on a visit to the camp from CTC.

They had got themselves into a spot of bother the night before in town and he wanted me to give them a message, but not a verbal one. A dozen of them had unfairly tried to pick a fight with two long-haired locals who looked a contrast to the short-haired, jacket-and-tie get-up of the young officers. The two locals turned out to be SBS operatives from MCT out for a quiet beer after a long day. It was obvious to the operatives who the 'yobs' were and they declined the fight without divulging their true identities. But they reported the incident to the adjutant. We did not appreciate out-of-towners who caused trouble on our local turf, especially those who would give the Marines a bad name.

'Take them for a little run,' the colonel asked. 'Early. And I don't care to see them at breakfast, either.'

When I met the young officers that morning at 6:00 a.m. for their unscheduled PT session, they had no idea, although they were obviously curious, why an SBS instructor was taking them. When I introduced my two assistants for the morning's activities, the two SBS men that they had picked on in town, their hearts sank. They had every reason to be concerned.

When I brought them back two and a half hours later, they were in a sorry state, some having to help others in through the main gate.

The colonel was an easy man to talk to and as we walked we got into a conversation. He asked me what unit I was originally from. I told him I had never been to a unit and that I had joined the SBS straight out of training. He paused to study me.

'Is that so?' he said.

I got the sudden feeling I had just made a big mistake.

'A man should have a balanced career,' he said.

And that was all he said on the subject; to me, that is. A few months later, I was called to the sergeant major's office, where he handed me my new draft orders. I was off to join 42 Commando for eighteen months.

My heart sank. How could this happen to me? I asked myself. But there was a little more to it than that. It seemed the Falklands conflict had shown that the SBS were a little too detached from the way regular Marine commando units operated. This included troop and company procedures, such basic things as conventional section attacks, artillery and mortar fire control. It would behove us to fill in that gap. To that end, I was not the only SBS rank sent to the units over the following few years.

Several months after receiving my orders, I drove through the main gates of 42 Commando to begin a year-and-a-half term as a regular fighting soldier. That was bad enough, but when I heard where the unit was going to spend the next four months, I could only shake my head in self-pity. We were headed for Northern Ireland – and not only that, to my old patch in South Armagh. After all the years I had done in that country as a grubby undercover operator, I was now going over as a regular gravel-belly, patrolling the streets and countryside, rifle across my body, and trying not to become a target. There were going to be some problems, especially when everyone in the unit knew I was SBS, including the intelligence officer, who was aware I knew more about the players in that area than he did and that I could not divulge any information.

As it turned out, the colonel had been right. I learned

a lot during those eighteen months and had some of the most fun times of my military career. I met many fascinating characters and got up to things I never could have in the squadron. Life was not as serious or intense in the regular units as it was in special forces. I found that a bootneck's solution to soldierly problems was always practical, sometimes Neanderthal, and although always professional in planning, concept and execution, they carried out their objectives, regardless of conditions, with stacks of humour and playfulness.

One day in Northern Ireland a reconnaissance troop patrol, that should have been away from the camp for four days, returned after only a few hours. They had been dropped off not far from the border by chopper just before dawn, and inserted into a ditch concealed by a thick hedgerow to observe a farmhouse several hundred yards away. Soon after first light, the first activity they recorded was the farmer moving his cows into the field they happened to be in. Animals are the bane of concealed observation positions because of their curiosity, and cows are among the worst.

The four Marines remained as still as they could so as not to attract the cows' attention, but this was clearly going to be impossible for the whole day. Sure enough, after a short time a cow wandered by, chomping at the grass, and saw the four lads in the ditch. As usual, with cows, she came over and stood and watched them with great curiosity from feet away. She was soon joined by another who stood alongside her, and then another and another, until finally every one of the fifty or so cows were standing in a semi-circle around the OP, heads down and looking in inquisitively. Apart from the fact that the Marines could no longer see their target because of the bovine obstructions, this crowd would attract the farmer's attention. He would surely come and investigate and the OP would be blown. The Marines tried shooing the cows and tossing stones, but all this did was scatter them for a few moments, after which they returned. The Marine in charge finally decided the only way to get rid of them all was to give one a sound smack and hurt it. This would scatter them but they would think twice about coming back. He pulled a large rock from the ground and launched it mightily at the head of the closest cow only feet away. The rock bounced off the cow's cranium and it instantly dropped forward unconscious with its head actually inside the ditch and its tongue hanging out. The other cows did indeed scatter and not return. However, the cow now lying out cold on the edge of the ditch was bound to attract the immediate attention of the farmer. The Marines had little choice but to close the op.

They called in a chopper to meet them a few clicks away, packed up their gear and pulled out. As they climbed a hill behind the OP they saw the cow come to and stagger off.

In the SBS it was impressed upon us to retain personal discipline at all times. A serious incident, getting in trouble with the law or civilians, could result in expulsion from the unit if it was our fault. This restricted our playfulness at times. This was not the case with the regular Marines. Much of the mischief they got up to was just for the crack. On one occasion, while in Norway with 42, I joined half-a-dozen members for dinner in Narvik.

We found an unusual restaurant, a thin, three-storey building with a dining-room on each floor. The waiter took us to the third floor, where we were shown a table by the window. After many hours of much food, wine and merriment we were given the bill. One of the lads, a Scot, was sitting at the end of the table with his back to the window. He was pretty drunk, more so than the rest of us, and joked that we should do a runner without paying. To enforce his suggestion, he leaned back and opened the window indicating it to be his proposed exit. A stiff, icy breeze blew in.

We all thought he was joking, and I believe he was, too. But when he dropped out of the window head first, his feet being the last part of him we saw disappear into the night, it was obvious he was the only one of us who had forgotten we were three floors up. We ran to the window and saw him lying on a hard-packed pile of snow that had been pushed up against the building to clear the pavement. We charged down the flights of stairs and out of the restaurant, thinking he must be dead. On the bank of hard snow his body had bent over in such a way that if he opened his eyes he could almost see the back of his heels in front of him. Amazingly, he had no broken bones, but he was in an awful mess, his face swelling up as if he'd had fifteen rounds in the ring with his back and hands tied to a post in the centre. One of the lads quickly ran back into the restaurant to ask the management to call an ambulance.

Meanwhile, on the middle floor, there was a flap on as a huge, fat, Norwegian lady was seemingly choking to death. She had suddenly broken out in convulsions during her meal, which had taken all the attention away from our friend lying in the street. I suppose as far as the restaurant was concerned, the Scot's problem was self-inflicted, whereas the choking fat lady was their direct responsibility. The truth of it was that the fat lady, surrounded by her family, had apparently been the only one facing the window at the time. She had just filled her face when she saw the Scot drop past the window and had started to choke.

When the ambulance arrived, we got the Scot ready for the stretcher, but the paramedics ran right past us and into the restaurant to deal with the fat lady. We ended up carrying the Scot to the train station and then on home. He was fine apart from hardly being able to see because the flesh around his eyes was so swollen, his face resembling a slab of red- and purple-coloured pumpkin. And his neck and back muscles were in such a tight spasm that he walked around the hotel ever so slowly and painfully, occasionally scaring civvies in the corridors who had not seen him before.

When I left 42 Commando and came back to the SBS I joined a team on their way to Scotland for more trials work with submarines. I was winding down my career with the SBS by now, preparing to start a new and exciting one elsewhere. But the trip was, as always, interesting, and provided me in my last few months, working directly with old friends, with yet more fond memories. Of the many fun submarine stories, this is one of my favourites.

Our job that week, in the deep waters around the Isle of Arran, across the North Channel from Northern Ireland, was to assist in preparing sub captains for some of the more clandestine work. Military Intelligence agencies as well as special forces sometimes had personnel who needed to be recovered at sea, having been on some foreign powers' territory for one reason or another. One of the techniques for locating and picking up people in these circumstances was the hook-and-line method.

The SBS used this system to collect divers, canoes or boats by submarine at night in most sea conditions, avoiding the really rough weather unless absolutely necessary. Like many of the things we did in the SBS, it looked straightforward enough on paper.

It required at least two people or two boats and had to be at a pre-arranged rendezvous with the sub. If two canoes were used, for instance, after paddling far out to sea to the approximate rendezvous point, the canoeist came together and connected a hundred-foot thin, nylon line between them strong enough to tow both boats. The line was passed through eyes at the bows of both canoes with the ends then fixed to quick-release devices within reach of the lead man in the front of the canoe. The canoes then backed away keeping their bows pointed at each other, until the rope was pulled into a straight line. Each canoe carried a device of a different frequency. The sub steered towards the canoes and, using the two different frequencies, carefully steered between them at periscope depth. The periscope snagged the line and towed the canoes out to sea to a safe location where they surfaced and brought the personnel inboard. I have used this technique with as many as six canoes at once.

On this occasion, there were four of us in two rubber hawks with no equipment. The hawks were small rubber inflatable boats with a small outboard motor, just comfortably large enough for two men plus their full equipment. It was midnight and the sea had a little chop to it. The sub was late and we had been hanging around for a couple of hours, but we were warmly dressed and prepared for foul weather. We'd already hooked up the hundred-foot line and paddled apart, our engines were disconnected and lashed inboard and our devices were pinging away. It was jet-black that night, cloud covered the stars and the only lights visible were from the small harbour village on Arran, miles away. We had been there from last light till 10:00 p.m., in the pub opposite the little jetty. We were no strangers to the locals – as individuals yes, but our types, no. For the past forty or fifty years, the SBS had been using the area to practise their secret trade. The islanders, mostly fishermen and farmers, were used to small groups of fit, weathered young men suddenly walking in out of the dark and often balmy night to order a pint or two, then most often at closing time, walking back out into the darkness towards the water and disappearing. They had no idea what we did, never had in all those years, and never asked.

Sitting there in the boats waiting for the sub did not mean we could relax our vigilance. We had to keep a constant eye open for the periscope. What the sub had to do was technically not quite as easy as it seemed to us. The sub, using sonar only, had an awkward perspective of the position of our boats since it could not see anything in reality, just 'hear'. It could not tell the precise distance from each boat itself and therefore could come at us from almost any angle. The angle could be so acute the periscope might even hit one of the boats, which had happened more than once in the past. And apart from the possibility of coming at us from any point on the compass, it could also come at any speed between two and fifteen knots. So we kept a constant vigil, even after hanging around for hours.

There was some incentive to not missing the U-boat, too. It took the sub a long time to position itself and prepare for its run-up. If it missed the boats, it had to describe a large circle back to us. If it was late, the captain was quite capable of calling it a day and sodding off without a word. We might not know till the wee hours that the whole thing had been cancelled. Such is life on the ocean wave.

Therefore it was with great enthusiasm and effort that we sprang into action when the shout went up, 'There it is!'

Zipper, in the other boat, had spotted it seventy yards away heading towards us at a difficult angle. Zipper was a popular operative in the SBS, bald as a peach and famous for two things: he was light and slight and could run like the wind for ever, an acclaimed marathon runner of international standing. He also had an awful stutter which, had he not been such a popular operative, might have been his downfall.

Zipper was an excitable chap, a northerner by birth, and never short of enthusiasm. 'The . . . there she blo . . . bloody is!' he cried. And then after a brief assessment, 'She's go . . . go . . . gonna fuckin' m . . . m . . . miss us!'

He was right. The sub was headed at a misleading angle across our front. It was going to cut past us on the outside of Zipper's boat.

'Paddle!' the shout went up, and we did just that – like the clappers.

The periscope was three foot out of the water and going fast – much faster than we could paddle. But we had the angle – or so it appeared. Zipper's boat might be able to get to it. What we were trying to do was paddle to a point across the front of the periscope's path. It did not have to snag us in the middle of the line that connected us. Anywhere along it would do. We could then pull and slide the rope up and down until both boats were alongside each other and then we'd sit back for the ride.

As we paddled for all we were worth, it became obvious to Zipper, in the front of his rubber boat, that we might not cut across the sub's path in time. The periscope closed on him at speed. At one point it looked like it was going to hit Zipper's boat, but then Zipper realised it was not even going to do that. The periscope was slicing through the water on a track that would take it just past the front of Zipper's boat.

As it went past, Zipper made his choice. He dumped his paddle, jammed his knees into the rubber boat, and lunged for the periscope. He grabbed just short of the top, but the periscope was moving, attached to several thousand tons of sub below, and it was not going to slow down. Zipper was dragged out of the boat, but his partner, reacting as swiftly as Zipper, managed to leap forward and grab his feet. He did it in such a way that he jammed his knees tightly into the forward corner of the rubber boat and off we went. I felt the powerful shunt forward in my boat, which nearly made me fall backwards.

And so there we were, steaming along, Zipper holding on to the periscope, his partner hanging on to his feet, the hundred-foot line, taut as a violin string, stretching back to my boat, and my partner and I being towed along faster than we could possibly paddle.

Inside the sub, after it had passed the pinging devices, the captain wanted to check if the boats had hooked up correctly. He looked through the periscope and all he could see was a bald man an arm's-length away wearing a bug-eyed expression – a mixture of pain and determination.

There was no way Zipper could hold on for the next ten yards never mind ten miles, and he had to release the sub, whereupon he and his partner ploughed into the drink. The sub never stopped, and left us in the middle of the black ocean to pull Zipper and his partner back into their boat.

Had an islander been out that late, and had he paused on the coastline to listen to the sounds carried on the night air, he might have heard another sound far out to sea that was not unusual when those strange folk were about. Howling laughter.

17

When the SBS were called to the Gulf I was in the USA on 'other work'. Once again it was a distressing time for me, for I thought I was going to miss yet another war. I was more than happy, but altogether curious, when I received a signal inviting me to return to take part in the war – but not to go to England, or even the Middle East, but Venice. I had no more information than that. I naturally accepted. I packed a small bag and caught a plane to Italy.

As I stood outside the arrivals lounge in Venice Airport, I looked around for my transport. I had no idea what to expect. I was a little miffed about the complete lack of information. They could have told me something. All I knew was that whoever was picking me up would have a description of me.

I was looking for a nondescript vehicle, or possibly even a military one, and therefore gave only a cursory glance to the stretch Mercedes that cruised past then pulled over across the road. However, it was a habit by now to watch everything else without appearing to, and I noticed a tall, casually dressed man climb out of the driver's seat and cross the road towards the lounge. He looked like he was heading for me. Indeed, he was staring at me.

He stopped, introduced himself and said everything required of him. This was my ride – the limo. It was obviously all they could find. This was a fun perk, I thought. He took my bags, I made a move to take them back, but he insisted. This man did not look or act like an operative of any kind. He looked and acted like, well, a limo driver.

He opened the door for me and I stepped inside and sat down in the spacious vehicle. It was very plush. The drinks' cabinet was full, but I was working.

As he climbed in and pulled away from the kerb, I asked where we were going.

'The harbour,' he said in an Italian accent.

I tried to figure this out. He was taking me to a boat, whereupon I would travel across the Med and be inserted into the Middle East. I wondered what I would be doing. I had visions of an OP somewhere, or perhaps a training mission. Hopefully not a BG (bodyguard) job. I disliked BG work. It was very boring and required only about 1 per cent of my expertise. I had no idea what the squadron lads would be doing in the Gulf, so it was all pretty much open.

We pulled to a stop on a long jetty. As the driver took my bag out of the boot I climbed out and faced a large ocean cruiser, a luxury yacht large enough to sleep a couple of hundred passengers. The driver handed my bag over to a steward in an immaculate white suit, who treated me like the President and ushered me on board.

It was like a floating Dorchester Hotel. I had known this was not some kind of mistake because the driver knew who I was and the reception had me down as a guest. I was shown upstairs to my cabin, on the top floor just behind the captain's. It was one of the suites, with a balcony and a small living-room outside the bedroom. On the table was a bottle of champagne in an ice-bucket beside a bowl of fresh strawberries. The steward left me without waiting for a tip and I checked out the bedroom. On the bed were a couple of suits, one of them a tuxedo and classic black tie with, fortunately, instructions on how to tie it. They were my size.

There was a knock at the door. I opened it. A short, oldish ship's officer in uniform walked in, more like scurried in, a little out of breath and carrying quite a heavy suitcase. He shut the door behind him quickly.

'Duncan?' he said and offered his hand. 'Jeff. I'm the head security officer.'

I said 'Hi' and nothing else, expecting him to be the man who would tell me what this was all about.

He carried the suitcase to the bed and unlocked it.

'I think there's everything you need here,' he said as he opened it.

I looked at the contents. I recognised everything inside. H&K 9mm pistol, shoulder harness, Sat-com, signal flares, torches, climbing harness, spare rounds, batteries and a bullet-proof vest.

'What is all this?' I said.

'You don't know what that lot is?' he asked, surprised.

'No. I know what all that is. What am I doing here?'

'You don't know?' he looked incredulous.

'I wouldn't be asking, would I?'

He shrugged. 'It's straightforward, really. There are a bunch of important people on board and their wives. They need to travel around the Med, all over the place, as far as Russia, and they're worried about terrorists. They put in a request to London for protection and here you are.'

He handed me a file from inside the case. 'It's all in there. I've gotta go, we're sailing in a few hours. If you need anything, contact me. The captain knows you're on board but not who you are. No one else on board has any idea about you. You're a journalist – a guest of the company. Other than that, have a good trip.'

With that he sneaked out of the cabin and left me alone.

I flicked through the orders. I wasn't going into Iraq or anywhere near the Gulf. I was to stay on board or close by, and in the event the ship came under attack and was taken by terrorists, I was to stay mobile, communicate with the SBS assault team that would move in to retake the ship, and help secure their landing. The reason I was in a top-deck suite was that the Sat-com would not work below decks.

Everyone on board, older couples mostly, were important dignitaries and wealthy businessmen. I wasn't sure if I was disappointed or not. I didn't mind the thought of leaping about doing a Die Hard on a boat, but I felt the odds of it happening would be slim. I decided to take a wander around the boat.

It was certainly luxurious. I wondered what I was going to do with myself for a couple of months, which was the initial plan for the voyage. I hoped they had a library on board as I had only brought along one book. I went below to check out the gym that was listed on the map of the boat. At least I could get a serious workout every day.

I had a master key for every lock on board, but the gym was open. I opened the door and stepped inside. There was a small pool and a Jacuzzi on one side of the room. I went further in to look at the mirror-walled weights room and stopped in my tracks apologetically. There, in various parts of the room, stretching out or lifting light dumb-bells, were six beautiful girls, members of a dance troupe that were on board to entertain the guests. And I was apparently the only eligible male guest on board.

If at this stage the reader is feeling somewhat sceptical about this story, sorry to disappoint you, but it's true. I had to sit down in my suite and smile as it sunk in, too. And it gets worse.

That evening, as the yacht cruised out of the Lido, past the bobbing gondolas, I stood on deck in the warm air wearing my tuxedo. Under my jacket rested my 9mm in its holster, and in my hand I held a slender glass of champagne. I had no illusions of being 'Bond'. But after so many years of hardship operations, which, don't get me wrong, I have enjoyed, even more so as memories, I was finally fulfilling the image of what many fantasise the job to be. I accepted it as a well-earned reward. I had arrived.

During the Gulf War, while the lads were up to their necks in sand, and frustratingly so for the most part, I could be found dining in Istanbul, watching a ballet in Odessa in my Armani suit (holstered gun hidden underneath, of course), or riding a camel to watch the sun rise over the Sphinx in Cairo (and yes, with a couple of the dancers in tow and a bottle of champagne just to rub it in). The phrase 'Oh, what a lovely war' sprung to mind. But someone had to do it.

The Gulf War was not all that it was hoped to be for special forces, which is why it was not such a personal disappointment to miss in the end. It was the Americans' war, and that meant a greater share of the work was done by technology. Military targets that once required a man to get close to them, photograph and describe them in detail prior to being attacked can now be reconnoitred by satellite or long-range radar, optical and listening devices. Where special forces were once needed to move in and plant explosives on that target far behind enemy lines, weapons can now be programmed to travel the distance and strike it. Special forces are generally only needed where technology alone cannot succeed.

This was the reason behind the first special forces mission of the Gulf War inside Iraq, and the SBS, above all others, were chosen by the Americans to execute it.

The American high command was originally reluctant to use any special forces in Iraq during the Gulf War apart from to assist smart-bombs on to their targets using laser guidance systems – the smart-bombs were not quite as smart as the media reported. This reluctance was probably based on the very poor combat record in recent decades of American special forces. Tehran was the most publicised abortion, Grenada goes down in history as one of the worst-planned military conflicts in modern times, and Panama and Somalia were chequered with screw-ups. The US Navy SEALs, for instance, the US's primary special forces unit and the most heavily funded, and some ten times the size of the SBS, had only one operative allowed to set foot inside Iraq during the entire war, and that was as a guest of the SBS during their first mission, and only then because he happened to have been attached to the SBS prior to the outbreak of war.

To argue the American side, their special forces have seen little action since Vietnam. Special forces need a certain amount of exposure to 'live' activity to maintain the high standards required of them and the Americans have not had the opportunities that we have had. The British have been fighting somewhere in the world every day for the last 500 years or more, with just a couple of days' break after the Suez crisis.

Another factor for American special forces' inactivity is the American government's reluctance to send them abroad, having suffered politically over the last few decades due to the notoriety of its clandestine operations. The American people are also highly vocal when it comes to losing even a single American soldier on foreign soil. America now has a very strict non-intervention rule. These factors irritate most American special forces operatives who, like all of us, joined up to be professional soldiers. The SEALs number one team do little more than bodyguard duties these days, but at least they get decorated for it. Excuse the little dig, lads.

The target for the first special forces operation of the Gulf War was a high-tech fibre-optic communications system that spanned the length of Iraq and was buried underground. American intelligence discovered that the system linked the Scud missile units and helped coordinate Iraqi attacks on Israel. The cable was also supported by microwave links to fill the gaps in any breaks in the flow of important data. The system could be disabled if certain sections of it were destroyed. The Air Force had made several attempts to destroy the buried cable with bombs, but every mission had failed. This operation is an example of men having to be used where technology fails.

The original plan was to send in teams that would destroy these links over a number of days, but there was an increase in political pressure to neutralise the Scud threat right away and so a team was hastily put together and sent out at the first opportunity.

The total flight-time there and back was estimated at five hours and therefore, taking into consideration the hours of darkness, fuel and load capacities, the team had less than two hours on target to locate and destroy the cables. This was not a lot of time. Satellite photographs revealed that the cable ran parallel to an oil pipeline and its service road, but its precise distance from these landmarks and depth below ground was unknown. It was going to have to be found before it could be blown up, and that was going to take as much luck as effort.

Another factor was the high possibility of attack from any of a number of mobile enemy troop concentrations in the immediate area. Reconnaissance flights a few days before had indicated that the cable was constantly patrolled. It was decided that the Chinooks were to remain on the ground within sight of the teams, their rotors disengaged but engines running so that the men could bug out in the event of an enemy assault.

The operation was carried out by twenty-seven heavily armed SBS operatives (and one US Navy SEAL guest). They left under cover of darkness in two Chinook CH47 helicopters from a forward base a hundred miles south of the Iraqi border. They flew a tight, pre-planned, zig-zag route to avoid enemy radar and anti-aircraft missiles for a distance of nearly 300 miles to a point just thirty miles south of Baghdad. This was a particularly hazardous flight because the radar and anti-aircraft missile sites were mobile and constantly changing their positions.

The choppers flew fifty feet above the ground for most of the journey and when they arrived they touched down within 200 metres of the pipeline. When the rear ramps of the Chinooks opened, the SBS stormed out and spread to their pre-planned positions. Most of the men were deployed to form a circle to protect the target area from assault while the rest hurried to the pipeline carrying shovels, electric cable locators and, of course, explosives. The ground was flat and featureless and no Iraqi troops were in the immediate area at the time. The flank parties dug in heavy machine-guns, lightweight mortars, rocket-launchers and grenade-launchers. If the

Iraqis did arrive, they would get a warm welcome for at least the first few minutes, after which ammunition would run low and the teams would have to get out before the enemy recovered and counter-attacked.

After a quick recce, the demolition team chose a spot and started digging into the sand. Within thirty minutes they found a cable. But after an inspection it was discovered not to be the fibre-optic they were after. Time was moving on and there were already fears that this somewhat hit-and-miss operation might be a tough nut to crack, mainly because it was dependent more on luck than judgement. The SBS have a long, unbroken string of successes to their name and they did not want to start off this war with a miss.

A few miles away American B52s bombed a couple of Iraqi troop locations, which the Iraqis answered with anti-aircraft batteries. The bombing was part of a diversionary attack to keep the Iraqis occupied, and it was working like a charm.

The men started another hole, but again, after many precious minutes of digging, it was a false call. Yet another hole was dug, but after an hour and a quarter on the ground the cable had not been found. With only forty-five minutes left, there was a distinct feeling of concern for the success of the operation.

The pilots were also growing anxious: sitting inside their gently throbbing cockpits waiting to lift off at a moment's notice was probably more difficult than having things to do. But they waited patiently while the surrounding defensive positions kept their vigil.

Yet another hole was dug. This one also revealed

nothing – the time was ticking away to barely minutes left. A decision had to be made.

The team leader studied the pattern of holes and knew that one of them was within feet of the optic cable. With a minute to go, he decided.

'Fuck it. Shove all the explosives in this hole. We'll make it big enough to lose a truck in.'

The team placed all 500 pounds of high explosive into the hole then shovelled the sand back in to act as a tamp and direct the force of the blast further down and to the sides. The formula for this particular type of charge is known as 'P', for plenty.

They were ready to go. The time delays on the charge were initiated and the flank protection teams were ordered back into the choppers. The rotors were engaged and the explosives team ran on board, the last man on being the team leader. His last thought as the ramp of the Chinook came up was, had he chosen the right hole?

The two Chinooks lifted off and turned back towards the border. A few minutes into the air they heard a heavy boom behind them as the charge went off.

They flew their zig-zag route back to the border and arrived at the forward base unmolested. The choppers touched down and the teams walked off. Everyone was wondering the same thing. As they walked off the heli-pad the team leader was met by the operations officer.

'Well done,' he said calmly. 'The cable was cut.'

Because of the success of the SBS operation, General Schwarzkopf regained some of his confidence in special forces.

*   *   *

The rest of the war was disappointing for the SBS in general. The squadrons worked ceaselessly preparing many possible operations, few of which came to fruition, most being cancelled at the last moment for one reason or another. The SAS would have had an equally uneventful time had they not gone off chasing mobile Scud missile sites, another problem technology could not yet solve. Finding a mobile site through the camera of a satellite is like looking for a penny on a football pitch through a straw – you have to know where to point the straw within a few inches before you can hope to find the penny. The SBS might well have sent out its own patrols in search of the Scuds, which again was a more political than tactical move to keep the Israelis happy, but the SAS were up to their old tricks again back in special forces HQ in Riyadh. They successfully blocked all attempts by the SBS to get involved in that department. So much for the combined special forces concept. In retrospect, missing out on chasing Scuds was not such a bad thing as the missions mostly turned out to be either fruitless or suicidal. At any one time during the war the SAS had at least twenty-two men on the ground, and out of communication with their HQ, who had to be considered missing in action. Considering the relative size of the conflict, and what little there was to do for the strength of force the allies had put against the Iraqis, this seemed amateurish. The SAS were acting like a bunch of soccer hooligans leaping all over the desert looking for someone to bash and getting lost in the process.

The Americans seemed content to let the SAS have their little adventures and continued to provide the technological security dome over the war zone, ready to react in the event of any emergency. When Bravo Two Zero had its fateful encounter, an American AWAC, the large flying surveillance craft with its huge saucer on the roof, happened to be in the area and picked up their emergency beacons. On board the AWAC, along for the ride with the American crew, was a single Brit from the Royal Corps of Signals, a man I met several months afterwards.

When the AWAC picked up Bravo Two Zero's emergency signal, it changed direction and headed for their area. It hoped to monitor the direction and location of the team and vector a helicopter pick-up on to it. As it headed towards the area at 15,000 feet, the emergency siren sounded on board and the white lights in the main cabin went to red. An Iraqi Mig had 'locked on' to them and was coming in fast for an attack.

Neither the signaller nor the American crew had ever been in an air-combat situation before and, needless to say, there were some terrified expressions on board. The AWAC pilot went into immediate evasive action and lurched the heavy craft into anti-pursuit patterns. Everyone buckled into their seats and held on. There was nothing else they could do: the AWACs have no offensive capability. It was a frantic moment.

A voice boomed over the intercom, 'Missile fired!'

The Mig had released an air-to-air missile and it closed on the AWAC at a rapid pace. The AWAC is not exactly an agile craft, but the pilot threw it violently about in an effort to lose the missile. For the Mig, the AWAC was a sitting duck.

Suddenly there were two very loud 'pops', as the signaller described them, followed seconds later by two explosions that shuddered the aircraft as it banked steeply.

'We're hit!' cried the signaller as he clutched his seat with white knuckles.

'Chaff!' shouted an equally frightened US crewman strapped in beside him.

He was referring to the anti-missile devices released by the AWAC, designed to explode behind its tail sending out thousands of tiny shards of foil and heat to confuse the enemy missile's guidance system. The AWAC dived and turned back to level flight and headed towards a pair of American fighters which were already responding to the attack. The aircraft ceased its violent movement as the pilot brought it under control. Then his voice came over the intercom again.

'He's a-runnin'.'

A cheer went up and the crew applauded. The signaller sat back totally exhausted by the experience.

The irresponsibility of Bravo Two Zero's mission would have been highlighted even more had the AWAC gone down.

The SBS's final piece of action came with the retaking of the British Embassy in Kuwait. This was a combined operation in so far as American and French special forces moved in at the same time to take back their own embassies. This was mostly a show, as little or no resistance was expected. But it is worthy of a mention because of one amusing and ironic incident.

Ron, an old friend, led the SBS team that roped down from choppers on to the embassy roof (photographed by the media and once again credited to you know who). Members of the British civilian diplomatic detachment were 'in the wings' to 'take possession' when the SBS had made the building safe and clear – there was still the very real danger that the Iraqis had left mines and booby-traps.

The heavy wooden doors that sealed the main entrance to the embassy were ancient and ornately carved and had been securely locked by the Iraqis before they left. Not willing to take any chances and risk his men's lives forcing open the doors, for fear they might be booby-trapped, Ron ordered them to be blown open. This was a standard enough procedure using a small charge.

The doors were blown in and, naturally, they sustained some damage. The embassy was searched thoroughly for charges, none were found, and it was declared clear. Ron, an SBS sergeant, felt somewhat honoured to have been selected to claim the embassy back. When the senior diplomat arrived to take possession, he approached Ron, who, in full SBS combat gear, was waiting to welcome him.

When the diplomat saw the mess at the entrance, instead of thanking Ron in an official capacity for retaking his building, he looked aghast and exclaimed, 'What have you done to my doors?'

Ron could not believe the ignorance and audacity of the man as he went on about the ancient carving and how it would cost thousands to repair. Ron did not bother to explain how he regarded the lives of his men more highly than this man's doors.

'Oi,' Ron said instead.

The diplomat looked at him with a sneer.

Ron extended his middle finger at the diplomat, held it there long enough for the man to get the message, and walked away.

Within a few weeks the teams were back in Poole and it was business as usual. There was a new job for them to do, one they were perfectly trained and equipped for, but which had never been considered before. The drug wars.

18

British Customs were having problems dealing with the trafficking of drugs into Britain by boat. The smugglers were getting smarter and Customs did not have the skills or technology to deal with them. They went looking for SAS assistance, but the SAS passed on it, thinking it was too small to get involved with. They did not have the expertise to fulfil the task anyway.

The SBS took on these small jobs at first because they did not drain the service's manpower and also because they served as rehearsals for one of the squadron's primary roles. But after many initial successes and the arrest of several drug smugglers and the seizure of their merchandise, the Customs authorities realised they were on to a winner and pushed for greater SBS involvement. London gave the OK. This was followed by the biggest single drugs seizure in Britain's history, carried out by the SBS at sea using MAT techniques.

Another operation, in the Thames, resulted in over a

ton of cocaine being captured and several arrests. This one was photographed by a woman from her apartment overlooking the raid and made the front page of the papers as an SAS operation. The SBS have never cared that the papers credited its successes to the SAS – in fact, as I've said, it has usually worked in the SBS's favour.

In all, over the past few years, close to a hundred drug smugglers and sixty tons of drugs have been captured as a result of SBS operations. The SBS have always taken great care to protect their techniques and to be on their guard against any attempt to counter them. So in spite of any efforts smugglers may have made to do so, often they have been completely unaware that they were being tracked until the SBS have burst on to the bridge of their ship.

Prince Andrew was a helicopter pilot in a naval squadron which flew in support of the SBS. A handful of Navy pilots work with the SBS in their MAT role on a rotational basis. The pilots are recruited because of their skills, which have to be no less than exceptional. The SBS cannot afford them to be otherwise. Prince Andrew flew for the SBS not because of his rank, but simply because he was a good pilot, having gained a lot of experience flying in the Falklands conflict.

Not long ago, the Prince was flying two SBS snipers in his Lynx to a firing range in northern England. I have explained the familiarity between officers and men in special forces but this does not apply in quite the same way to Royalty. However, the Prince was like most other special forces pilots: easygoing and approachable within the confines of the job.

The two snipers were dressed in their standard black MAT one-piece overalls, carried their ammunition in a bag and held on to their sniper's rifles, G3s, known as 'widow-makers' or 'barking dogs' because of the distinct sound they make when fired. They had flasks of coffee and offered a cup to Prince Andrew, who declined it.

'There's no laxative in it, sir,' they said.

He was used to SBS humour and smiled, but still refused it.

'Don't you like our coffee then, sir? It's instant.'

'I'd rather have a cup of tea, actually,' he said.

'We haven't got any, sir. It stews in the flask and doesn't keep.'

'Would you prefer a cup of tea?' he asked.

'Well, yeah, sure,' they replied.

'I have some friends nearby. Let's pop down and see if we can get a cup.'

The two operatives thought he was joking, but the Prince suddenly banked the chopper and started his descent. Even then they didn't believe he was serious, and when they saw where he was heading they sat there speechless. They were touching down in the courtyard of an immense country estate.

The Prince turned off the engines and climbed out.

'Come on, then,' he said.

They stepped out of the chopper carrying their sniper's rifles, still not quite believing their eyes. Then half-a-dozen security men in civilian clothes appeared from the buildings and surrounding gardens. The head of this security team hurried over to ask the Prince what was up, assuming that they'd had engine trouble, as no warning of their arrival had been given. The Prince explained they were just stopping for a cup of tea and headed for the main house. When the two SBS operatives set off to follow him the security officer stopped them and said they would have to leave their weapons in the chopper.

'We don't leave our weapons anywhere, mate,' they replied. They might have been a little overawed by the event, but they never forgot their own rules and responsibilities.

'Oh, come on,' said the Prince. 'They're SBS. Who's better qualified to carry arms into Sandringham than them?'

The security head could not argue with the Prince and let them pass.

The Prince led them around to a side door, and as they approached it, it opened. This time they really could not believe their eyes. Standing in the doorway, smiling and waiting to greet them was a short, elderly lady in slippers with blue-rinsed hair.

'Andrew! What a nice surprise,' she said.

The prince kissed her on the cheek. She then looked at the two operatives and smiled at them.

'These are men from the SBS, Mama. We're just stopping by for a quick cup of tea.'

The Queen stood back to let them enter. 'Do come in, please, won't you?'

She never acted like a Queen for a second – she was just like any other mother welcoming her son and his friends into her house.

Inside the hallway, she paused to consider their sniper's rifles.

'You can put those in there if you like,' she said, pointing to an umbrella stand.

It was unlikely that their weapons would be nicked here, so they plonked the rifles in the stand and followed the Queen into a beautiful library.

'Please make yourself at home.' And at that she left the room with her son.

The operatives sat there quite rigidly, wondering if this was really happening. Then the door opened and an old retired colonel walked in carrying a brandy snifter. It was 11:00 a.m. He seemed a cheery old fellow.

'How are you chaps doing?' he asked.

The men stood up. 'Fine, sir,' they said in unison.

'Good. Good. Sit down, please, please.'

They did. The door opened again and the Queen returned, leading a butler carrying a tray of tea and sandwiches. The men stood up again. The Prince returned and the Queen asked them to sit down while she poured everyone a cup of tea. They were joined by a Duke and Duchess. The operatives couldn't remember afterwards who they were but they described the Duchess as 'essence', meaning 'gorgeous'. They all sat around together like one big happy family, chatting away as if this was all quite normal. The Queen spent most of the time talking with the two men, asking them all kinds of questions about their work and families, and where they were from. At one point she realised that the two men were uncomfortably warm in their one-piece heavy-duty fireproof MAT suits.

'Please undo your tops if you're too warm,' she said.

One of them stood up thankfully, unzipped his top and rolled it down to reveal a plain white T-shirt underneath. The other operative remained sitting and perspiring.

'I'm fine Ma'am,' he insisted.

He could not undo his top because underneath he was wearing a T-shirt with a detailed drawing emblazoned on its front of a man with his head up his arse and some slogan about being kept in the dark.

When tea was over, the Queen escorted them to the door where they retrieved their sniper's rifles. She wished them luck and waved goodbye to the Prince and his guests as they headed back to the helicopter.

The future of the SBS now seems to lie alongside that of the SAS, and amalgamation appears inevitable. This has already happened to a degree and will increase in time. But it has its problems.

For one, an SAS trooper is paid more than his counterpart in the SBS, another indication of the SAS's 'pull' upstairs. Today, an SBS rank has to pass the SAS selection before he can move on and attempt SBS selection. On passing the SAS selection, he is technically qualified to join the SAS and therefore to receive their higher pay. By continuing on and passing for the SBS, a more selective process involving diving, boating and MAT training, he qualifies for less money. And if he fails to get into the SBS he can always go back to the SAS. Little wonder there is some discontent amongst the SBS ranks. These days it seems to be a much more money-orientated world than I remember, or perhaps it was just me. When I joined, I had no idea how much I would be paid and I hardly thought about it. When I was a noddy in training, after my second week, we were lined up outside the paymaster's office and, to my surprise, handed fifty pounds. Naïvely, I hadn't realised we were going to be paid at all until we finished training. With so many lucrative jobs in civvy street for ex-special forces these days, some men join for just long enough to get the basic skills, and of course the name and the kudos that goes with it, then leave to find a job outside.

Another problem is the conflicting attitudes of the two groups. The SAS still regard themselves as distinctly superior to all. Recently an SBS friend was training in Hereford alongside members of the SAS. He realised that, in the evenings, they blatantly avoided social-ising with him. He was informed by one somewhat embarrassed young trooper that they had been told by their senior SAS NCO not to fraternise with SBS ranks after working hours. The SBS, on the contrary, are well known for socialising even with non-special forces attached ranks when they are working together.

The SAS have recently adopted a new nickname for themselves. It seems many of them prefer to be known as 'Blades', obviously derived from their winged dagger. It sounds more like a gang name, which is perhaps poetic irony.

If a pie chart were used to show the contribution of man-power provided to undercover operations such as 14 Int, past and present, by the many individual military units in all three armed services, the Royal Marines would represent the greater slice by far. In a similar pie chart showing the contribution to special forces, the SBS and SAS, again the Marines would be the greater slice. This impressive statistic is a tribute to the organisation, its character, its unparalleled history, and the philosophy with which it imbues its manpower.

By telling these stories, I have tried to show a slice of life in one of the world's most élite – if not the most élite – military forces. In the highly specialised arena of MAT there is no unit on the planet that can better the SBS, and it makes me feel good knowing I contributed to that.

Many in the SBS will argue they don't care for anyone to know what they do or how well they do it. I have chosen to ignore them for reasons I feel are more important now. I believe it is time the SBS received their true appreciation, since they are no longer such a mysterious entity and will inevitably garner more media attention in the future. Also, if some of my anecdotes in any way help to humble both us and the SAS, that can only be a good thing.

It's impossible to describe the exploits of the SBS without sounding vain and egotistical, but I hope the overriding tone has been one of sheer pride in an exceptional team of men of which I had the honour to be a part. Those who don't agree with me writing about the SBS will get over it. This is already just a history book.

I monitor the future of the SBS with interest. I'm a civvy myself now, and my time is over, but they are part of my everyday existence. They trained my confidence, issued me with a set of principles, taught me the true meaning of loyalty and gave me a bunch of friends I will have until the day I die. It doesn't come any better than that.

Glossary

acquaint   pre-SBS selection course
ampho   home-made explosive mixture
ASU   IRA active service unit
ATO   ammunitions technicians officer
to back   support
badged   bona fide member of special forces
basher   sleeping quarters
beasting   punishing physical workout
bivvy   camp
blown   an undercover operative is un-
                      covered
bootneck   Royal Marine
BU   breathing unit
bug out   withdraw
click   one kilometre
CO   commanding officer
comms   communications
contact   live fire exchange with the enemy

CQA	close-quarter assassination
CTC	Commando Training Centre
cuds	countryside
the Det	14th Intelligence Detachment (also 14 Int)
dog's watch	short period of time
DS	directing staff
DSF	Directorate of Special Forces
DUCS	divers' underwater communications system
E&RE	exit from and re-entry into submarines
flash-crash	disorientation grenade
14 Int	*see* **the Det**
DZ	drop zone
GPMG	general-purpose machine-gun
gravel-belly	American term for infantry soldier
green lid	green commando beret
grots	accommodation
GSG9	German special forces unit
HALO	high-altitude low-opening (parachuting)
head	Navy toilet
H&K	weapon made by Heckler & Koch
INLA	Irish National Liberation Organisation
Int	intelligence (information)
IO	intelligence officer
Kampschwimmer	German Navy frogman
killing house	indoor shooting range

LO	liaison officer
LUP	lying-up position
LZ	landing zone
MAT	maritime anti-terrorism
MCT	maritime counter-terrorism
ML	mountain leader
mob	military
MOE	method of entry
MPK, MP5	weapons made by Heckler & Koch
MRF	Military Reaction Force
M10	small rapid-fire sub-machine-gun by Colt
nobber	ineffective person
noddy	Royal Marine recruit
nutty	chocolate or sweets
OC	officer commanding
ogin	sea or water
one up	alone
OP	observation post
oppo	friend
ops	operations
pinged	seen or discovered
PIRA	Provisional IRA
PNGs	passive night goggles
PSO	personnel selection officer
PWI	Royal Marines platoon weapons instructor
QRF	Quick Reaction Force
RABA	rechargeable air breathing apparatus
racing snake	fast runner

R&R	rest and recuperation
rate	rating
remount exercise	no-notice exercise
resup	resupply
RFA	Royal Fleet Auxiliary
rib	rigid inflatable boat
RPG	rocket-propelled grenade
RTU	return to unit
RUC	Royal Ulster Constablulary
rupert	officer
sat-com	satellite communications
sausage-bag	yard-long, tubular kitbag
SC	swimmer-canoeist
SEAL	Sea, Air and Land (US Navy)
serial	cycle
shiny-arse	clerk
sit-reps	situation reports
skeg	observe
SMG	sub-machine-gun
SOP	standing operational procedures
snake	soldiers moving along the same track
squadron lines	area of camp for which SBS is responsible
SSM	squadron sergeant major
stick	group
tab	Army/SAS term for **yomp**, but of a shorter distance carrying lighter weights
tout	IRA informant
tout-maker	person who recruits **touts**

2IC	second in command
UDR	Ulster Defence Regiment
UVF	Ulster Volunteer Force
VCP	vehicle checkpoint
webbing	belt and pouches carrying immediate-use equipment
wrap	quit, as in fail
yomp	long walk carrying heavy pack

Time Warner Paperbacks now offers an exciting range of quality titles by both established and new authors. All of the books in this series are available from:

Time Warner Paperbacks
P.O. Box 121, Kettering,
Northants NN14 4ZQ

Fax No: 01832 733076
Telephone No: 01832 737525
Email: aspenhouse@FSBDial.co.uk

Payments can be made as follows: cheque, postal order (payable to Time Warner Books) or by credit cards, Visa/Access. Do not send cash or currency. All U.K. orders free of charge. E.E.C. and Overseas: 25% of order value.

NAME (Block Letters) ....

....

ADDRESS ....

....

....

☐ I enclose my remittance for ....

☐ I wish to pay by Access/Visa Card ....

Number ☐☐☐☐☐☐☐☐☐☐☐☐☐☐☐☐

Card Expiry Date ☐☐☐☐